THE KING'S STATE

THE KING'S STATE

Proprietary Dynasticism
in Early Modern France

HERBERT H. ROWEN

Rutgers University Press
New Brunswick, New Jersey

Library of Congress Cataloging in Publication Data

Rowen, Herbert Harvey.
    The king's state.

    Bibliography: p.
    Includes index.
    1. France—Kings and rulers—History.   2. Monarchy,
French—History.   3. France—Politics and government—
16th century.   4. France—Politics and government—
1589–1789.   I. Title.
JN2341.R68   944′.03′0922   80–13572
ISBN   0–8135–0893–2

CONTENTS

PREFACE

THIS IS a short book with a long history. Its central idea came to me decades ago, when I was still in graduate school. I was struck then by an anomaly in our historical picture of the politics of early modern Europe. On the one hand, the narrative histories were full of events and statements by the politically active indicating that the kings were considered as the owners of the state. On the other hand, almost all the general histories were missing this element, or represented it at most by a brief remark noting how kings looked on their realms "as if" they were private estates. The question struck me, What was the truth of the matter?

Although my principal scholarly investigations moved into the history of the Dutch Republic, I remained fascinated by the problem of what I eventually called "proprietary dynasticism." I accumulated materials as I went along, most of them found in the course of other reading. However, during a fruitful year as a visitor at the University of California at Berkeley in 1959–1960, I was able to concentrate on this subject, making use of the rich materials in its research libraries. But I turned back again to my major work, a biography of the Grand Pensionary John de Witt. Not until it was done, many years later, was I in a position to pick up the threads of this study and put my ideas on paper. I had discovered unsuspected subtleties and significances since the writing of two early articles, "A Second Thought on Locke's *First Treatise*" (*Journal of the History of Ideas*, 1956) and "L'Etat c'est à Moi: Louis XIV and the State" (*French Historical Studies*, 1962).

Although I accumulated materials on proprietary dynasticism in many parts of Europe, even in the Dutch Republic,

I decided to focus on the phenomenon in France only. The Dutch aspect will form a part of a study of the stadholderate which I am now beginning. Elsewhere, I soon realized, my findings were spotty and suggestive rather than sustained and based upon close familiarity with the general history of the countries. If this book is persuasive to my fellow historians of early modern Europe, those who know other countries better than I do will employ its insight and its formulations as they find them useful.

The first encouragement to work on this theme along with my Dutch studies came to me from my doctoral adviser at Columbia University, Garrett Mattingly. Friends continued that encouragement over the years. Some, notably Helli Koenigsberger, helped by discussing its ideas and problems, without ever being called upon to read the manuscript as it emerged from the study. Others who added reading to their earlier comments have contributed notably to improvement of this work. Their erudition saved me from mistakes, and their close scrutiny of my argument enabled me to tighten and sharpen it, even when I did not go all the way with their criticism. None of them—the late William F. Church, whom I remember with special affection, Andrew Lossky, Ragnhild Hatton, Ralph E. Giesey, John H. M. Salmon, Melvin Richter —should be held responsibile for the ideas presented here, a disclaimer that in this case is not pro forma. My wife, Mildred, has lived with this intellectual concern of mine for more than three quarters of our years of marriage. To say that without her this book might well not have been written is true and trite, but, truth being more important than triteness, I must thank her again for her love and support all these years.

INTRODUCTION

In Quest of the Invisible

B Y ONE of the anomalies historians come to expect in their study of the past, it is perhaps the most characteristic political institution of early modern Europe—dynastic monarchy—that is the least studied and understood. The problem for our understanding of dynastic monarchy is that we are reluctant to accept it on its own terms. The modern mind rebels at the notion of the state as the *property* of the ruling family—the "dynasty" in the specific sense.[1] The very notion of ownership of political power has long since ceased to be significant, and we now distinguish absolutely between power and property even as we dig deeply into the relationship between them. Medievalists, to be sure, have long recognized that the institutions of feudalism and manorialism were simultaneously political and economic in character; but early modern historians, although increasingly willing to acknowledge the persistence of medieval institutions and attitudes into their own period, have seldom observed that *proprietary dynasticism* continued, unabated and even intensified, in the monarchies of the old regime Europe. Indeed, the influence of a work of great erudition and brilliance, Ernst Kantorowicz's *The King's Two Bodies*,[2] has only heightened this neglect, for Kantorowicz demonstrated the existence of a powerful current of hostility to proprietary dynasticism in medieval and early modern Europe. But he did not look at the practice to see how the idea of kingship as office was actually applied, or indeed, whether it was applied at all.

The chasm between theory and practice was recognized

more clearly by the Dutch historian Johan Huizinga. "In practice," he wrote, "princes and statesmen continued to navigate by a political compass of extreme primitiveness. . . . With all respect for the skill of the leaders, the politics of a Philip II or the last Valois, considered as intellectual accomplishment, cannot be rated any higher than bungling with elements they neither understood nor controlled."[3] It is undoubtedly true, as William F. Church has written, that the development of political thought and constitutional doctrines, although influenced by and running parallel to social and political evolution, was also shaped by intellectual trends.[4] How far astray a purely theoretical approach can lead even highly informed historians is shown by Olivier-Martin's affirmation that the French kings of the early modern epoch "made a perfect distinction between their own interests and those of the state [chose publique]."[5] This flies in the face of the facts, as any narrative political historian knows full well.

Yet, what is significant to observe is how much, or how little, and in what way, practice was influenced by theory. Indeed, it is part of the purpose of this book to attempt to see theory in terms of the known and felt experience of the time, so that we may read into the intentions of the thinkers not merely the plain (or apparently plain) meanings of their words, but also the implicit characteristics of the institutions and events that they were trying to understand and no doubt to shape to their own desires, or those of their patrons.[6]

The principle and practice of proprietary dynasticism in France in the early modern period, and the running battle against it by adherents of the antiproprietary principle, are the subject of this study. My concern is neither for the history of the idea of proprietary dynasticism or of its various contradictions, as such, nor just for the events of dynastic history, important though they were in the actuality of early modern times, but for the interplay between the two factors. This is, in a sense, an institutional study, but of an institution that is neither wholly formal, established by specific conventions and maintained by explicit arrangements of law, nor entirely informal, a practice so widely accepted and so deeply imbedded in the notions and feelings of the period that it requires no constitutive enactments at its origins nor any legal sanction to maintain it. It was an institution that was usually taken for granted; little explicit attention was given to it except at times of tension and crisis involving its fundamental elements—disputes over royal succession, wars of conquest, and republican revolutions. What I have done therefore in these pages is to trace the course and development of the institution of proprietary dynasticism as it was reflected both in political and legal debate and in key episodes. Places and times have been selected partly because of their inherent interest, as with the succession struggle over the accession of Henry IV or the wars over the Spanish succession during the later seventeenth and early eighteenth centuries, and partly because they have an illustrative quality, enabling us to observe proprietary dynasticism at work.

The materials upon which this study is based are the result both of deliberate investigation and of serendipitous discoveries in the course of work directed to other topics. Indeed, my conviction that the theme of proprietary dynasticism was not a quest for the obvious resulted from the realization that even the most perceptive historians sought to handle the problem on an "as if" basis, treating proprietary dynasticism as essentially something else, something more "real" and at least more familiar,[7] while for the most part it was simply not observed at all. It was also encouraging to find materials that could be understood directly and without the necessity for elaborate explanation: historians wishing to display their abilities at *hineininterpretieren* have more than enough occasions when straightforward understanding is not possible. Furthermore, a historical vision that brings clearly before us structures and events that we have previously overlooked and that enables us to see them plain, without twisting the patent meaning of our sources, is likely to be both true and useful.

3

The judgment as to whether this has been achieved in this book belongs of course not to its author but to its readers.

An aspect of proprietary dynasticism that has special significance for our study is the way in which it involves so many other aspects of political life. Most of all, it brings down from the realms of abstract theory the debate over the role of the state in society: whether it is defined essentially by its assigned moral role, or is no more than an instrument of human action, as value neutral as a tract of land or a hammer; and, in either case, which human group or groups it serves. Other questions concern the delegation of authority and the nature of political representation; the relation and the distinction between political and nonpolitical obligations and compulsions; the distinction between public and private, the community, the family or other intermediate group, and the individual.[8] This is not to say that all or any of these questions can be wholly comprehended from the perspective of the ownership of political power. Quite the contrary: our aim is only to add a view of the matter that has been missing from historical investigation and that was significant to contemporaries. Without this view the specific character of early modern political history cannot be fully grasped or understood, and hence the full nature of the change to the modern political order cannot either.

CHAPTER I

PROPRIETARY DYNASTICISM
IN ANCIENT
AND MEDIEVAL TIMES

T HE SEARCH for understanding what in our definition is a modern phenomenon takes a historian back to origins.[1] Yet, in looking for beginnings of proprietary dynasticism too far back, it is difficult to be sure that what we are observing is anything like what we are studying. One historian of ancient Egypt, asking whether the country was "the personal property of its sovereign, who exploited it as he would a private estate," or "a state . . . which he had received the mission of administering," goes on to note that the two ideas coexisted, or rather that the contemporaries were not aware of any conflict between them. Yet there was one, potentially, in the idea that because the sovereign had moral obligations, there was a state that existed independently of the person of the ruler, even if he was a man-god.[2] In classical Greece, of course, the ruler was all man and not at all god: not until Alexander conquered Asia (obviously in its limited contemporaneous sense) did the notion of the divinity of the ruler take hold in the West. It was Alexander's teacher, Aristotle, who provided, however, the fundamental ideas about the state upon which political thought in the West was to build for all subsequent ages. He laid down, as Plato had done before him, that the state, like all other associations, was established with a moral aim.[3] The aim of a king was to act as "a guardian of society," unlike the tyrant, who sought only "his own pleasure."[4] This distinction between good rule and misrule was incorporated into his matrix of forms of government, along with the number of rulers in a state.

The Romans, adding a sharpened sense and definition of property, built upon the Greek ideas to establish their own political theory. Private property was defined as patrimony, the wealth possessed by the head of a family with the rights of use, abuse, and free disposal.[5] The bounds of such property rights lay not so much in countervailing rights of members of the family as in the interests of neighbors and the state.[6] Property rights were essentially rights over *things*.[7] Such *dominium* was distinguished from property rights over persons, that is, slavery, not by Aristotle's metaphysical definition of slaves as living tools (that is, things), but as explicitly analogical, under the term *potestas dominica*.[8] Private property was therefore set absolutely apart from public property, which the Roman people (or their successors, the *principes* or emperors) held in their common, political capacity.[9] Indeed, the very term by which public property was called, *res publica* (public thing), came in time to be used for political power in general, that is, the state or "republic."[10] The emperor or prince ruled over the state, but he did not own it, as he did his private property (patrimony). Yet political power passed to a successor in office, an heir, somewhat like a patrimony.[11]

The great change came about with the conquest of the West by the Germanic peoples that formed the bridge between antiquity and the middle ages. During the medieval period the institution of proprietary dynasticism came into existence as a specific and explicit problem, and the terms in which it was understood in the succeeding centuries of the early modern period were defined then. Because the phenomenon we are studying was in the medieval period broadly European as well as specifically French, we observe in this chapter first the general and then the French developments, the latter as a specific case of the former.

THE GERMANS before their conquest of the Roman world in the West did not possess a clear notion of the state, for their "king" was a war leader rather than an administrator of a system of public order and law. Their notions of property were fixed upon the family rather than the individual.[12] Their institutions and their ideas had to change, however, when they became the new rulers, especially in Gaul. On the one hand, they were conquerors to whom their realms were simple objects of exploitation. To the extent that they understood the notion of property at all, they considered their new kingdoms as their property, and the distinction between public and private would have baffled them.[13] Had they continued on this road without diversion, their rule would not have been essentially different from that of the Ottoman Turks some centuries later, who chose to exact tribute from subject peoples without any notion of obligation to them, rather than to collect taxes conceived fundamentally as payments for the services of the state made by those it ruled. When, however, the Germans were converted to Christianity as part of the process of assimilating to the countries they had seized, this meant accepting the Christian principle that the public power is established by God for the sake of the ruled. The conquering German kings could play for some centuries the part of warlords enjoying their loot in traditional fashion, battling among themselves for greater shares; but slowly and surely they came under the influence of bishops who saw the kingship as an office like their own, at the service of those who served them. (The office conception of regal power was reinforced by its description as a "dignity," a hierarchical rather than a functional notion, but with an almost identical content.) This trend was strengthened with the establishment of the Carolingian empire, which applied its synthesis of Frankish and Roman institutions not only in Frankish Gaul but also in the old Germanic homeland beyond the Rhine. The tension between their old, exploitative, self-serving notion of rule and the Aristotelian–Christian conception was softened but not dissolved during the Carolingian period. It was not until the breakup of the Carolingian empire, whether from the effect of internal forces or the shock of the Viking incursions, giving rise to the political-economic system we call feudalism, that we enter into the high middle ages and see the problem of proprietary dynasticism come to the fore.

The proprietary character of early modern dynastic monarchy arose out of the feudal element in medieval kingship. Feudalism was the key fact of later medieval monarchy; the higher was formed by the lower.[14] Feudalism was significant in the rise of proprietary dynasticism not so much because it meant the grant of almost all rights of regional and local government to vassals, who obtained their fiefs as recompense for the performance of (primarily military) services, as because the fief, like the ancient Egyptian pharaonic monarchy, was both political and economic in character. Indeed, until the revival of Roman law made men trained to theoretical thought able to distinguish economics from government, property from power, the fief did not really combine distinct political and economic elements; men simply did not make such a distinction. Therefore, as the king became the capstone of the feudal pyramid, he became part of the system of feudalism, with all its implications. The royal power was at once political and economic in the same way that a vassal's was.

The merging of economics and politics is conceivable without the idea of property (as in modern socialist societies, although there are those who depict the power holders in such countries as in fact, if not in name, the property owners as well). But in medieval Europe the notion of property was omnipresent and virtually unquestioned in its essence.[15] What could be described as "mine and not thine" was property—and in fact property means literally the quality of being one's own. By contemporary conceptions, to say that vassals could have fiefs as their own while the kings held their crowns by no greater or even by lesser right would have been to malign monarchy. Yet this followed inescapably from the theory that kingship is an office. For an office is defined by its function, and if the function of kingship is, as Thomas Aquinas wrote, to "guide the people of a city or a country for the sake of the common good," if, as Thomas's continuator Ptolemy of Lucca wrote, "the kingship does not exist for the sake of the king, but the king for the sake of the kingdom," then the conclusion clearly followed that failure to perform this duty warranted removal from office or at least punishment by God.[16] The crucial question, of course, was who passed such a judgment. The great medieval conflicts between popes and the emperors and the kings of France revolved precisely about the claims of the popes, as Christ's vicars, to hold secular rulers, even the loftiest, to account, and to depose them if their offenses were sufficiently grave. The imperial and regal resistance to these claims had been the specific occasion for the development of theories of princely sovereignty to set against papal pretensions. But sovereignty was directed not only against the princes' external rivals but also against their competitors from below within their own countries. Theories that gave to princes a monopoly of all legitimate power conflicted with the vassals' sense of their right to participate in important decisions. Baronial rebellions were a reminder that vassals' rights were a matter not only of theory but also of hard practice.[17] There were many ways of defining these competing rights, but important among them were those set in terms of property. Princes claimed that supreme power belonged solely to themselves; barons and towns replied that they too had a share in power, which ultimately belonged to the people.

With the right to political power defined in terms of property, the meaning of property-in-power depended upon the character of contemporary property conceptions. But the medieval world did not evolve a clear doctrine of property, one that distinguished it in particular from lordship or political rule.[18] Far and away the predominant kind of property was land; most movable objects were consumption goods, not means of producing income; and dignities, offices, and sums of money were equated to land as "tenures."[19] The legists attempted to apply the rediscovered Roman law to landed property, but even their most brilliant efforts could not make the essential Roman idea of freehold property (to which they gave the name *allodium*, derived from a German word for "whole property" or "directly inherited property")[20] fit the case of feudalism and manorialism. For in freehold there was only one owner of any given piece of land, subject, it is true, to payment of taxes to the government; the use of land might be granted out, but the tenant who paid for its use in no sense whatever shared in its ownership. In feudalism, on the contrary, all land was considered to be held conditionally (and even kings were considered to hold their realms of God, the only true absolute owner), and there were multiple holders of rights, some of tillage and other forms of direct exploitation of the soil, others of revenues from the land in the form of dues, rents, and taxes, all of which were considered to be property. Thus the notion of property shifted its object from land to rights connected with the land.[21] (It might be held, in precise formal analysis, that property always has to do with rights and not with the things over which rights are held; but we are concerned here to note what people at a given period and place considered property to be.) During the late medieval age and down through the early modern period of European history, feudalism in the strict sense, as the grant of fiefs, came to be more and more of a legal fiction, with fiefs held in practice on a permanent basis, with only nominal requirements of service. In the manors, on the other hand, the multiplicity of rights continued little shaken in most countries of western and central Europe until the revolutionary age at the end of the eighteenth and the beginning of the nineteenth centuries. But even here the principle that manorial dues were paid in exchange for the grant of rights of exploitation came to be a dead letter, and the payments were considered to be impediments upon the effective owners rather than shares in ownership. This was part of the large-scale commercialization of

European life over these centuries, taking place not only in the towns but also in the countryside. The significant point is the emergence, within the framework of feudal-manorial property forms, of a sense of property that was essentially allodial. There was a reversion in fact if not yet in law to the old Roman principle that land ownership was indivisible, that a tenant in no sense shared in ownership.[22] It is a central argument of this book that the property notions that helped to shape dynastic monarchy in early modern Europe were allodial, but that the institution itself remained essentially a vestige of feudalism,[23] and that the conflict of these two notions, although not glimpsed in these terms, nonetheless was an important aspect of the undercutting of dynastic monarchy at the end of the early modern epoch.

At the same time that this was happening, the elements of the notion of an abstract, impersonal (or suprapersonal) state, distinct from the person and the will of the ruler, began to be sharpened and strengthened.[24] It arose, however, not immediately from the experience of monarchical states but from that of the Italian city-state republics, where the term "state" (*il stato*) shifted its meaning from the status of holding power to the power itself.[25] Although feudal law might treat office as proprietary, it was an institution whose very character tended to undermine the attempt to make it an object of ownership[26] (or, at the least, required the development of an idea of hereditary obligation). There was a gradual, if only partial, differentiation between the king's private purse and the public treasury, which the legists dubbed with the Roman name of fisc. The prince held the public treasury not by his own right (that is, as property), but by virtue of his regal office.[27] The rejection of a proprietary attitude toward kingship (or the imperial crown) was made explicit in a famous anecdote about the emperor Frederick Barbarossa and two legists, Martinus and Bulgarus, with whom he was riding horseback. "Am I lord of the world?" he asked. Martinus, referring to the passage in the Code of Justinian saying that everything should be considered as belonging to the prince, affirmed that he was such indeed. "No," Bulgarus replied, "the prince is not master of his subjects' property." The anecdote, an apocryphal adaptation of an episode about an earlier ruler and the legists Azo and Lothair, was to remain central to the debate over proprietary dynasticism for centuries.[28]

To assert, as one medieval historian does, that the kings came to "treat their rights as private property,"[29] is not literally correct, not because they did not consider themselves owners of their crowns, but because the distinction between public and private was not clearly made in the medieval world as it was in either the Roman or the modern.[30] The distinction began to be seen, partly under the influence of the revived study of Roman law, but also under the impact of struggles between rulers and ruled, which came to be restated as struggles between public and private rights, and because the transmission of the royal crown was overwhelmingly guided by private-law practices.[31] The hereditary transmission of the crown was an embarrassment to the legists who upheld the theory of kingship as an office. They developed all sorts of subtle ways to get around the problem, principally the notion that the kings were somehow not heirs of their predecessors but merely successors.[32] But both public and private dominion alike represented, if not absolute property rights, at least the right of lawful possession.[33] If tyranny was defined, therefore, as unlawful possession, as was done by the famed legist Bartolus of Sassoferrato, it could be criminal for either of two reasons: because the tyrant was a usurper, who did not have rightful possession of the crown even if he used his powers to rule his people for their benefit; or because the tyrant ruled against their interest and to his own advantage, even though he might be the lawful owner of the crown.[34]

———— •◆• ————

THE PATTERN of development presented in the previous

pages applied generally throughout Western Europe, although with many variations and according to the specific historical conditions of each country. There were significant differences from it even in France, the country of our special attention in this book and the one that most strongly shaped the general picture. Perhaps the most important idiosyncrasy in the French situation was that the most highly advanced feudalism and the strongest monarchy were both found there. In addition, it was the country in which the combination of Roman and Germanic traditions and institutions was most complete. It was the country that practiced customary law in one part of the land and a modified Roman law (*droit écrit*) in another part. Paradox and contradictoriness were therefore characteristic of the French political scene.

France came into being as the kingdom of the Franks late in the fifth century under Clovis. Although newly Christianized, the Franks could comprehend well enough the power of the Roman state that they took over in Gaul, but they had no grasp of what the Romans meant by *res publica*.[35] They saw it only as power over men and land, and themselves as the new Roman ruling class; but they understood Rome in the light of their own national experience, not as the Romans themselves had thought of it. The abstract notion of the state that the Romans had evolved was mere words to them. To them, Gaul, now Frankland, Francia, was theirs to use for their own advantage, without any particular obligation to the population they ruled. It was their booty which belonged to their king and which they shared with him as his followers. Olivier-Martin, the outstanding French historian of law, has summed up their attitude in a phrase: "the kingdom of France was the king's thing; . . . there was no 'public thing'; the state belonged to him." It was what the Romans called a patrimony. The king did what he wanted with it, as he had done with what was his own before the conquest, subject only to the ordinary customs of his people. He did not divide the kingdom as such among his heirs, because that had not been done before; but he did divide its rule among his sons and heirs, because that was what had been done before; and he excluded his daughters because Frankish custom excluded girls, who could not serve in the army, from inheritance of land.[36] The proprietary and even patrimonial vision of the kingship was not one that would disappear easily in the history of France,[37] although it would be attacked directly again and again and adapted to other notions by those who would not or simply could not abandon it. But there was also a consequence that later generations would not forget. The partition of rule among Clovis's sons and descendants led to the fiercest internecine war, with the danger of breakup of the realm.[38] It was a peril that was increased by the practice of outright gifts of land to leading followers along with the titles of count and duke. The land came from the royal domains, the land that had been owned by the state under the Romans and was taken over by the Frankish kings.[39] So long as the Merovingian dynasty descended from Clovis remained on the throne, this wild policy, which could ill distinguish rule from plunder, continued.[40]

A clearer family commitment, preserving and improving the present for the sake of future generations, and a sense of public duty—the idea of kingship as office—were required to bring about a change in the relationship between kings and their realms.[41] This was the work first of the Carolingian dynasty, which displaced the "do-nothing" Merovingians in 751, and then of the Capetian dynasty which took over the crown from the decrepit late Carolingians in 987. With the coronation of Charlemagne as emperor at Rome in 800, the Carolingians established themselves as the heirs of the Roman empire in the West, and deliberately modeled themselves upon the Roman emperors. In this capacity, the Frankish king-emperors saw themselves as supreme lords. They accepted and to some degree—certainly to a large degree with Charlemagne himself—understood the notion of their post of supremacy as an office. This was implicit in the use of the rite of unction in the coronation of the first Carolingian, Pepin, for it made of the kingship, if not a priestly office, something that was at least in part ecclesiastical, by making explicit and visible the theory that the king and his line were divinely chosen.[42] But they continued to look upon the kingdom as something owned by their family. To be sure, Pepin himself had been elected by the magnates and the bishops, with the approval of the pope, and the form of election became part of the coronation ceremony for the kings who came after him; but the election was more an acclamation than a choice. That it removed the patrimonial character of the kingship, as one historian suggests,[43] is dubious. The crown passed down the line of masculine descent, and partition continued to be practiced as it had been under the Merovingians. The combined electoral and proprietary character of the crown was expressed in Charlemagne's testament of 806, dividing his realm among his three sons: in it he talks of the "election" of a grandson to the "heritage of the kingdom."[44] But the royal "vocation" belonged not to an individual, but to a lineage.[45] It was an argument that was not to the liking of the churchmen, and in 829 the council of Paris proclaimed that the king did not hold his kingdom from his ancestors but from God.[46] The principle had to be reaffirmed when Hugh Capet was elected to the kingship in 987. At the assembly of Senlis, Adalberon, archbishop of Reims, admitted that the partisans of Charles of Lorraine, uncle of the late Carolingian king, "claim that the throne belongs to him by right of birth." No, he replied, "the kingship is not acquired by hereditary right."[47] The formula "by the grace of God," by which the idea of divine gift of the kingship was later expressed, did not therefore imply in the eyes of those who bestowed it on the kings a hereditary right; but it did so already in the eyes of those who received the grant.[48] The conflict of beliefs could not be more clear, and it would not be solved during the eight hundred years that the Capetian dynasty would reign over France.

It was during the first centuries of their rule that feudalism became the predominant political form in France. It represented an alternative form of state. To assume, as does Olivier-Martin, that only a central and centralized national government, represented in this period by the institution of royalty, embodies the "idea of the state," and that under feudalism there is almost no "state organization,"[49] is to commit the historical sin of anachronism, to fail to understand an earlier age on its own terms. Feudalism was a different form of political organization, and it shaped royalty to its own characteristics for a long time.[50] But feudalism did not end political conflict—far from it!—and in the competition of power and for power, the king represented the only significant potential for the unification of government throughout the land.[51] Feudal dispersal of power was in itself hardly good for the kingship; feudalism happened to kings, they did not deliberately create it.[52] But they accepted it as part of the conditions of the time. In any case, for centuries they had no real alternative. The kingdom became the highest feudal tenure, held of God himself but of no human being;[53] it was a lordship (seigneurie) like that of vassals and rearvassals down to the holders of manors, and therefore held as property. Even more than other lordships, however, it was held not as patrimony (in the Roman sense of wealth at the free disposal of the owner)[54] but as a family possession, which the living owner could not sell or give away, or otherwise disperse. The same limitations were placed upon the royal domain; although the king held these lands (and other rights) not as supreme overlord but in the same capacity as any vassal (that is, his revenues were received and his rights exercised not as king of France but as, say, duke of Aquitaine or count of Soissons), he could not alienate them any more than the crown itself.[55] It is revealing of the tendency of the kings to merge their personal and public capacities that the terms "royal domain" and "domain of the crown" came to be used not only for land, but also for the ordinary revenues of the crown.[56] But the character of the property rights of the royal domain is not really central to the problem at hand, because of the equivalence of the domain's rights to those of private proprietors. What concerns us, rather, is whether or not, and if so how, the crown itself as the symbol of the power of legitimate kingship, the kingdom not as land but as the right of rule over the land, was the property of the dynasty. It is a distinction with a very large difference.

Whatever the practice, the theory of kingship became more insistently than ever a doctrine of royal office. Even when the kings began to extend their claims within the feudal system, they would do so upon the basis that they, and they alone, served the general, common interest.[57] It is in the light of these claims that Olivier-Martin asserts that Hugh Capet was not a feudal king but a feudal lord (*féodal*) who became the king, and that as king he still incarnated the idea of the state.[58] Churchmen continued to expand the idea of kingship as an office created by God to serve the public welfare and the needs of the churches.[59] Yves de Chartres expressed the idea when Henry I ascended the throne of England in 1100: "Never forget it, Prince: You are the servant of the servants of God [priests] and not their master; you are the protector and not the owner of your people."[60] This idea could easily conflict with the hereditary character of the monarchy. Why should we obey an infant king? asked the barons when Louis IX, a minor, came to the throne in 1226. That a child who could not govern himself reigned over them obviously ran athwart the notion that the king served his people by ruling them.[61] However, at the level of popular belief, far more important, and even contradictory to this utilitarian notion, there continued to exist the feeling that kings possessed supernatural, even magical, qualities, as transmitted in the coronation and demonstrated in their power to cure scrofula by touching the victim.[62] This sacral notion conflicted, however, with the tendency to look at the king as distinct from the state, to "depersonalize" the state, in the words of one historian.[63] It was a tendency that was not followed through in the medieval period. The legists, after all, were servants of the monarchy interested in strengthening the king's powers and dignity, and, as the notion of the state as the formal and explicit political organization of a country began to emerge, they identified it with the king.[64]

To set the office theory of kingship against the proprietary attitude was to argue over principles; the crucial fact that had to be contended with was that the throne was inherited and that the inheritance followed broadly the rules for the devolution of property that held sway in the civil society. Under the Capetians the rules were adapted to the special requirements of effective rule, which had been made clear by the experience of the Merovingian and Carolingian kings. One was that the realm was not to be divided among the heirs but passed to the oldest son. This simple rule worked well enough if the oldest son was alive to take over his inheritance; complications arose when he had died before his father. Over the centuries the rule was clarified to take care of a whole variety of contingencies as these arose. The principle evolved of exhausting each line of male descent in succession through all the generations before moving across the line of surviving sons, each of whom provided a sequence of male descendants that had to be exhausted before the next line was taken up. During the first three centuries of Capetian rule, the question of succession of of a woman did not arise.

It was recognized by Olivier-Martin, who is one of the most notable modern supporters of the office theory of Capetian kingship, that the hereditary character of the monarchy conflicted with the view that kingship was an office. He sought to get around the problem by subtle analysis. Since the kingship was by definition an office, it could not be property; therefore it was passed down to the king's descendants "according to its own ends, in the interest of the people and not that of members of the royal family."[65] Only one who takes a theory to be more real than reality would be persuaded by such an argument; it may be doubted that the members of the royal family would have accepted it. And one wonders how much more persuasive it would have been, presented in the form that there were "two distinct personalities, the king and the royal dignity made incarnate in the crown," and bound together by a "mystical and indissoluble marriage," with the crown the stronger partner, because it imposes its laws upon the king.[66] This is, of course, the theory of the king's two bodies, expounded with vast erudition and subtle analysis by Kantorowicz.[67] But it possesses the same weakness as the office theory of kingship, a wealth of evidence that it was held by theorists but very little that it affected concrete action, because it disregards the common practice of human beings of accepting a theory that they think they follow but going their own way nonetheless, unaware or unconcerned that they are violating their own principles.[68]

The most important of the limitations upon the king's rights over the crown was, as we have seen, that he could not change the law of succession. During the early fourteenth century this law was clarified because of the crisis over the succession of Louis X, who had not even reigned two years, in 1316. His posthumous son, John I, lived less than a week, and his only living survivor was Jeanne, a daughter by his first marriage. An issue arose that had not been posed for three hundred years because there had always been a son to inherit from his father. It had never been questioned that sons inherited ahead of daughters, but what if there were no surviving direct male descendants but only a daughter? Did she inherit the throne, in the same way that women could inherit fiefs in most parts of France in default of qualified males? The elder of the late king's two brothers took the issue in hand by proclaiming his own accession as Philip V, and he was supported by a national council of barons, prelates, burghers, and professors, who enunciated the principle that "a woman does not succeed to the kingdom of France." To defend what supporters of Jeanne called an illegal innovation, the king's lawyers found two fundamental arguments. One was that the

French kingship was equivalent to the imperial throne, which was barred to women (they did not urge, however, that the French throne be made elective, like the emperor's!), but this was too contrived a theory to carry much weight. More important was the principle that only men could inherit land. Was it mere accident that there had been no queen regnant—a woman who reigned by her own right, not as consort of a king regnant—since Clovis? Or had the rule of royal succession bowed to contemporary feudal law and practice?[69]

It was a question that would not go away, for Philip V died in 1322 with only two daughters and no surviving son to succeed him. His brother, Charles IV, hereupon took the throne, but himself died in 1328 with only a daughter to follow him. In the case of both Philip and Charles, the rule of male primogeniture had been applied, but usage had not been long enough to put the question beyond doubt. The throne was now claimed by Philip of Valois, first cousin of the last three kings, because he was the closest male descendant of Philip III (reigned 1270–1285), the father of Philip IV, and by Edward III, king of England, because his mother, queen Isabella of England, had been the only surviving daughter of Philip IV. There could be no clearer confrontation over the principle of male primogeniture. If a woman could succeed to the throne or transmit to her progeny a claim to it, then the line of primogeniture had not been exhausted and Edward would succeed to the throne of France, bringing the two kingdoms of England and France into personal union. On the other hand, for Philip of Valois to succeed, not only must the rule of male primogeniture bar women from inheriting the crown; it must also keep them from transmitting a right to its possession. And this was what was decided by an assembly of French barons, that "no woman *nor her son* could succeed to the monarchy [emphasis added]." Robert of Artois affirmed that the crown "is not a patrimonial possession [*bien de patrimoine*]," but not upon the basis of the office theory of kingship; he cited rather the principle that princes do not have "free disposition" of the crown but only its "enjoyment" (jouissance)—what is known in property law as usufruct— and that they were called to the throne by the fundamental laws.[70] Even when the office theory of kingship was argued in the future, it was to face important competition from the usufructuary theory, which treated the crown as property of a special kind.

The issue of male primogeniture came to the fore again early in the fifteenth century. King Charles VI, angry at his heir, the Dauphin, declared him to be disinherited; at the same time, Henry V of England invaded France to reassert the claims on the French throne made almost a century before by Edward III and won the great victory of Agincourt in 1415 to buttress his pretensions. Around 1418 or 1419, a legist named Jean de Terre Rouge came to the defence of the Dauphin's cause in a treatise on "the law of legitimate succession in the inheritance of the crown of France."[71] The realm of France, Terre Rouge asserted, was possessed not as patrimony or even as an inheritance, but by a right of "power and royal authority." During his father's lifetime the Dauphin already shared with him lordship "over things which belong to the latter." The living king had no right to control the succession to the kingdom; the law of succession followed the ancient custom of the kingdom and had been decided according to the interest of the public welfare. "The right which the king has over his realm is of a completely different nature from the right of a proprietor over his estate."[72] This was a valiant effort to reconcile the office and the proprietary conceptions of kingship. Even as he denied that the kingdom was a patrimony, Terre Rouge allowed the terminology of ownership to slip into his formulations. But that, after all, was all that was necessary; he was not trying to assert the right of the "nation" to choose its ruler (although the possibility lay implicit just below the surface of the office theory), but only the rights of the Dauphin against his father and a would-be usurper.

The point of Terre Rouge's argument became all the more

clear in 1420 when Charles VI accepted the treaty of Troyes with Henry V, which declared the "so-called Dauphin" to be illegitimate and the English monarch, "our son," the rightful successor. The treaty proclaimed the eventual union of the two kingdoms under the same person to be perpetual. As if this were not enough, the king gave his daughter Catherine to Henry for his wife (for if the rule of female exclusion did not hold, she could bring her own rights of succession to her husband).[73] With Henry still a conquering hero—his army continued to march across France, driving the Dauphin's forces before it—the Sorbonne and the Estates General approved the treaty in 1421. (The struggle had been complicated by the party passions of two contending factions, the Burgundians and the Armagnacs.)

Charles VI died in 1422, shortly after Henry V, but the Dauphin could not go to Reims, the traditional site for the coronation, because the English victories on the battlefield continued. Charles VII could do no more than maintain himself at Bourges until the startling emergence of Joan of Arc in 1429. The peasant girl from Lorraine, stirred by her visions to take up the cause of the "true king" of France, obtained from him the right to lead an army to the relief of Orleans, which the English had put under siege the year before. She succeeded, Charles was crowned the next year, and the course of the war was fundamentally changed, although the English did not finally withdraw from France until 1453, retaining only Calais. Joan, although abandoned by Charles after her capture by the Burgundians in 1430 and her burning at the stake by the English in 1431, had undone the treaty of Troyes.[74] She had explicitly defended the principle that the kingdom did not belong to the Dauphin or the king, but to "the King of Heaven," and the king of France held it only *in commendam*, in trust.[75] It was an ecclesiastical term taken from the ceremony of coronation, and it emphasized the religious character and obligations of the monarch; it was consonant with the office theory of kingship. Yet, as Joan's words about the realm belonging to God indicated, the notion of the country as the property of someone who ruled it was not utterly rejected. To cynical modern man, God's ownership may seem too ethereal to be taken seriously; but it was an idea that was anything but strange in Joan's time, and John Calvin a century later was to say much the same thing. Nonetheless, the overall effect of her achievement was beyond question. The English claim to the French throne was not made good; the principle of male primogeniture was reaffirmed in practice; and the office theory of kingship was immensely strengthened. It did not, however, succeed in totally displacing the proprietary conception.

The doctrine that the kingdom was not a patrimony implied that the king had no right to give up any part of it. In 1440 Charles VII was ready to make peace with England and to cede Normandy as the price for it. Jean Juvenal des Ursins, the bishop of Laon, opposed peace on such a condition. You have no right to cede Normandy, he told the king: it does not belong to you but to the crown, "of which you are only the administrator, tutor, curator and procurator."[76] The crown, as the symbol of the kingship, might own the province; but the crown itself did not belong to the king. Yet even in this case we find a subtle interplay of office and proprietary theories. For Des Ursins, like Joan and so many before him, still acknowledged that the relationship between rulers and their realm was proprietary, but they put an intermediate term, the crown (or what would later be called the "state"), between king and kingdom. An imbalance was introduced, however: the crown was the owner of the country, but the king was not the owner of the crown. His role was usually defined, as Des Ursins had done, as that of an administrator of an inalienable inheritance.[77] The term "administrator" itself came from property law: property notions still permeated the office theory of kingship, although the use of the terms "tutor" and "curator," which came from the law of persons, showed that the sense of property did not operate in isolation.

The final French victory in 1453 settled the matter. The principle of male primogeniture became a fundamental law of the French monarchy, and although the English monarchs carried the French fleur-de-lys in their coat of arms for centuries, they made no effort to enforce their claim to be rightful kings of France (and queens—for if Henry VIII was in law king of France, then his daughters should have been queens of France). It was the French, after all, who, short of military defeat and conquest, decided which law held in their country, and they accepted the law of male primogeniture in the devolution of the crown.

What was also decided by the acceptance of this principle was that France would not be ruled by a foreign king who married a reigning French queen, or by one who succeeded after her marriage. The rule of male primogeniture did permit personal union with another kingdom in the case of a French king's inheritance of a foreign crown—a possibility that was to be a central problem in the conflict over the Spanish succession in the late seventeenth and early eighteenth centuries. In both cases it was obvious that the interest not only of the reigning dynasty but also of the nation at large was involved, but to give that interest force in determining who would reign and rule was to introduce a limitation upon the strict right of possession of the crown, to emphasize the office theory of the crown at the expense of its proprietary character.[78]

The same troubling use of contradictory conceptions was present in 1483, when Charles VIII came to the throne at the age of scarce thirteen years. At the Estates General called the next year, the jurist Philippe Pot argued not only against the willingness of the regent, the king's elder sister Anne de Beaujeu, to give away portions of the kingdom; he also raised the question of the residual right of the nation to determine the future of the country in the absence of any effective king.

Indeed, he affirmed, when the king is a minor, "the government and the right to dispose of it return to the people, not to a prince or a part of the people but to all Frenchmen, because in the last analysis a long vacancy or a bad regency turns to the detriment of them alone. I do not mean that the right to reign or ownership of the supreme power passes to other persons than the king, but only that the regency and the administration of the kingdom are not his property and belong temporarily to the people or to those they elect."[79] However powerful a statement of the ultimate rights of the people over their government this may be, it is not an unequivocal statement of the office theory of kingship. There is in it no denial that the supreme power is property, but only a statement of whom it belongs to, both ordinarily and under special conditions. There is no denial, either, of the hereditary character of the kingdom.

And it was well that there was none, for both the new king, when he was grown, and his successor, Louis XII, launched wars into Italy to gain possession of lands (Naples in the former instance, Milan in the latter) that they claimed by rights of inheritance, through women, it may be noted.[80] Significantly, Louis XII resisted the customary merger of his privately owned lands (those not held as royal apanages) into the royal domain, for he wanted to give them to his daughter Claude as a dowry in a proposed marriage to the archduke of Austria. But he withdrew this project and married her instead to his heir, count Francis of Angoulême, who succeeded to the throne in 1515.[81] The principle that the king had no private property was confirmed.[82] He owned nothing but the state itself! Yet the same Louis XII could speak of himself as an "officer of the crown."[83] But he was an officer who managed to spend the last years of his reign in a project for dynastic marriage with little or no visible advantage to the "state," that is, the French political entity.[84] What is an office that does not put its mark upon the man who holds it but on the contrary is shaped by him? The problem would confront the French monarchy for the next three centuries.

———————•◆•———————

BY THIS TIME the principle of male primogeniture in the transmission of the throne was acquiring a name, the Salic Law. This was the popular law of the Salian Franks as set down under Clovis and modified under his immediate successors; its original text has not been preserved. One of its provisions excluded women from inheritance of lands, especially the estates of the magnates. The Salic Law passed into disuse and was forgotten for centuries. By mid-fourteenth century it had been rediscovered, but it was not until the 1380s that it was applied to the exclusion of women from the French throne and used to explain the case of 1328. During the fifteenth century use of the term became more frequent, and by the sixteenth century it became commonplace for the principle of the exclusion of women from the throne. So popular was it that it became a cover-all term for all the fundamental laws of the French monarchy on the royal succession, but by the seventeenth century it declined to merely learned usage among jurists and historians.[85]

CHAPTER II

THEORY BEFORE PRACTICE
The Debate on Kingship
in Sixteenth-Century France

F RANCE ENTERED the sixteenth century with just two fundamental laws governing the kingship that were established in both principle and practice. The first was that the
succession to the throne followed the rule of male primogeniture, the second that the royal domain was inalienable. There
was no law concerning the king's religion; it was taken for
granted that he would be a Roman Catholic, although with
the advent of Protestantism in the form of the Huguenot
party later in the century the question was opened wide.
There was much discussion of the nature of kingship itself,
building upon earlier ideas but adding to them the novel
term of "the state," taken from the Italians, for political
power in the abstract.[1] Because apt names enable men to fix
and isolate their experience, the new word became a political
fact of increasing importance; it helped the politically aware
class in France to grasp more surely the idea of an impersonal
and even permanent, changeless institution embodying the
quest for the common weal, the public good.[2] When applied
to the continuing tension between the office and the proprietary notions of the kingship, the term "state" split into
two meanings. One, building upon the abstract implications
of the word, reinforced the office theory by emphasizing the
ethical functions of the state; the other, bringing forward the
institutional character of the state, made of it something that
could be externalized not as an abstract purpose but as a tool
men used to achieve their actual goals.[3] Nowhere did the two

meanings of state come into collision more strongly, and with greater implications for the development of both political theory and political practice, than in France. The creation of an effective state for rule over men reached its greatest height during the early modern period in France; but it was also there that the idealization of the state—the word *Etat* in its political sense is always capitalized in French—was most advanced.

The new word reflected the growing strength of the royal power in France during the first six decades of the century. The country was involved in repeated foreign wars, the beginning of the rivalry with the House of Habsburg that was to last more than two centuries; but it was able to escape civil wars and thus hold off the threat of Habsburg power on all sides. The twin processes of modern state formation—professionalization and bureaucratization—continued steadily, bringing the country more and more fully under effective royal rule and giving flesh to the idea of the state. All but one of the virtually autonomous fiefdoms of medieval France passed out of existence. After the ill-fated Constable Charles of Bourbon was driven by the machinations of Louise of Savoy, the king's mother, to rise in rebellion against Francis I in 1523 and failed utterly to win anything more than sympathy from his fellow vassals,[4] there remained only the Foix and Albret counties in the southwest, bound in personal union since 1484 to the tiny independent kingdom of Navarre and the independent viscounty of Béarn.[5] Royal justice and royal administration were everywhere present, although seldom moving below the level of seigneurial rule in the manors to interfere in the governance of simple people. The number of paid royal administrators increased; however few by modern standards, they represented at the time an instrument of central power that was not matched anywhere else in Europe. The potentialities and perils that became visible in this emergent modern state furnished much of the impetus for the political debate that continued during the century, as well as the causes it took up.

Economic developments, too, had their impact upon the

debate, although more indirectly. Perhaps the most important was that the feudal system, in the strict sense of the holding of land conditionally upon the performance of military (and other) service, was enormously weakened. Most fiefs had become the virtual outright property of their holders, passed on by inheritance. The distinction between "useful domain," the right to the products of the land, and "direct (or eminent) domain," the right of property as such (ultimately belonging therefore only to the king), was changing. Useful domain was becoming the real ownership of the land, subject to certain traditional obligations, while direct domain was being reduced to the right to such dues and services.[6] Most of the requisite services had become nominal; the essential military obligation, the *arrière-ban*, proved ineffectual against highly professionalized mercenary armies and was seldom invoked except as a kind of tax on the nobility. Even within the manors, where the performance of services and the payment of dues were maintained unabated, the *laboureurs*, holders of land with rights of tillage, became virtual proprietors and their lands their hereditary patrimony. The tenant too was becoming a proprietor of a kind.[7] Thus the allodial sense of property, although generally absent in law, became more and more pervasive in fact. Feudalism—for the term continued to be current in France for both the system of vassalage and the underlying manorial-seigneurial order—ceased to correspond to the actual relations of property for which it was a formal juridical and economic system.[8] The *seigneurie* was becoming predominantly an economic entity, whose political functions therefore came to seem anomalous and unjustifiable.[9] This allodialism was not gainsaid by the fact that property owners seldom had free disposition of their estates by will, that is, patrimonialism in the strict Roman sense. Either the laws and customs of a region laid down limits within which the rights of the testator operated, or, especially in the country districts of northern France, it was rare to use wills at all.[10] Thus, modern historians who deny that the king was proprietor of the realm because he did not have the free testamentary disposal of his kingdom, which was the property of his family rather than his own individually, use an argument that carries too far: a claim that private Frenchmen did not have property—familial if not individual—would be obvious nonsense.[11] That the king owned his own realm was assumed by the Venetian ambassador Michele Suriano in a well-informed commentary upon the kingdom of France in 1561, in which he described the rule of primogeniture in force not only in the royal family but also in all the great noble houses. It was, he said, in accordance with the law of nature.[12]

This incipient allodialism brought about an essential shift in the elements of the property theory of the state. Property, which during the high middle ages had been conditional in character, now began to take on an absoluteness which was reflected in political debate, although the debaters were not usually aware of the change. During the next three centuries the question of royal absolutism was to become entangled in the question of the proprietary character of monarchy. Allodialism shaped the new absolutist theory of royalty by making sovereignty inherent in the king by right of birth, wholly personal although coming to him through his family. As the modern political theorist Carré de Malberg has put it, "This personal sovereignty of the prince therefore did not come to him from the state nor the juridical order established by the state; it belonged to him as an innate right prior to the state and any constitution." Sovereignty, the crown, was the gift of God: the theory of divine right was shifting its meaning from justification of royal authority to explanation of how it came to be in the hands of the reigning prince.[13] As Chancellor L'Hospital expressed it to the Estates General at Orleans in 1560–1561, "The king holds the crown not from us but from God and from the ancient law of the kingdom."[14] The parallelism to the changes in feudal property was remarkably precise. But it was in direct contradiction to the idea that the kingship was an office "confided to the king," in Olivier-Martin's language[15]—except that, in purely human terms, that which is confided by God is effectively innate![16]

The fact of inheritance rather than the particular pattern of rules controlling it created the sense of ownership. And the desire to bequeath what one possessed, even civil and military offices, was very powerful indeed. Even the legists who maintained most vehemently one or another form of the office theory of kingship found it difficult to avoid using proprietary terms when discussing specific cases. Claude de Seyssel, who had served Louis XII in high office, summed up his vision of the kingship in his *Grand Monarchy of France*, published in 1519, the year before his death. It was a traditional work, emphasizing that the king, although absolute within his own sphere, was bound by divine and natural law as well as by the fundamental laws of France. The monarch, Seyssel affirmed, was not the proprietor of the crown but only its executor.[17] Yet, arguing against unjust wars, which he identified as "for greediness to rule, for human glory, or other immoderate passion," Seyssel went on to call the only just war one fought to "regain one's own that has been improperly occupied."[18] As if this were not clear enough, in his *In Praise of the Good King of France, Louis, Twelfth of This Name*, Seyssel observed that the king held various duchies, counties, and lordships "in property and right [en propriété et droict]."[19] The same formulation was used by the papal nuncio, Ardingello, in making proposals for French reconquest of Milan: "if he [Francis I] desires that which is his own [chi desidera quel che à proprio]."[20] The French royal chancellor during the next reign, Olivier, admitted that Louis XII had received the duchy of Milan as a fief from the emperor in 1509. But a "right of inheritance" (hoirie) had been established thereby, even though the fiefs of the empire were not hereditary but benefices. But, he went on, French law made fiefs "patrimonial, passing by right of inheritance in succession like other heritages," which could be alienated without the permission of the bestowing lord, and could even be inherited by women.[21] To invoke the principle that

31

the laws and customs of the native land of the invested duke, when he was a king of France, controlled the succession of an imperial fief, rather than those of the empire itself, was certainly stretching the argument to the breaking point. But at the same time it displays dramatically how even jurists, when they were not arguing against the patrimonialism of the crown in the strict sense of the term, assumed its broad proprietary character.

In 1536 a member of the Parlement of Paris summed up the legists' position in a plea before the king: ". . . by the law of France we call Salic, and by the common, divine, and positive laws, the sacred patrimony of the Crown and the ancient domain of the Prince are not property for sale [ne tombe au commerce des hommes]." The king was "political husband" to the state (la chose publique), which brought him as her dowry at the coronation the royal domain, which he solemnly swore never to alienate.[22] The jurist Du Moulin, writing about 1539, could formally assert that the crown "is not properly hereditary, because the new king is not the heir of his predecessor and does not succeed him in the possession of his property [biens] nor in the heritage abandoned by the deceased, but he does succeed to the crown by right of blood, according to the Salic Law."[23] The assertion that the king did not inherit the crown but merely succeeded to it was a common way of attempting to overcome the ordinary view that nothing defined property more certainly than its being inherited, whether by law or by testament, and to take the kingship out of this class.[24] But Du Moulin himself, denying that subordinate magistrates had property in their offices, did so on the ground that imperium—the right of command—belonged only to the king and could not be transferred to them. Not only did this conflict with the developing practice of venality of office,[25] it also undercut Du Moulin's assertion that the crown was not proprietary.[26] Du Moulin was therefore another in the continuing chain of theorists who were forced into twisted logic by the effort to reconcile an accepted doctrine with contradictory practice.[27]

One of the strangest, yet often surprisingly perceptive minds in sixteenth-century France, Guillaume Postel, glimpsed one of the problems implicit in the proprietary theory of kingship. If ownership establishes the right to hold power and is transmitted by hereditary succession, then one would have to go back to the first owner; for, to as strict a mind as that of Postel, a right of conquest would be impermissible, being essentially the same thing as robbery. The first owner of the world was obviously Adam, to whom God had given dominion; but since the Deluge reduced mankind to Noah and his family, the sole survivors, it was necessary to trace dominion back to them following the rule of primogeniture. Noah's eldest son was Japhet, and his in turn was Gomer, who according to Josephus was the founder of the Celtic or Gallic nation and hence of France. The right of the monarchy of the world therefore "belongs by right only to the Prince elected by and with the consent of the Gallic people."[28] But Postel did not reconcile this view with another from his pen, that anyone who used the public power for his own profit was a "criminal."[29]

Another aspect of the influence of property ideas upon political thought was the contract theory of the origin of kingship. Contracts were primarily employed in the determination of property relationships, so that formally the theory of the political contract resulted from the transposition of the categories of property law to the relationships of public power (that is, as looked at from the modern point of view—we have noted that the medieval mind did not clearly distinguish the two, and they only began to separate in the early modern period). The theoreticians of emergent absolutism argued therefore that the power that may originally have been in the hands of the people had been transferred *irrevocably* to the kings, just as land that has been sold cannot be taken back at the whim of the seller.[30] How clearly this is a property theory of kingship can be seen if we set it against the pure office theory, for it removes the condition of the performance of a specific task from the right of possession.

The question of the proprietorship of the king was not only one simply of political command, the right to make policy, to name servants of the state, and to give justice to the people; it was also the right to tax. Chancellor Poyet under Francis I, in proclaiming that the king was proprietor of the kingdom, did so in order to affirm that the taxes he imposed were legitimate taking of subjects' property.[31] Michel de l'Hospital, the newly appointed chancellor at the beginning of the reign of Charles IX, used the same point in speaking to the Estates of Orleans. Kings, he said, should live as far as possible on their ordinary revenues and keep their taxes as low as possible, but he added an important distinction. Kings had the right to tax because "the wealth of their subjects belongs to them," but "as the rulers, not as the lords and proprietors [*imperio, non dominio et proprietate*]."[32] The distinction therefore fell between the king's claim to the throne and the sovereign's claim to the wealth of the nation: the former could be proprietary in character without violating subjects' rights to their own property; taxation was the taking of their wealth not for the king's own use but for the public welfare. The distinction was not made by Quintin, a professor of law at the University of Paris, speaking for the clergy. "Evil spirits" who whispered in the king's ear that everything belongs to him were "slanderous interpreters of the Judge Samuel."[33] That Quintin was arguing against proposals by the second and third estates that the crown tax the clergy is beside the point; what is to the point is the rejection of the view that taxation is the king's taking back his own property. Writing later in the century, another jurist, Du Haillan, held that even the levies that had originated in popular grant had become "patrimonial and hereditary to the kings."[34]

Proprietary dynasticism was displayed at its strongest in ordinary times in the conduct of foreign affairs, with the concern for family interests all too obvious. Francis I continued his predecessors' policies in this regard when he ascended the throne. His efforts to conquer Milan and Naples—which Charles VIII and Louis XII had failed to do—may not have expressed any clear or specific French "national" interest, but the political advantage to his family was undeniable.[35] The same was true of the peace that Henry II, Francis's son, made with Spain in 1559. Giving his daughter Elisabeth as wife to Philip II did not involve any territorial cession, but the duke of Savoy, on taking Henry's sister Marguerite for his bride, also regained possession of his lands on the western slopes of the Alps which had been conquered by the French. The advantage went to the dynasty, which made good marriages, but not to "France"[36]—if we wish to treat France as a living person, with interests like those of ordinary people. It was dynasticism such as this that prompted Charles IX to encourage the great poet Ronsard to write an epic, the *Franciade*, designed to trace back the king's ancestry through sixty-six sovereign rulers, to the most distant legendary antiquity. Indeed, the king was so in love with the project that he supervised the composition in person. It was not "ethnic" consciousness that prompted the work, a distinguished historian of ideas and literature writes, but "dynastic pride."[37]

———————◆———————

THE DEBATE over property dynasticism, as the account in the foregoing pages shows, remained essentially quiescent for the first part of the sixteenth century. Neither of the issues usually required to trigger active controversy over this theme—a disputed succession or accusations of royal misrule—was present in sufficiently strong form. Arguments were taken now and again from either the office or the proprietary theories of kingship to buttress one or another case, showing that both theories retained enough vigor to be worth arguing from. But the conflict between the two theories remained unsolved, and nothing essential was done to resolve it, either by bringing about the total victory of one side or by reconciling the differences in some higher synthesis. It was not until the Wars of Religion broke over France in the decade of the sixties that these questions were thrust forward again with immense cogency and passion. At first only the question of the relation of the Huguenots to a Catholic king was involved, giving rise to further debate over the tie between tyranny and proprietorship; but during the seventies and especially during the eighties, when it began to appear possible and even probable that the reigning king, Henry III, would not sire an heir to the throne, leaving as his successor under the Salic Law King Henry of Navarre, a Huguenot and head of the Bourbon branch of the French royal family, the issue of the law of succession joined the controversy over tyranny.

Huguenot political theory rested ultimately upon Calvin's reading of the Bible and the Christian tradition, and Calvin was anything but a revolutionary in his attitude toward government. If a king came to his throne legitimately (that is, was not a usurper), Calvin held, Christians had to obey him even if he were a "depraved and cruel tyrant," like Nebuchadnezzar.[38] Squandering the public revenue was tyranny, but taxation for public purposes and to maintain a life of splendor was not. Kings had the right to rule absolutely, but not to take the property of private persons; indeed, to see to it that "every person may enjoy his property without molestation" was one of a king's primary tasks.[39] But Calvin died in 1564, scarcely two years after the religious wars had begun in France; his political thinking had not been shaped by the new events but by the prior situation, when the question for Huguenots had been how to suffer repression and not how to defeat it by force of arms or even how to capture the state. His successor at the head of the Genevan regime and in the leadership of the international Huguenot movement, Theodore de Bèze (Beza), could not simply continue with Calvin's counsel of patience and prayer. It became necessary to play down the inherent

right of the king and to emphasize instead the office theory of
kingship, because one of the supreme tasks of a rightful
Christian king was to defend the true Christian church—
which in Huguenot eyes meant only their own. Bèze therefore
called the king only the highest of the magistrates, "the first
dignitary of the state."[40]

In France the Huguenots remained uncertain at first as to
how to define the relationship of the king to his crown and his
regal power. The Huguenot port of La Rochelle, in rebellion
in 1568, justified its action because kings who were enemies of
God "are no longer true kings but private persons."[41] But one
pamphleteer would not go so far: the king's power should be
upheld in its sanctity and inviolability, limited however by the
"majesty [which here means sovereignty] of his public personality, that is, making the welfare of his people part of himself."[42] (Note the little phrase "*his* people"—it required the
closest attention and extraordinary sensitivity to avoid the
possessive adjective of common usage.) For a brief period in
the early seventies, when the young king Charles IX accepted
the guidance of the Huguenot leader, Admiral Coligny, there
was reason to look for favorable treatment from the crown,
and perhaps even for more. The young Huguenot publicist and theorist Duplessis de Mornay early in 1572 wrote
an appeal to the king to urge that France undertake war
against Spain in the Low Countries. It would be a just war,
he argued, because the king of Spain had dispossessed Charles
of many of his "hereditary provinces," and then from taking his
"property" (*biens*) had moved to attack his honor. If Philip
II wanted to live up to his pretensions to justice, he should reestablish the French monarch "in his patrimonies."[43] But
Huguenot hopes built on royal favor turned to ashes in August
with the massacre of Saint Bartholomew's Eve in Paris and
the subsequent killing of Huguenots throughout the kingdom.
The Huguenots turned back to the arguments of arms, but
they did not abandon the war of words. Rather, they changed
their theories to emphasize that ultimate sovereignty in the

country rested in the nation, represented through its intermediate magistrates, who had the right to lead armed resistance to a tyrant and even to depose him. But even then they
could not escape putting the community's power in proprietary form, so that the question was not whether the state
power was owned, but who owned it.[44]

A brief civil war followed Saint Bartholomew's. It was
marked by the successful defense of La Rochelle against a
royal siege, and within a year the Huguenots were victorious—
in maintaining themselves, but not in gaining control of the
state. It was just then, in 1573, that the first major Huguenot
political tract appeared, the *Francogallia* of Francis Hotman,
a legist of sharp mind and potent pen. He built his argument
upon a historical premise, that what the Frankish kingdom
had been so many hundreds of years before determined what
should rightfully be at the time he was writing. The French
crown was "not subject to the law of inheritance as if it were
a private property," he wrote, "but was habitually transferred
by the votes and decisions of the estates and people." Even
though it was possible to speak of public property as belonging
"in a sense" to the king, it was at his disposal, not really his
property.[45] Nor did the rule of male primogeniture mean that
the kingdom was either hereditary or patrimonial; it "belongs
to the claimant by the mere right of filiation or of blood."[46]
The king owned only his patrimony or personal possessions
(which, since all fiefs and conquered territories became part of
the royal domain, meant in practice only movable objects);
the domain itself belonged to the "body of the people," and
the king had only its usufruct.[47] In the third edition, published
three years later, Hotman clarified his thought. The royal
domain was not the king's property but only a kind of inalienable dowry which he had the right to use but not to dispose
of.[48] The principle of male primogeniture in the royal succession did not derive from or depend upon the Salic Law, but
rested on "the practice and customs of the nation [which]
have acquired the force of written law." Indeed, it would have

been better to base the accession of Philip VI not upon the
rediscovered Salic Law but upon feudal laws excluding women
from the succession to fiefs (where they did succeed, these
should be called quasi-fiefs).[49] Hotman was here being too in-
ventive a debater, for by an appeal to feudal law he brought
back in through the back window the proprietary theory of
kingship which he had just driven out through the front door.
To admit that the right to the throne "belonged" to the
claimant by some objective rule, as he had just done in the
passage denying hereditary or patrimonial succession, was to
display how strong was the grip of the proprietary reality even
upon strong-minded thinkers.

Seven years after the appearance of Hotman's *Francogallia*,
another work came off the press written in far more powerful
language. Even its title was more explicit: *Vindiciae contra
tyrannos* ("A Defense against Tyrants"). The authorship, on
the contrary, was concealed behind a pseudonym, Stephanus
Junius Brutus. Probably two authors were involved, with
Duplessis de Mornay, now an adviser to the Huguenot King
Henry of Navarre, writing the first two parts, and Hubert
Languet, a Huguenot exile, the third and most important
part. The *Vindiciae* adapted to contemporary needs the old
principle of feudal law that bound vassals and kings in mutual
obligation; if either party violated what he was bound to do,
the other was released from his obligation. Thus, if the king
violated the rights of his vassals (and in the sixteenth century
this already meant his subjects), he lost his legal and moral
right to rule, even though the people might not be able to
depose him at the moment. But they had the *right* to do so.[50]
God, as the creator of the world, was its true owner. Kings
were only his servants and agents, and obedience was due to
them because of the master they served. The sharp Roman
distinction between authority, which belonged to the king,
and property, which belonged to subjects, was repeated. The
hereditary succession to the crown was not the consequence of
ownership but symbolized popular investiture; there had to be

at least an implicit election of the successor to the throne. The kingship was not the king's property but only either his posses sion or an office.[51]

The historical significance of the Vindiciae for our study lies in its connection of the rejection of the proprietary theory of the kingship with the doctrine of legitimate rebellion against a tyrannical king. The author of a Huguenot pamphlet of 1577 drew out the implications in plain words. There was a distinction between the person of the king and the state, "which is the right of command, authority, and majesty, that which makes the person no longer common but holy and sacred." Rebellion was not justified against a lawful king, but no one would be "so stupid [si abêti] as to deny it against a tyrant."[52]

The decade of the 1570s continued to be one of extraordi nary productivity for works of political theory of the first order of importance. In 1576, three years before the Vindiciae, France's most important political thinker of the century, Jean Bodin, who alone in all Europe approaches or matches Machiavelli's significance, put out his Six Books of the Re public. Unlike such Huguenot thinkers as Hotman and the pseudonymous author or authors of the Vindiciae, Bodin was a Catholic and a supporter of the crown.[53] He spoke for the party of those who called themselves the Politiques. Their program put the interests of the state ahead of those of the rival religious camps; they therefore favored strengthening the position of the monarchy and bringing about a compromise settlement of the quarrels over faith. Unlike the Huguenots, they were not rebels but the most extreme loyalists and had been encouraged by Queen Mother Catherine de Medici and (until his death in 1573) the royal chancellor Michel de l'Hospital; but, unlike Catholic extremists, they were ready to come to terms with the Protestant minority in France.

Bodin's single most important contribution to political thought was undoubtedly to clarify the concept of sovereignty, so much so that it is almost possible to speak of him as its inventor; and it is his formulation that has remained the common definition of sovereignty ever since.[54] Sovereignty, he held, was the ultimate power of legitimate command in a country; as such, it could not be shared or distributed—and his rejection of the political heart of feudalism was therefore total. There could be only one sovereign in a country, and he had to be hereditary, not elective. He possessed his power by right, not as an office or by conditional grant. But his rule was not arbitrary. He possessed his unshared or absolute power essentially in order to serve the welfare of his people, and he had no right to take their property from them except for the public need and good. Nor could he violate the fundamental laws of the kingdom, by which he came to the throne and by which he ruled.[55] However clear Bodin's concept of sovereignty, he left unsolved the problem of tyranny. To say that a prince who either usurped his throne or used his power against the interests of his people thereupon lost his sovereignty because he was a tyrant, as Thomas Aquinas had argued three hundred years before and as the Huguenots repeated in Bodin's own time, would have been to undercut his own doctrine. In the real world, rebels always presented their cause as the overthrow of tyranny; and if they won, their case was "proved"—wasn't God the god of battles?

What is significant to us in our present enquiry, however, is how Bodin handled the question of the proprietary aspect of royalty, not only because of his enormous importance as a thinker, but also because he specifically rejects the office theory of kingship. A magistrate who "continues in office by consent . . . is not a sovereign prince, seeing that he only exercises power on sufferance." Sovereign power came from the people, but it was an irrevocable transfer, as with "the man who gives to another possessory and proprietary rights over what he has formerly owned." It had to be not just for his own life, but also for that of his heirs, "in the same way that any proprietor, out of his liberality, can freely and unconditionally make a gift of his property to another."[56] He described the difference between prince and subject in proprietary terms: ". . . one is a prince, the other a subject; one is a lord, the other a servant; one is a proprietor and seized of the sovereignty, the other is neither a proprietor nor the possessor of the latter, and holds nothing except in trust."[57] Without strictly defining the kingship as proprietary in character, Bodin was driven to use the concept of property to make his point.[58] The relation of the king to his subjects' property was also one of the key ways of distinguishing the three kinds of monarchy: "royal, or legitimate," in which the prince obeys the law of God and "the natural right of property is secured to all"; "despotic," in which the prince is "lord and master of both the possessions and the persons of his subjects by right of conquest in a just war," so that subjects are like slaves; and "tyrannical," in which "the laws of nature are set at naught" and the property of free subjects is treated as if it were the king's.[59] The distinction is immensely important, but it does not bear on the question of whether the sovereignty itself is the property of the ruler and his family. This is deliberate in Bodin: differences in the method of succession in monarchies do not matter, only whether they are despotic, royal, or tryannical.[60] In this way Bodin brings back the premise of the office theory of the kingship, which is that the just king rules to "further the common good, and the welfare of his subjects," not for "only his own profit, vengeance, or pleasure."[61] Bodin also accepted the principle that usurpers were tyrants.[62] But there is no possible justification for rebellion against "true kings, . . . whose authority is unquestionably their own, and not shared with any of their subjects." Not even "all the evil, impious, and cruel deeds imaginable" would suffice as grounds.[63]

As the Wars of Religion continued, so did the political debate, although the level reached in these three masterpieces was not attained again. As it became evident that Henry of Navarre would be the probable heir of the reigning king of France, Henry III, the Huguenots veered away from the possible outcome of their arguments in outright republicanism, or even in the right of the people to share in the rule (it was a doctrine that was picked up by the Catholic League as they found themselves in conflict with Henry III and desperate to prevent the accession of the Navarrese).[64] Henry of Navarre had long taken it for granted that his family owned the sovereign power in his native country of Navarre and Béarn, a tiny independent kingdom and viscounty in the Pyrenees between France and Spain. He was also acutely aware from his youth that the Bourbons were next in line of inheritance to the French crown after the Valois, tracing back their descent to Louis IX, who had died in 1270; he was twenty-two degrees distant from his cousin, Henry III.[65] That was twelve degrees more than was permitted under the rules of acceptable consanguinity in private laws of inheritance! Some of the League publicists claimed therefore that the Capetian line was extinct (implicitly accepting the very equation of the laws of royal and private succession that they were denying in other writings) and that the people should elect a new king through the Estates General. This was therefore all the more reason for Navarre and his supporters to accept the principle that the royal succession was governed by a special rule, the Salic Law, which contained no limitation whatever of the degrees within which the inheritance was lawful. Thus, in denying (after Jean de Terre Rouge) that the crown was private property, they were affirming that it was dynastic property of a special kind.[66]

The immediate threat to the succession of Henry of Navarre came from the claim of the Guise family whose older branch reigned in the duchy of Lorraine. During the 1560s, not satisfied to dominate the reigning French kings, they had put forward a claim to be directly descended from Charlemagne, thus providing genealogical support to their aspiration to the throne itself.[67] In 1569, when Henry of Navarre was only sixteen years old, he denounced these claims in a letter to Duke Henry of Anjou, who was next in line of succession to the throne, while he himself was third, after Francis, duke of

Alençon (and later of Anjou, after his brother Henry ascended the throne as Henry III in 1574). The Guises, he wrote, "have dared to allege that this Crown was usurped from their predecessors by our ancestors," but it was we who are "the just and legitimate possessors of this Crown."[68] Is there any better definition of property than "just and legitimate possession"? From the time of his ascending the throne of Navarre in 1572, he spoke of "my sovereign countries" and "my subjects," using the possessive adjective in the same unconsidered, natural way that other sovereign rulers did.[69] That was in Béarn and (Lower) Navarre, lands "that he possesses in sovereignty."[70] In France, where he was duke of Bourbon, he acknowledged the same possessory rights of Henry III to "his state" and "his crown." These were not empty words, although Navarre was writing in 1580 to justify a rebellion he was leading against the king of France, for he did not abandon his place in the royal family as heir presumptive, second in the line after Francis of Anjou (who died in 1584).[71] In 1583 his closest adviser, Mornay, described his situation to Sir Francis Walsingham, Elizabeth I's secretary of state. His "patrimonial property" (*biens et moyens patrimoniaux*) consisted partly in "sovereign lands" (*souverainetés*) and partly in fiefs held of the king of France.[72] The next year, writing of Guise conspiracies against Henry III, Mornay put it simply: "the House of Guise claims that the crown of France belongs to it." As for their decision during the past two years to support not their own claim but that of the cardinal of Bourbon, Henry of Navarre's uncle, as coming before him in the line of succession, Mornay denied that the succession to the crown "was governed by the ancient custom of the Châtelet of of Paris."[73] Mornay was not denying the proprietary character of the kingship, but only that the customary law of Paris instead of the principle of male primogeniture held sway over it.

If the Guises' tactic of supporting the claim of the aged cardinal of Bourbon could win over people by its appeal to

dynastic principle, then Navarre's position would be danger-
ously undermined. The Navarrese chancellor therefore called
upon Francis Hotman to prepare a defense of Henry's right of
succession; but it was a difficult assignment, because in
Francogallia Hotman had attacked both the principle that the
royal succession followed the rules of inheritance in private
law and the Salic Law itself, which by this time had become a
holy of holies in the French political tradition. Instead of
basing his argument upon the general provisions of French
law, including the law of fiefs, Hotman set the theory of royal
succession upon a "royal birthright," which was the most
fundamental of all French laws. Normal rules of succession
did not hold against it, and there was no possible legitimate
way for men to amend it. He gave as his authority Jean de
Terre Rouge's fifteenth-century tract against the Burgundian
claims, and published it along with his own treatise. This
new work, *Disputation on the Controversy over the Royal
Succession between an Uncle and His Late Brother's Son*, was
presented to the king of Navarre in April 1585, and the warrior-
statesman, a man of action rather than of theory if ever there
was one, was satisfied: its conclusion favored him, and his
advisers, like Du Ferrier and Mornay, did not reject its
argument.[74]

An immediate need was served, to counter the possible impact of the cardinal of Bourbon's claim to inheritance of the
crown. It is I, Henry wrote to the queen of England and her
chief minister, who is being "deprived of the right that justly
belongs to me."[75] He called the League's claim that he was
also disbarred as a heretic, whom the pope, Sixtus V, had just
declared incapable of succeeding, a threat to all Protestant
princes. If the pope could make his declaration stick, they
would not be able to transmit their crowns to their descendants but would have their "ancient patrimony," their "wealth"
(*biens*), their "heritage" stolen from them.[76] He turned the
tables on the Catholic League, accusing it of armed rebellion
to "ruin both the House of France and the state, and the

45

fundamental laws of the state," on the pretext of religion, at the same time that he and the Huguenot party themselves again took up arms.[77] And he warned Henry III that if the pope could bar him (Navarre) from the succession, he could also declare the king on the throne incapable of reigning.[78]

Yet it was not only politics of the moment that was involved. A basic problem had been posed. The inherent birthright for which Hotman argued seemed on the one hand to be the highest form of property, based on a law so exalted that no human being could alter it, so that the king's ownership of the crown and the heir's right to it upon his death were the most absolute property conceivable. On the other hand, the right ceased to be of a piece with other kinds of property, because it could not be judged and upheld in the courts that enforced the known and established laws of the country. It was unique, so exalted that in practice a dispute over the succession could be settled only by God, or, in strictly human terms, by the god of battles in the judgment of war. Thus the crown would become the trophy of military victory. It was a conclusion that went much farther than anyone wanted; it violated the sense of law that was so strong in the country—the very sense that Hotman was called upon to bring to the side of Henry of Navarre. The deep problem remained. The king of France in some sense did own the crown and realm of France, and affirmations to the contrary were, and are, spiderwebs in a land of abstractions; but the crown was a different kind of property precisely because it symbolized the right of legitimate command in the country at a time when more and more the political side of property rights was being stripped away in other institutions, with the fief already a legal fiction and the manor becoming a source of income (the judicial functions of the lord of the manor were important to him more because they provided him with fines and fees than because he was performing a service to the community he headed).[79]

As the debate went on, by arms and by words, Navarre and his party continued to affirm Henry's proprietary right of succession. In November, an Association de Bergerac issued a declaration which was presumably drafted by Mornay. It was beyond doubt that the succession "belongs" to Henry of Navarre as head of the House of Bourbon and first prince of the blood of France, unless Henry III had an heir before his death.[80] Late in April 1589, Mornay drew up a declaration for Henry of Navarre in defense of his claim to inherit the throne. He could not believe, wrote Henry (or Mornay for him), "that France would be so degenerate [abâtardie] and false to itself [démentie] as to renounce, with premeditation and in cold blood, its fidelity and loyalty to its natural prince, that is, to the heritage and patrimony of its fathers."[81] Only a few months later, Henry III was dead from the knife of Jacques Clément, and Henry of Navarre was Henry IV of France—if he could make good his claim with the persuasion of words as well as of arms. The deathbed acknowledgment of Henry III that Navarre was his successor was utterly beside the point. Office or property, the crown of France was no man's to bequeath by testament; on that, all parties were agreed.

CHAPTER III

TO THE KING HIS OWN

Henry IV, Richelieu, and Mazarin

THE ACCESSION of Henry IV to the throne of France brought the issue of the proprietorship of the crown to a climax. As we have seen, it had already caused a reversal of political doctrines between the Huguenots and the Catholic Leaguers: it was now the latter who upheld the doctrine that the crown was in the gift of the people, the nation, and the former who emphasized the inflexibility of the law of royal succession.[1] Of course these were not the only issues involved: there were also such questions as whether a Protestant could reign and rule over a predominantly Catholic France; the attempt of the king of Spain to use Catholic resistance to accepting Henry as their king to put his daughter Isabella, whose mother Elisabeth was the daughter of Henry II, on the French throne, in violation of the Salic Law; and the bull of Pope Sixtus V barring and dispossessing Henry of the throne. Even more than upon his armies, Henry depended upon the absoluteness of the law of succession for his right to the throne.

Any possible tendency to consider the royal power as patrimonial—that is, as the full property of the king, which he could transfer and bequeath at will—was therefore eliminated from the start of the reign.[2] Instead, the divine right theory of the monarchy was stressed. On the one hand, it enabled the monarchy to be seen as legitimate; on the other, it portrayed the king as the protector of subjects.[3] Political writers in the king's party were concerned with the extent of his power, not with the earlier question of the best form of the state or the legitimacy of the state.[4] Their ideas developed upon the basis

49

of Bodin's formulations, either expanding or modifying them.[5]

The relationship between dynasty and nation remained fluid and uncertain. It is exaggerated and unjustified simply to equate king and nation,[6] and Ritter correctly reminds us that when French kings did so, it was primarily the interests of the dynasty they had in mind.[7] There is an extraordinary naiveté in Olivier-Martin's affirmation that the kings of France were "always ready to sacrifice their family interests to the general welfare of the nation." To add that "as a king he cannot but desire the welfare of all,"[8] is to accept a mystery of feeling for fact, to confuse what should be for what is.

Henry IV announced his accession in a circular letter to the principal cities of the kingdom on August 2 in his first public act as king. God had called him to the succession; he would do nothing "in what concerns the state" that was not good for the public welfare. "Hold my people in obedience to me [*Contenés mon peuple en mon obeissance*]."[9] All the key elements of our problem are here in a few sentences: the hereditary possession of the throne, expressed in the straightforward use of the possessive adjective, and the office theory of the state. Henry sought to persuade Catholics who had been in the service of Henry III to stay with him, because he was the rightful king, the lawful owner of the crown. I am the "legitimate and natural king by the laws of France," he told the keeper of the seals, asking him to remain at his post (which the devout Aubervilliers refused to do).[10] The duke of Nevers, whom the king asked to come into his army to help manage "the affairs of my state," took some months to decide, but eventually accepted.[11] The possessive adjective became a commonplace in Henry's correspondence. To Mornay, a few weeks later, he wrote that "if the fortification of my cities is an important task, the maintenance of my army, which today is the only foundation for my authority and the preservation of my state, is no less so."[12] Four times in twenty-five words (in the original French)—can we really doubt that Henry thought of cities, army, authority, and state as all his? To be sure, the possessive adjective could be used in a nonproprietary way: it had pleased God to call him to the throne as "your king," he wrote to one subject.[13] It was one thing for a subject to speak of "my country" or "my king," another for the king himself to speak of "my states" or "my people." It is worth noting, however, that Henry still used the word "state" primarily to mean the country he ruled, less often its political authority.[14] He usually indicated his right to rule by the word "crown," less frequently by "throne," and at least once by "scepter."[15]

The new king did not treat all fundamental laws as equal. He was reluctant to accord to the principle that a king on his accession incorporated his private estates into the royal domain, which neither he nor any successor could thereafter alienate, the same stature as the Salic Law, by which he had come to the throne. Less than a year after becoming king of France, on April 13, 1590, Henry issued letters patent separating his patrimonial lands from the royal domain. His sister, Catherine of Navarre, had been opposed to such a junction, and he wished to use the revenues from his private lands to pay off some of his immense indebtedness; he may also have wished to keep them as family property in the event he lost his throne, as Viollet suggests, but it is hard to believe that so tough-minded a politician as Henry would have expected to live a private life if he were dethroned. The Parlement of Paris (sitting at Tours because the capital was still in the hands of the League) stubbornly refused to register the declaration. Henry ceased his efforts to compel the judges to accept the declaration the next year, but did not formally incorporate his fiefs into the royal domain until 1607, when he felt quite safe and secure upon the throne.[16]

Writing to the government and people of Paris, who were still unwilling to acknowledge him in 1590, Henry accused them of resisting "reason, natural duty, and the ancient laws and constitutions" of the kingdom by not recognizing "our legitimate call [vocation]" to the crown.[17] If God punished him (Henry IV) for his sins with political defeat, he warned

51

the duke of Nemours, those who refused to accept their "legitimate and natural King" would suffer by falling under the yoke of the "proud" and "cruel" Spaniards.[18]

If "vocation" speaks the language of the office theory of kingship, Henry used far more often the terminology of the property theory. He described Don Antonio, the prior of Prato and pretender to the Portuguese throne occupied by Philip II of Spain, as "a king unjustly robbed [spolié] of his crown," of the kingdom that "belongs" to him.[19] This usage was matched by that of the Turkish sultan, Murad III, who offered Henry two hundred ships to use against Philip. The Spanish king, wrote the sultan, was trying to deprive the Frenchman of "the legitimate succession which belongs to you of the kingdom of France."[20] Henry (or whoever wrote his letter for him) could use the term "patrimony" to describe possessions of the crown—despite the principle of inalienability of the domain.[21] (The famed historian De Thou also wrote of "the king's patrimony, ordinarily called the domain.")[22] Yet, of course, Henry did not believe that the crown itself was a patrimony—as did the Spanish delegates to the League-sponsored Estates General which met at Paris in 1593. Applying to France a notion in common usage in their own country, they proposed on behalf of Philip II that the estates declare Isabella of Spain and a French prince whom she would marry "kings proprietor of this throne."[23] This was too much even for the League version of the Parlement of Paris, which declared only a week later that anything done against the Salic Law would be null and void.[24]

When Henry decided to abjure his Protestant faith, he informed the pope, Clement VIII, that his action applied not only to France but also to "our crown and kingdom of Navarre, which belong to us by right and legitimate succession on the maternal side."[25] In a circular letter on the decision of Paris to admit him after his conversion, he spoke of the "confusion" of those who wished to drive "the true and legitimate heirs" from France.[26] At the same time, he could describe himself as "he whom God has constituted [Frenchmen's] King and natural prince."[27] God, "by his holy Providence, [had] put in our hands the scepter over Frenchmen by legitimate succession," but he had to defend "our royal patrimony" against rebel usurpers.[28] He looked forward to the time when he would be "the peaceful ruler [dominateur] of all that belongs to me."[29] The kingdom of France, he snapped at the judges of the Parlement of Paris in 1599 who resisted registering the Edict of Nantes, "the kingdom of France . . . is mine by inheritance and acquisition."[30] In a dispute with the duke of Savoy in 1600 over the marquisate of Saluzzo (Saluces), he repeatedly identified it as "what belongs to me," "what is mine [à moy]."[31]

He was concerned as well with the proprietary rights of fellow kings—at least those with whom he was friendly. He warned against a papal plan to declare James VI of Scotland incapable of inheriting the English crown when Elizabeth I died. It would arouse the English against the Catholics and worsen their condition, and even if God had not touched the heart of the king of Scotland to recognize "the truth of our religion," as he had done to Henry himself, James was still "the true heir" of England.[32] In 1603, while the queen was in mortal illness, Henry instructed the French ambassador at London to reassure her, if she recovered, that rumors he was plotting with the pope to put someone loyal to himself on her throne, "to the detriment of those to whom it belongs by right," were false.[33] He had no compunction, however, about approving arguments by the French ambassador that in the Spanish Netherlands the law of succession, particularly in Brabant, excluded children of the second bed (that is, those born to a father's second marriage after the death of his first wife) from succession while those of the first bed or their heirs lived. He had in mind the case of the Infanta Isabella, just established with her husband Archduke Albert as sovereigns in the Low Countries, should she die without children. In that event the duchy would pass to her sister's children.[34] He did not have in mind any French claim (that would come during the reign of his grandson, Louis XIV), but he obviously accepted the principle that the civil laws of inheritance governed the succession to the throne in the absence of a special law covering the royal inheritance.

Overall, Henry IV's correspondence shows (and it does not matter whether the individual letter was drafted by him or someone else) that he accepted both the proprietary and the office theories of kingship. Discussion of specifically proprietary issues is very much bound by events; characteristically, it arises when a debate over a succession arises. This is, of course, the question of usurpation, or, as we might say, tyranny by misappropriation. The other occasion for the debate arises when the issue of tyranny by abuse occurs, an accusation that Henry faced from extreme Catholics and (to an extent after his conversion) stalwart Huguenots; but then it involved the policy of the state or ruler, and the issue of the crown as office stands out. In other words, in the case of tyranny by usurpation, the characteristic question is not whether the state is property, but whose property it is. In that of tyranny by abuse, the question is primarily whether the crown is office or property, although sometimes the question arises in the form of a discussion of whether the crown belongs to the king or the people (in which case, this is another form of the functional-teleological concept of the state and ownership becomes a functional way of defining interests by having those whose interests are concerned do the defining). Behind it all lay a reality that Mornay, who knew Henry so well, saw clearly. Anyone who undertook to write a history of this time would have to remember that princes are not just princes—that is, public men who lost their private life in their office, according to the doctrine that theorists were so fond of—but men, "and not so much strong men as strongly men [*non tant forts hommes que fort hommes*]."[35]

Henry IV not only accepted—and emphasized—his own proprietorship in the state; he also gave venal office, which institutionalized government offices as private property, full legality in the French state. He was not deterred by theologians, who argued that there could be no property in office, that it was a sign of tyranny.[36] The term "venality of office" encompasses the original sale of posts in government service by the royal authority to the benefit of the royal treasury, the inheritance of the offices, and their sale to outsiders. The evolution and formalization of venality of office was not completed until the beginning of the seventeenth century, with the institution of a tax on venal officeholders called the *Paulette*, but the process had begun well before the sixteenth century as officeholders sought to make their posts hereditary. At first it had been resisted by the crown, but the willingness of the officials to pay for the privilege of keeping their posts for their heirs soon broke through the crown's resistance, especially as such revenues proved easier to collect than traditional taxation. The details of the process are not of concern here,[37] but what is significant is that it marked an acceptance of property in public office below the level of kingship at the very time that jurists were striving to persuade their readers that the kingship itself was not only the highest office in the state, but also that it was not patrimonial property. Where in the medieval period pervasive feudalism had shaped monarchy to itself, in the new period venal office began to replace fiefs as a model of property in office—with the not unimportant difference that the crown was not in the marketplace. Furthermore, there was another implicit contradiction between political theory and the practice of venal office. It soon became evident that government officials who held their posts as property that could be taken away from them only if they were proved guilty of malfeasance or treason in formal court trials, or if the office was repurchased by the crown (an unlikely prospect with an ever-impecunious royal treasury), were effectively independent of the royal authority; if they could not always do what they wanted, they were able to refuse to do the crown's will and only very infrequently suffer for it.[38] This was a development of the greatest importance, because it put brakes on the creation of royal absolutism, a process that was occurring at the same time. The powers that the crown gained in thinning out the feudal system beneath it, retaining for itself the sole status of possessor of full power, were now given away again, not to vassals but to officeholders.[39]

It was late in Henry's reign that the problem of the property of the king or his dynasty in the crown was treated in depth by one of the most remarkable legists in French history, Charles Loyseau.[40] Where most jurists, however aware in practice of the facts of political reality, still preferred to present kingship and the state in the light of ideality, alluding to reality only to deny or denounce it, Loyseau sought to grasp reality in a way that fitted into the terms of the general legal and political theory that he accepted. Although a fervent admirer of Henry IV, "this incomparable and miraculous king,"[41] he was no sycophant. He did not admire venality of office, which exposed the public to the peril of bad administrators by the chance of the marketplace; it was the "plague of the state."[42] He recognized that "all things tend to become property and in the end do so [toutes choses tendent & s'établissent enfin à la propriété."[43] He bitterly applied to France Jugurtha's savage outburst in Sallust, that the state itself would be for sale if there were a buyer available.[44] He did not reject the notion of the office theory of public power, but sought to link it with the reality of ownership of some public offices. There were public dignities that had a public function only, and others that combined it with "ownership in the public power [puissance publique en propriété]."[45] He called the latter "lordship" (seigneurie) and noted that its essential characteristic was that a person held it because he inherited it.[46]

It was idle, he held, to try to define the existing situation of the king in France by a perfect analogy with the Romans. Only the sovereign prince had "full property" in the right of command, and it was subordinate magistrates whose right was not inherent, but given them by the sovereign.[47] The true property of subordinate offices was therefore in the state, "which consists principally in the ownership of the public power."[48] He recognized the fundamental equivalence of subordinate office and fief, the characteristic forms of delegation of authority in the modern and medieval states.[49] The king was an officeholder himself, to be sure, but one of a special kind. He was the "perfect officeholder" because he exercised all public power, and the "perfect lord" because he had "the full ownership of all public power." This did not keep him from being an officeholder and a fiefholder at the same time, under God and the people.[50] It did not matter whether the people had originally granted power to the kings or it had been won by ancient usurpation, for then it came under the rule of prescription (the conversion of possession of long standing into full ownership).[51] Yet, unlike lesser fiefs and lordships, kingdoms were not patrimonial in the strict sense of the term; the right of free disposal had been eliminated in the interest of the public peace and to avoid the mishaps and disorders of uncertain successions.[52] (It may be noted that Loyseau here describes fiefs without their original component of precarious possession). Even the countries that accepted testamentary control over the succession by the living king normally required that the crown pass to the nearest relative in blood; it was not transferable to strangers.[53] It was not in the public interest for kingdoms to be partitioned, because the people had a "notable interest" in their "integrity and perfection."[54] Loyseau accepted the principle that sovereign principalities were not established for the sake of the rulers but for that of the people who needed a leader to govern and defend them. Because of this, monarchies were different from other lordships; the office element in them was stronger.[55] Nonetheless kingship was both lordship and office.[56] Elsewhere Loyseau distinguished between lordship and office because the former had ownership of the public power and the latter simply its use.[57]

The king's property in his supreme office did not mean that

he owned his subjects' property.[58] The royal power did not extend to taxation without the consent of the estates, even though they did not share in the sovereignty. This was because sovereignty consisted in the right to command persons, not to use their property for public needs without justice.[59]

Loyseau followed earlier jurists in attempting to distinguish the hereditary power of the crown from that of private property. Princes of the royal lineage were properly so called because they possessed a right of succession; it was not "hereditary" in the strict sense because it did not carry with it the "burden" of a previously reigning king's "deeds and promises"; it was succession by "right of blood." Yet even here Loyseau used the language of property law to explain the significance. The crown was like a fief that had been limited on its establishment to certain families; it was like a trust (fidéicommis) held within a family. "From which it follows that the males of the house of France have a right to the Crown which is similar to that which reversioners [substituts] have to the property [biens] subject to the substitution, which is a much stronger right than the hope of a mere relative to the inheritance of his family's property." ("Substitution" here means the assignment of a property to fixed and designated successors rather than to ordinary heirs and is a form of entailment; it is more specific than ordinary entail [majorat].)[60] It was because the kingship was bound by fundamental law, which no reigning monarch could change, because it was entailed according to the law of male primogeniture, that Loyseau could say on the one hand that "sovereignty and universal stewardship belong to him as king everywhere in the kingdom,"[61] and still hold that the crown was "not in the marketplace."[62] This did not mean that the king was not the proprietor of the kingdom, and Loyseau observed the parallel between him and venal officers.[63] Feudalism he saw as usurpation of sovereignty, specifically of the right of command.[64] Only the king truly had "all power and all command in his ownership," and its usurpation by feudal lords was a "great absurdity."[65]

Examining the key idea of lordship more deeply, Loyseau noted the ambiguity in French as in Italian of the word *seigneur* (*signor*), which sometimes meant the master and owner and more properly the honorable title of the holder of public authority, which he called *seigneurie publique* (public lordship).[66] The term "*sieur*" was more properly used for ordinary owners.[67] Hence lordship could be defined as "property in power [*puissance en propriété*]."[68] Public lordship was exercised over subjects, private lordship over slaves.[69] This was a distinction that cut too deeply, for it made private lordship inapplicable to the conditions of France in his own day, when even the few remaining serfs were far removed from servile conditions and slavery would be reintroduced across the oceans in the future French colonies in the Caribbean, as it already existed in the Spanish. But Loyseau recognized these things too: there was no longer any slavery in France, "which is the country of the Franks [free men]," and private lordship was no longer effective over persons, but only over land. The public lordship, on the other hand, now held force "directly and principally" over persons, who could be given orders, and not over "inanimate things," except as exerted through persons.[70] He rejected seigneurial monarchies, in which the rulers commanded not only their subjects, but also their subjects' property and lives, as "barbarous and against nature," and unworthy of Christian kings who have willingly abolished slavery in their own countries.[71] France on the contrary was a "royal" monarchy, where the estates did not share in sovereignty and the crown was hereditary, not elective, although women were excluded from the succession.[72]

Sovereignty, which is "a very ticklish and important matter," Loyseau defined as "lordship of the state," the "form that gives being to the state."[73] He also defined the Aristotelian forms of the state in terms of property over lordship. Democracy consisted in the people's ownership of lordship, aristocracy in that of those ordinarily called lords, and monarchy in that of the king.[74] Sovereignty itself he defined as "absolute power," not any specific rights of the crown; but the sovereignty of princes was limited by divine laws, the laws of natural justice, and the fundamental laws of the state.[75] It was the king's ownership of the public power, which was "entire and perfect."[76]

During the next two centuries, until the fall of the French monarchy, Loyseau was to fascinate the more perceptive of political theorists because he attempted to come to grips with the reality of the French monarchy instead of merely defining it theoretically. He did not solve all the problems of the tension between the office and the property theories of the kingship, not least because they were insoluble, each theory being the contradictory of the other.[77] He wasted few words on moral injunctions to rulers, the usual means by which the relationship between the office and the property conceptions had been "resolved." What he had done essentially was to clarify the elements of the two theories in the light of practice. Both theory and practice would be put to the test of vigorous rulers during the reigns of Henry IV's son and grandson.

UNDER LOUIS XIII, who came to the throne in 1610, the strong hand at the helm of state was not that of the king himself but that of his famed chief minister, Cardinal Richelieu. But more than a decade of uncertainty and civil war intervened before Richelieu took over. Louis XIII's succession had not been in dispute, but the kingdom was not spared the rigors of a minority government until he came of age, first legally and then in fact. The struggle over the regency government between the queen mother, Marie de Medici, and the magnates, both princes of the blood and great nobles, with the latter claiming a share in the government, was of great importance politically and involved an important constitutional issue;[78] but it was not one that brought up the issues involved in proprietary dynasticism.

During the next half century, political thinkers concentrated their attention upon the supreme organ of state authority, the king, but in so doing they also intensified the notion of the state as an abstract, almost superorganic entity. The relationship of king and state became central, and the force of the office theory of kingship would create the concept of an abstract state—an abstraction that lived ultimately only in men's minds—guiding, controlling, perhaps even judging the king.[79] But what was really happening was that political struggle and political debate began to be recast in the form of a subordination of the king to the state, although the concrete meaning of the "state" remained inherently beyond specification: it was, inevitably, like the famed words of *Alice in Wonderland*, whatever the speaker or writer wanted it to mean. Yet the assertion that the king was not the proprietor but only the administrator of the state, which becomes more sharply presented in histories of the political thought of this period,[80] continued to conflict with the ordinary political actions of the time and with what we might call the unsophisticated political theory—that seen not in formal treatises but in day-to-day documents.

Even in formal treatises, however, the proprietary element continued to be present. Jean Savaron, in his *The Sovereignty of the King* of 1620, affirmed that the king's power was given by God alone and was "free of all domination but his [God's]," but only on condition that he neither accept any other sovereign over himself, nor alienate the royal domain. Sovereignty was an "inviolable trust," which "cannot be traded [*entrer au commerce*] by Princes without sacrilege."[81] Savaron held that such alienation was forbidden by "the royal law, the law of the state, the fundamental law, the law of the kingdom, the Salic Law."[82] Hence the king was "only the administrator, and as it were the usufructuary of his kingdom."[83] Yet Savaron did not actually deny that the king was proprietor of the state, but, citing a declaration of the Parlement of Paris of 1527, added that "while the kingdom belongs to the king, the king also belongs to the kingdom."[84] The proprietary and office notions are thus merged in a single image, but one whose false parallelism is significant. For the king's ownership of the kingdom meant his sovereignty over the people, his right to command them; but the kingdom's ownership of the king meant that he had to command his subjects in their interests, not his own, without providing them with any mechanism for defining and asserting their interest if he saw it differently from his subjects, or any group of them. Savaron also extended the doctrine of inalienability to the principle that the king could not resign or abdicate his crown.[85] Here we see the triumph of abstract principle over reality, for how an abdicating king could be prevented from giving up his throne, short of a rebellion to compel him to rule, is hard to imagine.

The relationship of king and state became more complex when Cardinal Richelieu undertook the government of France as prime minister for Louis XIII in 1624. This was no office that he held, but an assignment, a commission, from the king, to be his "man" in acting for him at the head of state. It was an intensely personal relationship, and historians who see Richelieu as having the state and not the king as his "idol,"[86] have been led astray by their own notions of an abstract state which they read into Richelieu's thoughts. What he had in mind was the notion of the continuing and permanent interests of the kingdom, rather than a personification of either the government or the country. Avenel was more on target in describing the cardinal's image of French government as that of a well-run house, with the king as master-father.[87] This patriarchalism, although distinct from the proprietary concept of kingship, is not at all necessarily opposed to it.

Richelieu's notion of the state is probably best indicated obliquely. One of the reasons things were not going well in France, he wrote, was that there was not a single post in the realm that had not been made into a *métier*. By this he did not mean a craft, as did Louis XIV in his famous statement on the *métier du roi* in his *Memoirs* almost half a century later.[88] He meant rather the other, less prepossessing sense of job, for such a *métier* was one whose possessor was not concerned with "what he must do to perform his assignment, but more with what he must do to make his assignment bring him profit."[89] He himself had a *métier*: "My first concern was the King's majesty, the second the greatness of the kingdom."[90] Around 1625, only a year after becoming first minister, he wrote of "the passion that I always had for the good of the state and the kingship."[91] The order is inverted, but it is enough to show that although he might put the king's majesty first, he was acutely aware of the state, probably not so much as an abstract entity but more as an instrumentality of power. He used the term "state" by itself much more than his predecessors.[92] By it he sometimes clearly meant the country ruled by the king,[93] sometimes the government itself.[94] He used the possessive adjective with regard to state and kingdom without embarrassment,[95] and would no doubt have been surprised to see its obvious meaning questioned.

He did not dispute that the king held his crown from God: one would have to be "a very bad theologian" to deny it.[96] But this was only to say that the king, in temporal terms, was an absolute proprietor, since in theology only God was the absolute owner of the world: but he who held only of God held of no man. But, as a "good theologian," Richelieu emphasized the need for the king to control his private feelings and interests for the sake of the permanent ones of the public and the state.[97]

When it came to the interests of state, Richelieu knew just what he meant. As Dickmann, the outstanding modern historian of the Peace of Westphalia, notes, Richelieu unabashedly had jurists and historians demonstrate French dynastic claims almost everywhere in Europe, treating countries and states according to the concepts of the Roman law of private property.[98] It may be that he was only playing a diplomatic game, frightening other governments a bit in order to gain much less than he seemed to want;[99] but the point of the tactic is that neither he nor the princes at whose states he pointed the publicists treated the argument as meaningless. They did not want their property taken from them by a rapacious and over-mighty France.

The tension between the office and property concepts of the kingship is only implicit in Richelieu's writings, because he did not doubt his own capacity to serve the king and the state at one and the same time. It is more evident in the political writers whom Richelieu put to work. Unlike many of the reigning kings, who were only dimly aware of all the debate and of the implications even of common phrases, Richelieu himself was theologically trained and concerned; if not a legist, he understood what jurists wrote and meant.

One of the most important of the legists was Dupuy, whose *Treatise of the King's Rights* was published about 1630. Denying that the duke of Mantua was fully sovereign, Dupuy distinguished his status from that of "absolute Princes who possess kingdoms and are absolutely sovereign." He was only a feudatory.[100] Treaties that transferred French territory even as part of peace terms were invalid, at least if the cession was of importance, because the territory was "a piece of property [*un bien*] of which our kings are only usufructuaries, and which is therefore inalienable."[101] This was an important claim, because this volume was a treatise upon the rights of the king of France elsewhere in Europe, and an invalidation of peace treaties was a most serious matter. In explaining this principle, Dupuy made it clear that usufruct was a kind of ownership: the domain of the crown "belongs to our kings only by usufruct." He cited as a parallel the argument of a Spanish legist that "kings cannot alienate their sovereignty."[102] But the distinction ran not between property and office, but between kinds of property: the kings received their crown not by the free disposition of their predecessors, but "solely by the law and custom of the kingdom."[103] Unlike some earlier writers who had accepted the notion that "immemorial possession" created proprietary rights in the sovereign power, he specifically barred prescription.[104] Yet he maintained that wars, if just, could result in conquests that would constitute a legitimate title of possession of sovereignty. It did not matter that conquerors were judges in their own case condemning those who were not their own subjects.[105]

Where Dupuy broke with tradition among royalist thinkers was in disputing the applicability of the Salic Law to the royal succession. It spoke only of private inheritance and not of the succession to the kingship, he observed, and the crucial clause *De Alodiis* applied to "patrimonial, nonfeudal property possessed by individuals." The law of royal succession was established by "ancient observance," not by written formula, and its "uncertain origin" made it "more august and venerable." The fact that mattered was that it had been observed without violation over many centuries.[106]

Two years after the publication of Dupuy's treatise, another work less concerned about scholarly precision came from the pen of Cardin Le Bret.[107] He was a vigorous supporter of absolute monarchy, but in the service of the public peace and welfare, not in its own self-interest.[108] Kings had been created by the "first men" of the country when they found themselves exposed to the blows of their enemies, the abuses of the rich, and disregard of the laws.[109] The immediacy of what Le Bret had in mind is strong, but this plain statement of contract theory pales beside the sophistication of Hobbes and Locke. Le Bret went on to say that kings were sovereign because they depended only on God.[110] Tyrants were those who usurped their throne.[111]

Defending the right of the king to make laws and give commands on his own, without participation of his council or of Parlement, Le Bret made the famous comparison that "sovereignty is no more divisible than a point in geometry."[112] The formula was taken over by Richelieu in his *Memoirs*.

Clearly referring to Dupuy's rejection of the Salic Law and the *De Alodiis* clause, Le Bret reaffirmed their central place among the fundamental laws of France. Objections like Dupuy's were "captious." The fact of the matter was that everyone knew that royal successions were always considered in the same way as allodial lands, "which are held only of God and the sword." The Salic Law had been confirmed by usage since the French monarchy had begun. The exclusion not only of women but also of their male descendants had been done according to the example of masculine fiefs. Indeed, "the Crown of France is a masculine fief."[113] This might seem a contradiction in terms, except that one definition of allodial property, as we saw earlier, was that it was a fief held of God. Le Bret also defined the king as God's subject, but no man's.[114]

The kings' usufruct in the domain of the crown, Le Bret wrote, was "recompense for the trouble and labors that they take in protecting and defending their people."[115] The point is a crucial one: the king's rewards came to him personally, not in his public capacity but as a private person for his public activity. Here Le Bret comes down to earth: kings are not depersonalized supermen, gifted with utter selflessness, as required by the office theory of the state, and they will not do what they are supposed to if they are not held to account by other men, their subjects. Like other offices, the royal office was good not only for what it enabled the king to do for his people, but for what it made them do for him. Similarly, Le Bret affirmed the absoluteness of the property rights of subjects. To claim that subjects possessed their own property only as a kind of usufruct, that it belonged in the strict sense to the king "by right of sovereignty," was "shameful and slavish flattery" and false.[116] The king could not take subjects' property, that is, tax them, for his own "private convenience, against their will."[117] Le Bret's lack of servility went so far as to refute those who claimed that absolute monarchy was not compatible with popular assemblies. Far from weakening the

66

king's power, they strengthened it and heightened its splendor and glory.[118]

————◆————

AFTER THE DEATH of Richelieu in 1642 and of Louis XIII in 1643, France again passed under the scepter of a minor king. A regency government was established for the five-year-old Louis XIV by Queen Mother Anne of Austria, who entrusted the leadership of the state to a prime minister, Cardinal Mazarin. Although the powers and policies of Mazarin were as furiously disputed and debated as any in the history of the French monarchy, the legitimacy of the king himself was never questioned in the slightest. Political discussion therefore veered off to the questions of the moment, involving the extent of the authority of the queen mother and her chief minister as well as the wisdom of their policies; but the controversy between the office and property theories of kingship slumbered.

The late king, in an effort to thwart the Habsburg sympathies that Anne of Austria had always displayed, had set up a regency council, dominated by Mazarin, in which her voice would be only one of several. But once Louis XIII was dead, the legists in the queen mother's service contested the declaration establishing the regency council, because the monarchy was "successory," not "hereditary," and hence the former king had no right to impose his conditions on the monarch who followed him.[119] The Parlement of Paris agreed, the declaration was declared null and void, and then, by one of the most stunning reversals in history, Louis XIII achieved his aim of continuing the policy of hostility to the Habsburgs through Anne's conversion to it, and through her use of Mazarin, who remained in the leadership of affairs as her prime minister, to carry it out.

The revolt of the Fronde, which broke out in 1648 and con-

tinued spasmodically until 1653, was directed against the authority of Anne and Mazarin. It employed slogans of struggle
for the public welfare—what rebellion in France did not?—
and so did the government—what government in France has
not?—but the level of debate remained extraordinarily low.
The Mazarinades, in which the Parisians sang of their con-
tempt and hatred for Mazarin and the queen mother, display
scabrous sarcasm and sometimes wit, but no lofty thoughts or
sentiments. Mazarin's propagandists sought to put his government in the best light, as serving the interests of the state, but
the element of personal service was if anything stronger than
ever.[120] Some Frondeurs, like Claude Joly, might go all the
way to republican theories, but for the most part even he remained within the boundaries of monarchical thought of a
traditional kind. He was not afraid, he informed the readers of
his *Collection of True Maxims*, that "those who sought to
make a legitimate kingship [*royauté*] into a perpetual brigand-
age" (shades of Alexander the Great and Saint Augustine!)
would attack him; they would not dare sink their "venomous
teeth" into him lest they also bite "great Personages" in the
country.[121] A legitimate kingship was "bounded and finite,"
"not absolute," and those who gave monarchs the notion that
"they have the right to dispose of the lives and wealth of their
subjects at their discretion" were guilty of "presumptuousness"
(*impertinence*).[122] The notion that kings were "absolute
masters of the lives and wealth of their subjects, so that everything that belongs to us is theirs and so that they have the
right to take it and give it to whomever they want, or put it to
use however seems good to them," was a "very dangerous
falsehood" taught to them by "greedy and ambitious Ministers."[123] Yet even Joly could not evade the grip of the habitual
language of proprietary dynasticism. Spanish Navarre should
be returned to its "former possessors" by the reigning king of
Spain because his father, Philip III, and his grandfather, Philip
II, had both ordered in secret codicils to their testaments that

this should be done if the acquisition of Navarre by Ferdinand and Isabella were shown to be neither "well founded nor legitimate."[124]

During the Fronde, the Huguenots, who avoided all involvement with the rebellion, were more royalist than the king's own jurists. One pastor, carried away by his rhetoric, accepted as truth what Joly had called a dangerous falsehood. He could hardly have meant literally the principle of seigneurial monarchy that he enunciated: "Our property, our bodies, our lives belong to the king, and reserving only our consciences, which concern only God, everything is devoted to his service."[125] Catholic preachers, like Mazarin's confidant, the Carmelite Léon de Saint-Jean, did not have to go beyond reaffirming that the king held his power directly of God, so that attacking the king was attacking God himself.[126]

The immediate origin of the Fronde lay in the efforts of the regency government to extract increased taxes from France so as to bring the war against the Habsburgs to a successful conclusion. It was a goal half won at the peace negotiations in Westphalia, for in 1648 the emperor made a separate peace with France. Spain fought on alone, but made its own separate peace with the United Provinces. During the negotiations at Westphalia the French representatives accepted the proprietary character of sovereignty without debate, as did their counterparts on the other side of the negotiating tables.[127] When a representative of the Alsatian cities, which considered themselves free republics, not part of the patrimony of any prince, complained that the emperor was transferring to France rights that he had only as provincial governor (Landvogt) and not as sovereign, the French negotiator D'Avaux replied bluntly that if this were true, then the emperor had given away someone else's property, but this did not concern France.[128] At the level of states, presumably, the receiving of stolen goods was not fencing but high politics.

The proprietary character of royalty was equally emphasized at home. It is plain in a statement given to the king to read in a *lit de justice* before Parlement on his eighth birthday. "Gentlemen, the needs of *my* state have led me to come to *my* Parlement to speak to it of *my* business. *My* chancellor will inform you of *my* will. [emphasis added]."[129] It is hard to conceive of more intense personalism than that, or a more clearly proprietary attitude. That was on September 7, 1645. Six years later, on September 6, 1651, the king returned to Parlement to inform it officially that he had come of legal age of majority: "Gentlemen, I have to come to *my* Parlement to tell you that, in accordance with the law of *my* state, I have come to take over personally [*moi-même*] the task of government, and I hope that God's bounty will enable me to govern with piety and justice [emphasis added]."[130] The attitude had not changed one whit. By 1657, the king was old enough to speak for himself without prompting, but the proprietary attitude was just as strong. During that year he gave an audience to the Dutch ambassador in connection with an incident in which a Dutch admiral had seized two French warships in the Mediterranean supposedly engaged in piracy. "Your people have gone too far," he told the envoy, "because they took *my* ships in *my* seas, which belong to me in sovereignty."[131] But the most famous episode in which the king spoke of his relation to the state is supposed to have occurred two years earlier, on April 13, 1655. Still wearing his hunting boots, he came to the Parlement of Paris to order the judges not to interfere in political affairs. It was on this occasion, so the story goes, that he used the phrase "*L'Etat c'est moi* [*I am the state*]."[132] There is no documentary proof that he actually spoke these words; if anything, he probably did not. They would have been quite in character, however, as a reply to assertions by the judges that they were acting on behalf of the interests of the state in rejecting certain fiscal edicts.[133] There is no need to read too precise theoretical meanings into the phrase, whether or not it was spoken then, as has so often been done; the king was not and would never be a sophisticated political thinker, although his power of analysis of political events would become impressive. What would be significant was that Louis XIV would rise to the notion of the abstract state, but never see himself as subordinated to it.[134]

Meanwhile, in exile in the Spanish Netherlands, Condé, the great loser of the Fronde, expressed the idea that the crown was a personal boon with all the fervor of a lost dream. He went in 1654 to a reception for Queen Christina of Sweden when she landed at Antwerp, on her way to Rome after her abdication. "Where is the woman," he asked, "who so lightly leaves what we fought for all our lives and cannot get?"[135] The notion of the kingdom as property was also expressed in a poem probably written by Tristan l'Hermite, which Gaston of Orleans, the forlorn, never-victorious rebel now obedient to his nephew, presented to Princess Marie Louise de Gonzague. It was an expression of rejected love, "my sovereign good [bien]," through the metaphor of a scepter that never became his.[136]

In June 1659, when the diplomatic preparations for the Peace of the Pyrenees were endangered by the king's infatuation for Marie Mancini, Mazarin's niece, the cardinal-minister, telling Louis that he had to break off the affair for his own glory, went on to say he wished to see him "the greatest king on earth by his personal qualities" (which would be displayed by this self-sacrifice), "as you are by the kingdoms that you possess."[137] A month later, as the king continued stubborn, he emphasized that God had established kings "to look after the welfare, the quiet and the safety of their subjects, and not to sacrifice their welfare to their private passions." His duty was to "make your state and your subjects happy" by taking the Infanta Maria Teresa as his bride.[138]

The principle that the crown was property permeated the negotiation of the treaty of the Pyrenees. The first clause of the peace treaty proclaimed that it bound not only the living kings of France and Spain, along with their "children now born and to be born," but also their "heirs, successors, and heirs-apparent [Hoirs, Successeurs et Héritiers]." It would apply to the "kingdoms, states, provinces, and countries be-

longing" to the two kings.[139] Lionne, Mazarin's right-hand
man, had already explained to the chancellor of the elector of
Mainz that France, in all its territorial acquisitions since
Charlemagne, had never kept anything by sole title of conquest, but only things "that in any case happened to belong to
our kings by succession, confiscation, exchange, or even by
purchase."[140]

It was clear to the negotiators from the beginning that what
was involved was the ultimate succession rights that a bride
brought to her husband. Don Luis de Haro, the chief Spanish
negotiator, warned Lionne, who had come to Madrid, that
Spain would not follow the Austrian example at Westphalia.
The Austrian Habsburgs, he said, had gotten out of a "tough
spot [*mauvais pas*]" by ceding to France "something that belongs to us by right, just as Madrid is the king's."[141] It was not
that the Spaniards did not recognize that other things than
ownership as such counted in these matters. Haro's secretary
rebuffed a French claim for Perpignan after the French defeat
at Valenciennes: "We will never swallow it . . . just as your
principal aim is to push your frontiers in Flanders in order to
protect Paris, we have the same interest in protecting ourselves
there."[142] And Mazarin himself could speak the language of
the office theory of monarchy when it came to thwarting
Spanish ambitions. His instructions to Lionne and Gramont,
the French plenipotentiaries to the imperial diet at Frankfurt
in 1657, on the occasion of the forthcoming election of a new
emperor, were to urge the electoral princes to vote freely and
thus to "show all Europe that the Imperial dignity is not the
patrimony of a single House which the Council of State can
dispose of as it pleases, which it has done until now."[143]

Article IV of the Pyrenees treaty, the weightiest in terms of
consequences, was inserted at the insistence of Lionne and to
the dismay of the Spanish negotiator, Coloma. It provided
that Maria Teresa, as a condition for marrying Louis XIV,
renounce her rights to the "greater properties, rights, reasons,
and actions because of the heritages and greater successions"

of her mother and father, "conditionally upon [*moyennant*]" payment of her dowry of 500,000 gold écus.[144] The property side of a marriage was represented with the utmost force by a dowry. It is possible to argue that the clause about greater properties, rights, etc., refers only to the private property of the Spanish king, especially since the renunciation in Article V of "kingdoms, states, lordships, dominions, provinces, adjacent islands, fiefs, captainries, and frontiers" does not contain the *moyennant* clause but gives the peace of Christendom, the benefit of Christianity, the common welfare of the kingdoms, and the preservation of the crowns as the reasons for the renunciation, without mentioning the dowry.[145] But it must be noted that this distinction was not made at the time, when the Spanish negotiators were fully aware of the French intention to use the marriage to strengthen an eventual French claim to the succession to the Spanish crown. Ambiguity there was, as there was in Austria's cession of Alsace to France eleven years before, but it was intentional ambiguity, and in both cases it would have momentous political consequences. Indeed, the French court later heard that Philip IV had himself declared that the renunciation was invalid, because he could not change the rights of succession to his throne.[146] And Lionne too, in his relation of his mission, denied that "a simple article" in a treaty could destroy the "fundamental laws" of the Spanish monarchy, specifically the one that had been in force for centuries "between the kings and their subjects" providing that women succeeded to the crown in the absence of males.[147] Valid or not, this claim upon the Spanish succession became one of the foundation rocks of the foreign policy of Louis XIV when he took over the guidance of the French government from Mazarin on the minister's death two years later.

CHAPTER IV

LOUIS XIV AND THE STATE

W ITH THE DEATH of Mazarin in 1661, Louis XIV came into his own. Having already reigned for eighteen years, he would reign and rule for another fifty-four, marking a whole age with his prowess, his personality, and his ideas. The very vigor of his mastery led to a renewal of the theoretical debate between the office and property concepts of kingship, and to a sharpening of the terms of analysis. Because he was a man of strong mind and purpose, but quite lacking in that power of abstract thought that could make consistency more important than practical success,[1] he himself gives us a clear, steady picture of how the king who was the very exemplar of early modern monarchy saw the problems in which we are interested in this book. The completeness of his absolutism—in the sense accepted by modern historians, not of totalitarian power extending over all social institutions and to all men, and enforced by terror, but of the full possession of a sovereignty that was limited in theoretical scope and in practical effectiveness—meant that the problem of tyranny by abuse would be explored as well, quite separately from that of usurpation, of which there was no question.[2]

Whatever was possible and right for a king to have and to be, he wanted, but no more. He therefore carried the potentialities of absolute monarchy to a peak; but he did not go beyond the boundaries of the Western concept of kingship, what was called "royal monarchy" in contradistinction to "seigneurial monarchy." On the one hand, because he possessed a powerful sense of acquisitive proprietorship, he displayed the property view of the kingship at its most extreme while remaining within the traditions of Western thought and prac-

75

tice. On the other, because he also had an equally strong sense of duty, he saw and accepted the office theory of kingship so far as it implied service to the state and the people: he did not forget the maxim he had been taught as a child, "The good of my subjects is my sole law."[3] But he made no concession of subordination and accountability to anyone but God. He was responsible *for* the people, not *to* them. The famous phrase, "*L'Etat c'est moi*," whether or not he ever spoke it, expressed his deep conviction that in practice no distinction could be drawn between himself and the sovereign power, that it was his will that moved the state.[4] He affirmed the principle in practice and theory without any of the timidity with which it had been expressed before.[5]

Although he accepted the principle of the abstract state, he hardly did so in its pure form; he was too committed to the unity of the idea of the state with the interests of his family and himself for that. True, the creation of a "pure and specific administration of public services,"[6] that is, the institutionalized form of the abstract state, made large progress during his reign, but it was not Louis's deliberate intention to create a political entity utterly distinct from himself. He did not "distinguish perfectly," as Olivier-Martin asserts, between his own interest and that of the state, and, significantly, the historian of the law can locate that separate identity of the state only in the rule of devolution of the crown and the special status of the royal domain.[7] There can be no question that the king sometimes did distinguish between himself and the state; but on other occasions his intense personalism washed that difference away. This personalism appeared in his very first official act after the death of Mazarin. Attending the council, he addressed himself to Chancellor Séguier: "Sir, I have brought you together with *my* ministers and *my* secretaries of state, to tell you that until now I was willing to permit the late Cardinal to conduct my affairs. It is time that I govern them myself [emphasis added]."[8]

In 1690, writing to his son, who was on campaign in the

Rhineland, he could advise that for "his own glory," it would be better to fight, "but not for the good of the state." The Dauphin should enter battle only if victory were certain.[9] A great self-sacrifice on the part of the Sun King, no doubt, but it probably tells us more about his quite human ability to paint his own desires, especially those of which he was a little ashamed, as imposed by duty to a higher cause: for during all of his administration the Grand Monarch was in the grip of an aversion to risk that was as great as his yearning for glory. Madame de Maintenon, who knew him so well, saw something other than self-sacrifice in him in 1698. Complaining that she had been compelled to go on maneuvers in the company of a twelve-year-old princess, she wrote that she would have preferred to attend an "assemblée de charité," but the king (whom she indicated with a decorous on [one]) "desires everything to be done with a regard to himself."[10] This personalism permeated his politics. In medieval times, fealties had been given to feudal overlords all up the ladder of authority; now Louis XIV wanted all his subjects to be bound to him by a personal as well as a political tie, and he held all bonds to lesser men in deepest suspicion, as Fouquet found to his cost.[11]

In evaluating the thought of Louis XIV we have recourse to a remarkable source, the memoirs he wrote for his eldest son, the Dauphin.[12] Most historical memoirs are suspect because they are written with an eye to posterity, and are usually more useful in telling us what their authors would like us to believe about them, than in informing us about what the writers were actually doing or thinking at the times they describe. But, much as Louis was concerned for his image in the future (and a modern historian finds himself both a little flattered that so proud a monarch should hold his opinion in so high respect, and a little amused that the king thought he could command it), there can be no question that these memoirs were designed for the education of the Dauphin, that they are just what they purport to be. It is no philosopher-king that the memoirs reveal; quite the contrary. Louis XIV had his eyes turned toward the sun that he took for his emblem, but not to the starry realm of abstract principles. His generalizations are at best edificatory warnings drawn from specific examples, at worst trite reiterations of the commonplaces of royal doctrine. But they are of no less interest to us, for they are the ideas that the king held to all his life, or thought he was following. We are not confronted, as we are with Frederick II of Prussia, with the thought of a subtle and wily mind fully aware of theoretical implications and able with a twist of phrase to persuade all but the wariest of readers—at least until the reader turns to what the roi-philosophe did rather than wrote.[13] Louis XIV comes to us plain, for it is a rare modern reader who is taken in by the flattery of the king's contemporaries. We read Racine's plays, not his pieces of royal adulation.

The balance of "I" and "the state" in Louis's thought may be gauged by a famous reflection of 1679 known as "The Craft of Kingship" (Le Métier du Roi). This passage, although incorporated into the memoirs for the Dauphin, was apparently not directed to him at all, but was written by the king himself as he debated with himself whether to dismiss Arnauld de Pomponne from the foreign ministry almost as soon as the final treaties of the Peace of Nijmegen (1678–1679) had been concluded. The published version is based on a final draft modified by Louis many years later to soften its acerbities.[14] The king's accusations against Pomponne that he had not been industrious enough, that he was stubborn and weak at the same time (and beneath it all probably rested Pomponne's unwillingness to call the peace concluded at the end of the long Dutch War a triumph to be emblazoned in painting and poetry), are beside the point of this study. What is significant is that in some one hundred fifty words Louis uses the first person singular ten times, and only at the end does he mention possible harm to the state.[15] If on the one hand he writes that "the interest of the state should come first," he continues with celebrated words about "the craft of a king" being "great, noble, and delightful" and ends with a key passage in which "I" and "the state" become virtually one:

When we have the state in mind, we are working for ourselves. The welfare of the one creates the glory of the other. When the former is happy, lofty, and powerful, he who is the cause of it has glory too and consequently should enjoy more than his subjects with regard to himself and to them everything in life that is most pleasant.[16]

In the *Memoirs* as such, Louis, to whatever extent he accepted the office theory of kingship, acknowledged responsibility only to God; subjects were bound to obey "without discernment."[17] Kings were the "sovereign arbiters of the fortunes and the conduct of men,"[18] they were "born to possess all and to command everything."[19] Explaining the origin of the Devolution War, he wrote that he had called upon Spain to give him "states that belonged to me." Yet, even here, he admitted that he had intended to take possession either of the Low Countries or of an equivalent.[20] This was realpolitik, of course, but if ownership of states by dynastic families was "not in the marketplace," as he urged, then the notion of exchanges or equivalents ought to have been barred. But the king did not quail before self-contradiction or tremble at merely logical consequences: he was concerned with the specific, the concrete, with what he wanted and what he could get.[21] He included among the things that were his "property" (*bien*) the lives of his subjects. Although the passage goes on to draw the conclusion for the Dauphin that he should therefore take good care of his subjects, nonetheless the stench of slavery—the heart of the seigneurial monarchy that theoreticians denied that France was—can be detected in such a phrase.[22]

Urging the importance of keeping the king's splendor (*éclat*) undiminished by not letting other members of the royal family become too grand, Louis described the danger of "desolating an inheritance of which they or their descendants may one day be the legitimate possessors."[23] Preeminence was not only a question of personal interest, "it is a property [bien] for which we are responsible to the public and to our successors." It was, in fact, one of the rights of the crown "which cannot be validly alienated."[24] Louis was not a logician, perhaps, but he must have possessed a certain gift for abstraction after all, if he could see preeminence as a kind of property!

In one passage, Louis uses the word "state" to mean both the kingdom and the public power.[25] In another, he aligns "love for my people," "passion for the greatness of the state," and "ardor for true glory."[26] He believed that "everything that is done or proposed in the administration of the state should have its principal relationship to the prince."[27] He saw the treasury as personal, "the purse of the master."[28] Sovereigns were "depositories of the public fortune" who had been made by heaven. They should not dissipate their subjects' substance in useless expense, but it would be "a misplaced economy [ménage hors de propos]" to refuse to spend for "glory of the nation or the defense of their provinces."[29] (One wonders under which of these two rubrics he placed his expenditures upon his mistresses.) In a well-known passage, he proclaimed that "kings are absolute lords and by nature have the full and free disposition of all wealth of both laymen and churchmen to use with wise economy, that is, according to the needs of their state."[30] Whatever "wise economy" may have been, and however obvious the point that he wanted to tax ecclesiastics, Louis nonetheless did consider all wealth in France in some sense to be his. The passage, taken literally, would have made the country into a seigneurial monarchy, but there is no reason to believe that such was Louis's intention. The passage does, however, also show that he was quite insensitive to the difference between taxation and tribute, that he confused eminent domain with true ownership. In another passage, he warns that "whatever he permits to be taken from his people in any fashion whatever is never taken except at his own expense."[31] "It is a great mistake for sovereigns to appropriate certain things and certain persons for themselves as if they were their own in a different way than the rest of what they have under their dominion [empire]. The moneys that are in their cashbox, those that remain in the hands of their treasurers, and those that they leave in their people's trade, should be treated by them with equal care."[32] Again the immediate purpose is to urge care in expenditure, but the distinction between public and private wealth, between the king's own and the people's, is blurred, with the king's interest obviously paramount.[33] That these were not mere words but expressed a real attitude in practice was demonstrated in 1710 when twelve doctors of theology at the Sorbonne assured the king, who was seeking more taxes in the final years of the exhausting War of the Spanish Succession, that all the property of his subjects was really his. When he took it by taxation, therefore, he was really taking back his own property.[34]

Louis XIV always had difficulty in understanding that he had not been made by God without the failings of other men. He had ministers and family in mind when he wrote, "Never make a mistake, my son, we have to do not with angels but with men to whom excessive power always in the end gives a temptation to use it."[35] Montausier, the Dauphin's governor, warned the young man against considering kingship "as a title of dominion and liberty to satisfy your passions and to keep men subject to your power."[36] The Dauphin's father would have approved the thought, but without being able to live up to it. He could turn around a statement of his duty to protect the people so that in the end it was they who were his property: "Finally, as we belong to our people, our people belong to us, and I have not yet seen that a wise man would take revenge at his own expense against those who belong to him."[37]

When we look beyond this private work to published political theory from the king's side during the reign of Louis XIV, we find remarkably little of importance. Where Richelieu had been eager to win over and hold public opinion, Louis seems almost to have distrusted political theory, even in the hands of adulators. It was as if he sensed that there are some questions that are best not asked, because the answers cannot be commanded.

Some of these perils can be seen in a work published in 1665 by the legist Béthune, *The Councillor of State*. He starts with the commonplace definition of the aim of the state: "the benefit of all in general."[38] To this he adds the notion of the service state, describing what he calls "royal principality" as a government in which one person rules according to the laws of nature and the country, "leaving natural liberty and the ownership of his property to each individual, and with its principal aim the public utility."[39] He defined legitimacy of government in terms of ownership: the legitimate state "is the one that belongs [*appartient*] to us, either by the gift of him who has the power to give it, or by just conquest, or it may be that one that is bestowed by the laws providing either succession, election, or lot."[40] The difficulty, however, of remaining with a purely proprietary definition emerged when Béthune came to discuss the Salic Law. Although the succession of females was accepted almost everywhere in Christian states, some rejected it for the state because it is a question "not of an inheritance but of commanding a people."[41]

Béthune did not accept the principle of absolute monarchy in its extreme form. Law was not simply the will of the prince; it was not "whatever may appeal to his whim and wish, but only what he should justly and honestly wish, because the Laws should be made and published to improve and bring about the things that they are directed to, and not to feed the appetite of the lawmaker."[42] This distinction is directed at the central dilemma of the proprietary state: for the legitimacy of self-advantage is the key characteristic of property that distinguishes it from office. But Béthune did not mean that subjects should have the right to determine what was to their own advantage[43] (that was the key tenet of republican doctrine, which would express itself in the form of the people's ownership of the state).

Another jurist, Fleury, was able to distinguish clearly between the royal domain and sovereign power. The former was the king's patrimony, but the king's relation to it was like that of any other owner of property, that is, he did not exercise public lordship. Sovereign power, on the other hand, extended over the whole kingdom, and here the king's rule was obviously different from the rights of private owners.[44] As sovereign, however, the king "should not be considered as a simple officer, but as a true lord." He was the "owner [propriétaire] of the whole public power, that is, of the authority to command Frenchmen and dispose of their persons and goods for the use of the state."[45] This was the nub of the question stated in its elements, but without the tension between them. If, however, what the king owned was "the authority to command Frenchmen and dispose of their persons and goods," how was this property in the same sense that ordinary people owned their wealth—which no longer included political authority as such, now the king's and the king's alone? Yet, if the king's authority was limited by the requirement that political authority and taxation be used for the sake of the state, not of the king personally, was it really property either, when all other property was legitimately used for self-interest, and self-interest extended to the right of abuse as well as use? ("Abuse" here means, of course, damage to the property itself rather than harm to others.)

The problem was not solved by the intellectually most powerful exponent of the royal cause, Bishop Bossuet. In his *Politics Drawn from the Very Words of Holy Scripture*, published posthumously in 1709, Bossuet pays little direct attention to the conflict of the office and proprietary theories of kingship. He is concerned rather with affirming both the divine grant of the crown to the king and the divine establishment of the royal authority. Although he views all legitimate government as established by God, he sees monarchy as the most perfect, because most clearly modeled on divine government of the universe.

He strongly affirms the right of private property, which he views not as existing before the state but as its institutional creation.[46] A key element for his view of kingship is the distinction he makes between men and the law: men are corrupted by self-interest and passion, but the law is without either.[47] The prince "by his quality has no other interest than that of the nation."[48] Yet, in defending the advantages of hereditary monarchy, Bossuet acknowledges the humanity of kings. "The Prince who works for the state works for his children; and the love he bears for his kingdom, merging with that which he bears his family, becomes part of his nature."[49] Part of divine right is God's establishment of dynasties ("reigning houses") and his determination of their duration.[50] The power of kings, coming from God, should not induce them to think that they are masters to use it "however they please [à leur gré]." It should be used religiously.[51] This is Bossuet's distinction between kingship and tyranny: "The true character of the prince is to provide for the needs of the people, as that of the tyrant is to think only of himself."[52] It is the distinction between absolute and arbitrary government.[53]

Bossuet uses the property image in discussing the relation of God, king, and subjects. The people are God's more than the king's. "It is he [God] to whom justice and judgment belong as property; and it is he who gives them to kings."[54] But the people's property is their own. Under arbitrary government men are no better than slaves; they own nothing for themselves, but everything belongs to the king and there is no right of inheritance, not even from father to son.[55] In an absolute monarchy, on the other hand, "ownership of wealth is legitimate and inviolable."[56]

A different vision of the royal cause came from the pen of another bishop, Fénelon. Although the tutor of the king's grandson, the duke of Burgundy, he was no admirer of the policy of Louis XIV; neither was he an enemy of absolute monarchy as such. Like Bossuet, he believed in moral guidance of the monarch as the only legitimate and effective way to ensure that the kingship was used for the sake of the people and the country. But he was far more vigorous in criticizing the personalism and the greedy arrogance of the Sun King than was Bossuet, who restricted himself to hints and allusions that Louis could always construe to his own advantage. Fénelon's retelling of the story of Telemachus in prose, published in 1699, was actually a roman à clef of contemporary French politics. It was no wonder that the king finally decided that the bishop was "the most intelligent and most chimerical man in the kingdom."[57] But he had already commanded him to leave the court and reside at his see of Cambrai for his role in the Quietism controversy and his quarrel with Bossuet.

Seven years earlier Fénelon had written a scathing letter to the king. It may or may not have been delivered, although Madame de Maintenon and Cardinal de Noailles certainly read it, but it did not reach the eyes of the public. If it had, Fénelon's disgrace would have come earlier, for in it he denounced the monarch's personal absolutism and put the blame on ministers who "speak no longer of the state or its rules but only of the king and his good pleasure."[58] He decried the king's love of conquests: "You should restore the countries that do not belong to you."[59] It was no argument that these conquests were "necessary to your state . . . other men's property is never necessary to you."[60] But to keep one's own state as property was in itself no crime. Fénelon did not call the proprietary concept of the kingship as such into question.[61] Indeed, a decade after his disgrace, in the "Examination of conscience upon the duties of kingship," written about 1711 or 1712, although he criticized the blind application of laws of royal succession, he did not deny that "municipal laws," applying to ordinary property of ordinary people, usually held for kings as well—but their application had to be subordinated to political needs.[62] Kings should not wage wars that concerned only themselves personally, although the people had to pay for them.[63] Fénelon thus accepted one side of the office theory of the kingship, the obligations placed upon the monarch, and one side of the proprietary theory, the ownership of the state, but he rejected the other sides, in the former case the institutional controls upon the king, in the latter the principle that an owner had the right to use property for his own advantage. Like Bossuet, therefore, he posed the dilemma of the co-existence of the two theories, but did not advance its solution.

Another moralist who accepted the absolute monarchy but not the notion that the king should seek his own advantage at the expense of the people was La Bruyère, the author of the biting *Characters*. He held that the sovereign and his subjects had duties toward each other. The king was the depository of the laws and justice, not the absolute master of all the wealth of his subjects. Those who said he was were flatterers.[64] He was only the people's shepherd and should not live a life of luxury which did not benefit them.[65]

Marshal Vauban, not a moralist but the greatest military engineer of his age and in his late years a critic of royal policy, accepted the notion that the king was the master of his subjects' lives and wealth. This was conceding much, although he had only the monarch's political authority and power of taxation in mind, and for a royalist pen it was a rare proviso that followed. The king, Vauban added, was not master of subjects' opinions; these were "*intérieurs*," beyond his power, and only God could direct them as he wanted.[66] Even less adulatory was a pamphleteer of 1680, who denounced the brutal war minister Louvois and urged the Dauphin to depose him, lest the people or foreign princes do so. It was a question of the safety of the kingdom and of keeping "a crown that belongs to you."[67] The proprietary character of the kingship was still taken for granted; it could be used by critics no less than flatterers.

It was from the camp of the Huguenots that the principle began to be called into question. During the mid-century crisis of the Fronde they had remained staunchly loyal to the crown, but their royalism went for naught when the king decided on a policy of conversion, first by bribery and then by force, culminating in the revocation of the Edict of Nantes in 1685. When they went into exile, as virtually all their spiritual and intellectual leaders had to do, they faced their new relationship to the crown with reinforced religious convictions but shattered political principles. In England they could read the works of Sir Algernon Sidney, beheaded after the Rye House Plot in 1683 for his writings. Sidney, more a moderate monarchist than an outright republican, hated Louis XIV and his state with undiluted fury. His description of France under the Sun King—"the whole body of that state is full of boils and wounds and putrid sores."[68]—may be pure savage rhetoric, but Sidney's assertion that the kingdom of France "neither was, nor is, disposable as a patrimony or chattel,"[69] is a sober restatement of what had been said and resaid hundreds of times by French legists.

A quite new avenue of political debate was opened up, however, by an argument from the pen of a Huguenot exile, La Combe de Vrigny, who was a grandson of Henry IV's Duplessis de Mornay. Absolute monarchy, he wrote, reduced subjects to the status of slaves.[70] This was not rhetoric at all, but an equation of absolute monarchy with seigneurial monarchy that was of the highest significance. For no serious political thinker upheld the Ottoman empire as a model for Western countries, and if it could be shown that absolute monarchy in practice was indistinguishable from seigneurial monarchy, then the only respectable alternatives that remained were either some form of limited monarchy or an outright republic.

The latter option was not suggested even by those exiles who emigrated to the Dutch Republic. One of these, Pierre Jurieu, produced the most important critique of absolute monarchy by any Huguenot. Unlike his great contemporary and rival, Pierre Bayle, who managed to combine the most corrosive philosophical skepticism with a continuing belief in the superiority of absolutism as a form of government, Jurieu turned all the weapons of his intellectual armory upon the rule of Louis XIV. The problems of proprietorship of the state permeated his principal political work, *The Sighs of Enslaved France.*[71]

Jurieu broke ground from the very beginning, defending the Fronde as an effort on behalf of the public welfare and freedom.[72] The kings of France had risen to the height of tyranny where the prince "looks at everything as belonging to himself." He imposed and collected taxes without consulting the people, the magnates, the estates, or the Parlements. Under Colbert's administration, he asserted, there had actually been a discussion of whether to make all the monetary holdings and lands in France part of the royal domain (there is no evidence that such a discussion ever happened); this was parallel to what had been done by the Mohammedan princes of Turkey, Persia, and the Mogul empire. Some day a finance minister a bit bolder than Colbert would wrest away all inheritances; the prince who ruled France was already convinced that he had the right to do so.[73] The old emphasis upon the needs of the state had been replaced by stress on those of the king. "The king has taken the place of the state." Only the personal interests of the king counted any longer.[74] Earlier kings of France had claimed despotic and absolute power; Louis XIV exercised it. He believed he was bound by no laws, because he was obliged to give account of his actions only to God; he was convinced he was the "absolute master" of the lives, freedom, persons, wealth, religion, and conscience of his subjects—"a maxim that causes us to shudder with horror when we consider its consequences and see with our own eyes its present effects."[75] Jurieu brought to the fore the antipersonalism implicit in the office theory: "A wise king should have no private quarrels, no private interest. For it is not permitted to him to spill the blood of his subjects solely to satisfy both his ambition and his vengeance. All those who have defined tyranny have made one of its characteristics that everything is done for the king's own interest and not for the people's."[76] A case was the War of Devolution, which was waged for a private interest of the king.[77] Jurieu castigated the whole school of theologians and jurists who taught "a mad theology" and "a mad juris-prudence" on the power of kings. Among their false teachings was the doctrine that the kingdom belongs to the king in the same way as private property to individuals, including the right of sale and disposition, so that "successive crowns are family property like other inheritances."[78]

Thus far Jurieu might have been only an extreme example of the kind of criticism we have seen at its most cogent in Fénelon. But he went beyond to argue for a right of resistance to an absolute and tyrannical monarch.[79] He rebuffed and re-butted the argument that subjects had no recourse against a king who was a tyrant because he abused his power. It was his duty to rule on behalf of his subjects, and if he did not, they could correct him.[80] They had no obligation to provide him with all kinds of needless luxuries and "filthy pleasures of the senses." Why should the people pay for "the wild passions of the king"?[81] This is the argument not of a forthright republi-can but of a passionate believer in the office theory of kingship. The time had not yet come for the argument that kings by their very nature are incapable of ruling well—for that would have been to abandon the office theory, forgoing the oppor-tunity to use it as a weapon against tyrannical abuse of the royal power. Indeed, Jurieu used the proprietary notion in 1689 to defend the sovereignty of William and Mary in Britain. Replying to a work by Antoine Arnauld, the great Jansenist who, although himself in exile in the Spanish Nether-lands, nonetheless denounced William as "a new Absalom, new Herod, new Cromwell, new Nero," Jurieu asserted the legitimacy of the new king and queen across the sea. James II had become a tyrant, forfeiting his right to the throne. Public affairs and property are not controlled by the same rules as private matters. Private persons may do what they want with their patrimony, but public persons who govern states and societies may not. Yet William's right to the throne was dynastic, hereditary: he was acting as heir to the throne (it will be recalled that he was both James's nephew and son-in-law) to save the state that belonged to his family.[52] The people might have been the original sovereigns, but when they created a monarch by contract, the public power still belonged to him "as his property."[53] Still he was obligated to use it for the benefit of the people, at the risk of forfeiture. The revolutionary potential of the office theory of kingship was beginning to predominate over the proprietary attitude. Yet, how persistent this was was shown when the author of a Huguenot pamphlet, *French Policy Unmasked*, which openly called for Louis's overthrow, phrased it in terms of "dispossessing" him.[54]

The test of the king's own commitment to either or both of these principles lies, of course, in what he did rather than in what he wrote. Particularly revealing is his conduct in 1714 in declaring in his testament that his already legitimized bastards, the duke of Le Maine and the count of Toulouse, were princes of the blood, with the right of succession to the throne immediately after the Orleans line and the Condés. It had been a never-questioned rule of the royal succession that only the king's sons on the right side of the bed inherited a claim to the throne; illegitimate sons might be given high titles and vast estates, they might be wed to future duchesses and countesses, but they were barred from the throne itself.[55] The rule rested both on the common family law of Western Christendom for many hundreds of years, and on the political fact that illegitimate claimants were an irrepressible source of civil war. Louis's action seems to have rested in part upon strong affection for the sons Madame de Montespan had given him. But it was a flagrant violation of what was universally recognized as part of the fundamental law of the French monarchy. It was unconstitutional, to use an anachronism, and it displayed Louis's discomfort with even those limitations upon his power that consolidated absolute monarchy as a dynastic possession.[56]

Saint-Simon was wrathful: the king had acted as if he could dispose of the crown, forgetting that it was an entail that did not belong to him "in his own right [en propre]," that it was not a "free heritage."[57]

But Louis does not seem to have taken the act very seriously. In giving his testament on August 26, 1714, to De Mesmes, first president of the Parlement of Paris, to be opened on his death, he was frank: "The example of the kings my predecessors and that of the testament of the king my father do not leave me unawares of what may happen to this one; but they wanted it, they tormented me, I was left no rest no matter what I said. Well! I bought my rest. There it is, take it away; what will happen to it will happen; at least I shall be patient, and I will hear no more about it."[58] The next day he made a similar statement to the widow of James II: "Madame, I have made my testament. I was tormented to do it. . . . I have bought some rest. I know it is powerless and useless. As long as we are alive, we can do anything we want; afterwards, we can do less than private persons; we have only to look at what happened to the testament of the king my father, and that right after he died, and those of so many other kings. I know it very well. Nonetheless they wanted it; they gave me neither peace nor patience nor rest until it was done. Well then, Madame, it is done! What will happen to it will happen; but at least they will not torment me any longer."[59] These are the statements not of an imperious king violating the fundamental laws as if they did not exist, but of an old man, almost another Lear, whose bastards were his Goneril and Regan.

Although when Louis XIV died the next year, the right of the legitimized bastards to the crown would have been an empty one, because the king's legitimate great-grandson survived and followed him, the late monarch's will was soon undone, as he had predicted. On September 12, 1715, the Parlement of Paris declared the legitimization of the bastards null and void. The Regent Philip of Orleans claimed that Louis had said to him: "I recommend the Dauphin to you.

Serve him as faithfully as you served me, and work to keep his kingdom for him. If he should pass away, you will be the master and the crown will belong to you."[90] There is no reason to doubt that the king had said it.

Actually there would have been a closer heir than Philip according to the strict rule of inheritance, the regent's nephew Philip, duke of Anjou and since 1700 king of Spain. But the possibility that Philip V might rule simultaneously over France and Spain had been one of the central issues in the War of the Spanish Succession, and peace had not been possible until both Louis and Anjou had accepted the Allies' demand that Philip renounce the French throne in perpetuity for himself and his descendants. The struggle over the demand for the renunciation had brought into the clear not only the question of the immutability of the fundamental laws, but also—and from the point of view of this book—more importantly, the subordination of the private to the public interest in the conduct of the state.

CHAPTER V

LOUIS XIV AND
THE SPANISH SUCCESSION

OUIS XIV looked at war not only as a fact of political life
L but also as a positive good. What Barker says of wars in
this period—that they were for absolute rulers the "greatest of
games," with territorial aggrandizement the prize of victory[1]—
holds especially true of Louis XIV. By war he hoped to make
the France he ruled larger and stronger, more than ever domi-
nant among the nations; by war he hoped to assure his own
everlasting glory. War in his reign centered on the question of
the Spanish succession, and we can see in the diplomacy of
that question how the issue of the proprietary character of the
monarchy came to the fore. Issues that had been only sporadically important during the struggles over the successions to
Philip IV and Henry III and during the episode of the treaty
of Troyes now became crucial. But they were not quickly
solved, so that the debate ran on for decades, permitting and
impelling the political implications of theoretical principles to
be worked out in unusual detail. The modern reader must
guard against stretching such territorial questions beyond personal and dynastic interests to include the deliberate creation
of a united French nation, as is so prevalent among modern
nationalist historians.[2] This is to assign to a man of the seventeenth century the goal of building the nation-state of the
nineteenth and twentieth centuries. Similarly, to say that the
king conducted his foreign policy more along dynastic lines
than according to the interests of the state, as does Näf,[3] is to
assume not only the ethical rightness but also the factual
reality of the office theory of the kingship; it is to assume that
the abstract state actually exists. Hill, the historian of

European diplomacy, is more on target in equating dynastic policy like Louis's with the proprietary theory of the kingdom.[4]

The diplomatic documents of the time speak of sovereignty as property in the most matter-of-fact way. Duke Charles IV of Lorraine ceded to Louis XIV in 1662 the "ownership" of his duchy of Lorraine and Bar to pass into the king's possession after the duke's death, "with all the rights of sovereignty," to be incorporated forever into the crown of France.[5] That the struggle between Louis and the slippery duke continued for more than a decade is beside the point here. The duchy of Lorraine was property, and was so seen after the French seized it in 1670, both by the French themselves, who claimed that Prince Charles of Lorraine was the "true owner," and by the Dutch ambassador in Paris.[6]

The property claim of the French king that mattered far more than the eternal contretemps with Duke Charles was the right in the succession to the Spanish monarchy that Louis XIV claimed on behalf of his wife. The French ambassador in Madrid in 1662, the archbishop of Embrun, told the duke of Medina that the Low Countries "belonged" to the French queen even ahead of the infante of Spain, her brother, just as Isabella had received the territory in 1599 with her husband, Archduke Albert, from her father, Philip II. The comparison was invalid, Medina replied, because Isabella had been invested with the sovereignty. Embrun, writing to Louis XIV, said it was no refutation because "gifts" between living persons do not suppress a right of inheritance but rather assume it."[7] Neither Frenchman nor Spaniard doubted that the sovereignty of the Low Countries was proprietary in character, although they differed as to who the owner was.

Although Louis XIV lusted after the whole of the Spanish heritage, his strongest interest was in those Low Countries immediately to the north of France and so uncomfortably close to Paris. Many decades earlier French jurists had noted that the law of succession in Brabant and some other provinces of the Low Countries (Malines and Namur) established a difference in the rights of inheritance between the children of the two marriages of a father who took a second wife after the death of the first. The rule, known as the "right (or law) of devolution," was that the children of the first bed inherited all the existing estate of their parents when their father remarried; he retained only a life interest in it, and the children of the subsequent marriage could inherit only property brought by their own mother as dowry and whatever wealth accrued to the family after the new family was formed. (Different in its mode of operation, this law was not too different in intent and impact from a rule in force in France, the Edict on Second Marriages of 1560, as it was applied in practice.)[8] The problem of whether a law that held force in only some of the provinces could control the succession in all of them was not made central, although the question it raised would be one to which Emperor Charles VI would address himself in the next century with his Pragmatic Sanction. Indeed, since the last surviving son of Philip IV by his first marriage, Philip Prosper, died on November 1, 1661, and Charles Joseph, the future Charles (Carlos) II of Spain, was born only five days later, for a brief time Maria Teresa had been the heiress of the whole Spanish monarchy. Under the principle of the devolution law the Spanish Netherlands should have passed to her at once if her renunciations were void. But, as the Spanish ambassador at The Hague pointed out sardonically, if that rule held, the Netherlands should have gone to the descendants of Charles Emmanuel of Savoy, since his third wife, Catherine of Spain, was born of the third marriage of Philip II, while Philip III was the issue of the fourth marriage.[9] The debate that ensued, however, was centered not on the rights of the House of Savoy but on those of the House of Bourbon.

Jurists on both sides wrangled over whether Louis XIV was stretching a law that applied solely to private individuals (a "municipal law") to cover possession of the sovereign power. French jurists were hard put to support their case, because only three instances were found where there had not been male heirs to the duchy of Brabant in the direct line of succession. In the first, Philip the Good, duke of Burgundy, had been preferred to his aunt, Margaret of Holland. In the second, Mary of Burgundy had been her father's only heir. The third was the case of Isabella of Spain, and, as Embrun had found it, the transfer of sovereignty here was considered to have resulted from a father's gift, not the operation of a law.[10] In the face of the obscurity of the situation, Louis felt it was legitimate to make his claim on behalf of Queen Marie Thérèse (as historians call her after her marriage), especially since her dowry had not been paid and there was not the least likelihood that it ever would be. He was doing no more than to make good in the Low Countries what had been denied him in violation of the marriage contract. But behind this desire lay, of course, the strategic advantage that he sought there.[11]

The question could not be put off to the future because of France's relations with the Dutch. Louis made an alliance with the States General in 1663, but it was in danger from the beginning because of the continuing Dutch fear that French occupation of the southern Netherlands would give them much too mighty a neighbor. De Witt, the Dutch leader, at first conceded that the French queen's renunciation of her inheritance rights might be invalid because her dowry had never been paid, but he hoped to obviate the anticipated French attack on the Spanish Netherlands by gaining acceptance of either of two alternatives that dated to the time of Richelieu. One was the formation of a separate Low Countries republic in the south under the protection of France and the States General (called "cantonment"); the other was the partition of the country between its southern and northern neighbors.[12] Either measure would give France security against invasion down the north French plain from the Low Countries, but only the latter would give any satisfaction to the desire of the French monarch for territorial aggrandizement. Louis wanted to take the Low Countries as his own, and the devolution law was his grounds for immediate action when Philip IV died.

De Witt tried, however, to disprove its applicability; it had force, he told the French ambassador at The Hague, D'Estrades, only for the inheritance of private persons, not for the crown of Brabant, but he also asked for an exact statement of the French claims.[13]

Louis was forced to play a subtle game of diplomatic maneuvering, because he needed the Dutch as allies to prevent their becoming the allies of England at his expense; but he did not want to pay the price of abandoning his ambitions in the Low Countries. He therefore did not reject cantonment out of hand, but at the same time he reaffirmed his queen's rights in view of the invalidity of her renunciation and the Spanish failure to pay her dowry, and left the devolution claim unmentioned for the moment.[14] De Witt became openly skeptical that failure to pay the dowry was adequate cause for invalidation of the renunciation,[15] and he told the French ambassador that the Dutch would accept the devolution right only if it was shown to be effective in law and practice, which had not yet been done.[16] He also turned to studying the histories, laws, and customs of Brabant, or, more exactly, asked the historiographer Wicquefort to do it for him. Wicquefort informed him that the histories of the Carolingian period were too vague for any reliance to be put on them in matters of such detail, except for the fact that Charlemagne had had no children by his first marriage.[17] De Witt thereupon told D'Estrades that he did not see how any right the law of devolution might bestow upon the French queen could arise before the death of her brother. He repeated, too, that the preference for the children of the first bed, which was the law of Brabant, applied only to private persons; it had not been used for fiefs formerly held of the crown since the late fifteenth century. The Dutch were willing to accept a French claim based on a legitimate title to the succession, confirmed by marriage contracts, testaments, laws, or examples.[18] The king had his ready reply: well briefed by his legists, he informed De Witt that there had been no case since the fifteenth century for the good and sufficient reason that there had been no such double marriage, but that there had been instances of the application of the devolution law before then.[19] De Witt was not impressed. He told the States of Holland a few weeks later that he could not imagine that there existed testamentary treaties or other similar dispositions that could give the French the right they claimed. For one thing, Flanders and other provinces "were not at all the property of the late queen of Spain" who could dispose of them by will, but "belonged to the patrimony of Philip IV."[20] Once again we see the pattern: what was involved was not whether the southern Netherlands were the property of the reigning dynasty, which everyone granted, but only what kind of property, held under what special conditions.

In any event, war broke out between England and the Dutch Republic early in 1665, the French came in on the Dutch side, however reluctantly, and the issue of the Spanish Netherlands slumbered. Even the death of Philip IV on September 17, 1665, did not seem to stir the French, although he left a testament dated September 14, establishing the succession to the Spanish throne to the exclusion of Marie Thérèse.[21] Only in 1667, when the English were obviously defeated and peace was only a matter of time (it was concluded at Breda in July), did Louis at last reveal his hand. D'Estrades came to De Witt in mid-July with the official announcement of a French invasion of the Low Countries. (The war of 1667–1668 between France and Spain is known in history, of course, as the War of Devolution because its primary ground was the queen's rights under that law.) D'Estrades gave the councilor pensionary a copy of the *Treatise on the Queen's Rights*, written by the French legist René Bilain and published by the king's own press.[22]

Bilain's treatise is a work of key importance in the history of proprietary dynasticism. It has no significant originality as political theory; but, after all, that is not what we are looking for. It does state with unusual candor the views that held sway in the court of Louis XIV, which is what interests us. It is also significant that Bilain was willing to speak plainly of things that most legists avoided like the plague. He wrote to defend the king's action in sustaining "all the privileges of blood and law" possessed by Louis XIV in his person or that of his wife or son. In language that carried the spirit of the court remarkably well, he observed that the king "lacks neither the power to maintain his rights, nor affection to preserve them, nor courage to assure them." The remark that Louis's silence would make men believe he had fallen into "a kind of lethargy" rings like the king's own words.[23]

The invasion of the Low Countries, Bilain affirmed, was not a war of conquest but a war to assure the king's son of his patrimony.[24] Centuries of argument that sovereignty was not patrimony were swept away with a single stroke of the pen. True, the Burgundians and their Habsburg heirs had always called their Low Countries provinces their patrimony; but Bilain does not ask whether, once these territories passed under the crown of France, they became inalienable parts of the royal domain. Would they then cease to be patrimony? He neither asked nor answered the question, because it was too precise.

The king was duty bound to protect his peoples, Bilain continued. Was he to do less for his own family and himself?[25] What was involved was not an ordinary act of royal legislation, "but a right, an inheritance. . . . We are not treating sovereignty as sovereignty but as an inheritance, a succession that comes into play with the death of the last sovereign."[26] Louis was only obeying the law of God "which adjudges to each his own" (as well as the law of nature which inspires kings like other men with love of their family).[27] Successive monarchies were like other property, except for particular characteristics, such as independence, inalienability, and indivisibility. As sovereignties, they were distinct; "as fiefs or heritages, they follow the same rules as the succession of ordinary fiefs and heritages."[28] Hence hereditary sovereignties are "veritable patrimonies which are transmitted [se déferent] and follow the customs, like other successions."[29] Bilain did quote, however, without rebuttal, the statement of Pimentel, a Spanish negotiator at the Pyrenees, to Mazarin, regarding the French queen-to-be's renunciation, that "the right of scepters is not in the marketplace of private arrangements, and it belongs only to Heaven to distribute them by the order of Blood and Birth."[30]

The queen was asking only for "what belongs to her by the strictest rigor of customs in the successions of their common father, mother, and brother. . . . She is a daughter, and consequently an heiress; nature is her title, and law her reason; she needs no other favor than that of common law, nor other eloquence than the voice of blood."[31] Her dowry consisted of two parts: what her father gave her, and what she inherited by the death of the queen her mother and Prince Balthazar her brother, which included a number of "sovereignties" in the Low Countries.[32] Being the only child from the first bed, on these deaths she had inherited according to the law of devolution the "property" of the duchy of Brabant which belonged to her father.[33] The rule of devolution did hold for the family of the sovereign and for sovereignty; it had been so applied in the empire, and "in any case it is an error of principle to deny that sovereignties follow the customs like other fiefs, unless there is a special law in the state disposing of them."[34]

Bilain then turned the argument of inalienability of royal successions against the Spanish Habsburgs, because Marie Thérèse had had no right to renounce her patrimony.[35] She had been compelled to abandon "everything that belonged to her that she did not retain either as dowry or as personal property." Could there be anything stranger than to despoil a young princess of "her patrimony, her sovereignties, and all her hopes?" Could a father be so unjust?[36] To reign "is the highest of all Heaven's blessings upon earth."[37] Was it more legitimate to despoil sovereigns than other men, when they were otherwise the special recipients of heaven's privileges?[38] The importance of royal successions was shown in the severity of wars of succession, civil and foreign.[39] How could the king of

France ratify a renunciation that was null, and that "embodies the alienation of so many states and sovereignties that belong to his wife?"[40] Sovereignties were inalienable and could not be renounced, except in a solemn assembly of the estates and with the consent of the whole people.[41] One may imagine how likely such an assembly would have been in the France of Louis XIV. But any stick was good enough to beat the Spaniards with, and Philip IV had not submitted his eldest daughter's renunciation to the Cortes in Spain or the States assemblies in the Low Countries.

Succession was an obligation that an individual could not divest himself of: "The authority to reign is no less a servitude in its way than the necessity to obey is for others,"[42] and the prince could not withdraw from the body politic of which he was the head.[43] In Spain there was an "inviolable maxim" that the children of the sovereign came to the throne not by a right that they held from him, that is, as a patrimonial inheritance, but "by a sacred entail of the law of the state." The successor was a "substitute" or reversionary (in the special legal sense of one who holds an estate in a particularly tight kind of entailed trust). The will of the predecessor had no part in the succession. Sovereignty was the greatest of entails (*majorats*).[44] Not only was this Spanish practice parallel with the French theory, it was a view of the Spanish royal succession law that would conflict with the French attitude toward the testament of Charles II some thirty years later.

Bilain could not avoid inconsistencies. He could hold that the ducal domain of Brabant could not be alienated or diminished,[45] and then that it was sovereignty that was indivisible by its nature, although this was not true of domains, "which are divided every day."[46] Renunciations are forbidden by public law because the crowns were given to kings not for their own sake but for that of the peoples they ruled. "Religion cannot tolerate them [renunciations], since the right of the scepter and the crown is not like possessions that are for sale in the marketplace and are subject to all the vicissitudes produced by the self-interest [*l'interest*] or inconstancy of individuals. Rather it is a kind of priesthood [*sacerdoce*], a wholly sacred calling and mission, which forms a conjugal and indissoluble bond between the Prince or Princess and his or her state."[47]

Throughout these passages Bilain, although acknowledging various other principles or theories of kingship, reverts constantly to the proprietary approach. There is, too, a clear conflict between the proprietary principle, with its emphasis upon what the crown does for the holder, and the office theory, which stresses what the holder does for the people, even if the discordant statements are found in different portions of the same work.

Louis XIV knew that these arguments, however cogent, would lack persuasiveness without the reinforcement of arms. Years before he had admitted to his own envoy at The Hague that the Dutch demand for an exposition of "clear" French rights was asking for the impossible, "for there are hardly any claims in the world so clear, in any conflict whatsoever, that exceptions and contrary arguments will not be found which everyone will accept as good depending on his passion or interest."[48] No wonder, then, that Wicquefort wrote that the devolution law was important not for its theoretical force but as a basis "for preserving the queen's property [*bien*] by the means that sovereigns customarily use in such circumstances."[49]

Although modern historians usually dismiss the devolution argument as a mere pretext or worse—André calls it an unscrupulous transposition of private law to the public sphere[50] and Tapié asserts that no one took it seriously[51]—the contemporary arguments against it were somewhat different in character. They denied not the proprietary element in the Habsburg patrimony in the Low Countries but only the application of a particular municipal law to its inheritance. The transmission of the princely power in the Netherlands had long been frankly proprietary in character. The "natural lords" had been called "prince-proprietors of their states"; there had been cases in which they had disposed of their principalities by gift, sale, and testament.[52] Philip the Handsome on taking over the government in person in Hainaut in 1494, swore to be a good lord "as true heir and proprietor of the country."[53] Charles V, in proposing the formation of the Burgundian Circle to the Reichstag, had argued that his lands in the Low Countries and Burgundy had always been free allods and not imperial fiefs, coming to him by legitimate succession from Charlemagne and Lothair.[54] After the battle of Crépy in 1544, the duke of Alba and other Spaniards had proposed that Spain divest itself of the Low Countries, but the key argument for retaining them had been that they were part of the "ancient patrimony" of Charles V, and this had been decisive.[55] Elizabeth I had told Dutch delegates in 1575 that she did not believe those who told her that the forefathers of Philip II had had the "ownership" of the Low Countries not by inheritance but by election of the people.[56] In 1607, ratifying an agreement with the Dutch, Philip III spoke of the Archdukes Isabella and Albert as princes and sovereign proprietors of all the Netherlands.[57] The archdukes, in fact, had considered that they possessed the sovereignty of the Low Countries only in usufruct, because the future ownership reverted to the king of Spain.[58] In 1646, at the Westphalian negotiations, Peñaranda, the Spanish envoy, had protested to the imperial negotiator, Trautmansdorff, that peace was being bought with his master's property, because the lands of Hither Austria were Spanish property left to the Innsbruck line only in usufruct.[59]

Bilain's treatise raised special problems in the United Provinces. It was not that the Dutch rejected the very notion of proprietorship of the state because they were republicans; they were reluctant to see France in the Low Countries by virtue of any principle. On the one hand Wicquefort called the devolution claim a chimera, because the renunciation had destroyed whatever rights Marie Thérèse and her husband had in the Low Countries.[60] Yet he considered the rule of the Low Countries to be proprietary in character, even if the devolution law was not applicable to it. Isabella, he informed De Witt in a private memorandum, had held the Low Countries by gift of her father and not by the right of the first bed. There was no law in Brabant expressly forbidding sons of the second bed from inheriting where there were daughters of the first, unless the daughters were private heirs of their mother's wealth. It could be assumed that the succession of the duchy of Brabant followed the order of the common law. Significantly, this admission was crossed out, although it remains easily readable in the copy in the archives at The Hague.[61]

The chronicler Aitzema took the devolution right more seriously (and sardonically). It was "plausible" for the French to protect the rights of a child of the first bed against one of the second, "and it was notorious that Spain and Austria had made most of their acquisitions by marriage, *par la Lance de Chair* ["by the Lance of Flesh"; italics in the original] so that the Queen could claim with some reason a right to her father's heritage."[62] Peter Stockmans, the leading jurist in the Spanish Netherlands, had already written a pamphlet, *A Brief Proof*, rebutting the French arguments, with less wit but more weight of erudition, and it was reprinted now.[63] Stockmans questioned whether private inheritance laws could apply to political power, especially if it meant that a woman would inherit ahead of a man.[64] But he admitted the patrimonial character of the Low Countries. Charles V had "freely disposed" of them in the marriage settlement of Philip and Mary Tudor which favored their eventual (and never born) children over Don Carlos, Philip's son by Mary of Portugal. He could not have done this if the succession had been controlled by the law of devolution in Brabant, Gelderland, and other provinces. The same principle held sway in the accession of the archdukes.[65] Thus Stockmans assumes that the ducal dignity was property.

He took Bilain to task for assuming that the private inheritance law that applied in political affairs and political things corresponded to laws for private persons. The argument that the customs of Brabant in private property, called the right of devolution, should be followed in the public succession of the duchy had no force. "For, as affirmed by authors on politics, there is no direct reasoning from private to public successions."[66] Even if Brabant had no laws of succession, it would beyond question be governed by the general law of nations, which always provided that in cases where women are admitted to a succession, they follow men.[67]

In England the earl of Arlington told John Meerman, the Dutch ambassador, that when he had been in Spain most of the members of the king's council there had placed little importance upon the Low Countries, and those who did "cherish" them to some extent did so because they were "the old patrimony of the family and the House of the King," but even they preferred a village on Spain's own border to a whole district in the Low Countries, because Spain drew no profit from this "expensive stepchild."[68]

Lisola, the imperial diplomat who was the most implacable diplomatic foe of Louis XIV and wrote the most important rebuttal of the devolution claim in his *Buckler of State and Justice*,[69] nonetheless admitted that these provinces were part of the "ancient patrimony" of the Habsburg house. Charles V had been the "proprietarie Prince" of the Low Countries.[70] Would Marie Thérèse "out of a frolick throw at their faces Eight of the most flourishing and rich Provinces of the ancient Patrimonie of her Family?"[71] He noted that the same kind of claim could be extended to Germany and elsewhere.[72] (In other works, he observed that the dukes of Lorraine had given the duchy "hereditarily and as property" to the counts of Brabant,[73] and that in recent times Isabella had been its proprietress.)[74] But there was no reason to follow the usages of subjects in settling the affairs of sovereigns, especially since they had the right to change and abolish these usages. "The Princes and the people have their separate laws." The French had to acknowledge this, since it was the only basis of their Salic Law.[75] He pointed out the danger to other states in the doctrine of the French jurists that the crown and its domain were inalienable and that therefore all that Charlemagne had possessed still belonged to the king of France.[76] As for the Low Countries, if Louis wanted to base his claim on his status in private law, then the rule of private law that favored the occupant in peaceable possession should hold.[77] He mocked the application of the law of devolution in this case as "imaginative."[78]

Five years later, when the French invasion of the Dutch Republic began, Lisola wrote in another book that the assertion of the French ministers and writers that the invasion of the Spanish Netherlands in 1667 had been "a simple taking of possession," was an "elegant, ingenious, and well conceived" turn of wit that would amuse later generations of readers but would not please those who now felt the pain in their own guts and asked God for peace in their own time.[79] He mocked Aubéry, author of The Just Claims of the King in the Empire, who had been arrested in 1668 for publishing his work without permission and at an embarrassing time. "These things should not be talked about until they're done."[80] Aubéry did not claim just the imperial crown for Louis XIV but the empire itself, "the patrimony and ancient heritage of French princes," because Charlemagne had possessed it "as a king of France and not as an emperor."[81] He was put in the Bastille not for calling Germany a patrimony of the French kings but for blurting out ambitions that could only frighten the German princes.

Aubéry was also attacked during the Dutch War of 1672–1678 by a Dutch publicist, Petrus Valkenier. Valkenier denounced the Salic Law as a "pure fabrication," and noted the political purpose of its use: to prevent any alienation of French territory while incorporating into the French domain for perpetuity whatever was acquired by the French kings. By establishing the principle that anything given up (as in peace treaties) could be recalled as invalidly granted, despite the rule of prescription, or treaties, or military defeats, or whatever, the French made usurpers of those who possessed anything that Charlemagne had ever had.[82] This would make most of Germany part of the patrimony of the French monarchs.[83] Valkenier, in this attack upon Aubéry, does not hesitate to use the term "patrimony," but he does not take advantage of its Roman law meaning—that the proprietor had free disposal of his property—to attack the French argument, which in this case rested precisely upon denial of the alienability of the French realm or any part of it. This is another instance of the broad use of the term, which legalistic historians tend to forget in their concern to make Louis XIV a hero of the abstract state.

It was a crime in France to read Lisola's *Buckler*, and the son of a celebrated physician, Guy Patin, had to flee Paris because it was found in his home.[84] The book so worried the French that Pellisson was assigned to write in rebuttal a history of the causes of the War of Devolution and an exposition of the king's claims that would be more effective than the lawyers' threats. The *Buckler*, Pellisson wrote in his prospectus, "is the work of an able man which has caused much ado in foreign countries."[85] Years later, when an imperial diplomat bitingly asked the French foreign minister if anyone had ever totted up what Louis had spent in honor and money to rebut the *Buckler*, Croissy replied, "We fight with arms, not books." The imperial diplomat was "satisfied" with the reply.[86] William of Orange agreed. In 1698 he told the French ambassador at London that although it was generally held that Marie Thérèse's renunciation had been valid, such matters were decided not by jurists and lawyers but sword in hand.[87] It may be that the devolution claim was monstrous, as a Dutch Catholic historian of the nineteenth century called it, because it equated a country of hundreds of thousands of dwellers with a private estate and the farm and cattle on it.[88] But he was thinking in terms of his own time. After the War of Devolution was over, Lionne, the French foreign minister, described the French conquests inscribed in the peace of Aachen (Aix-la-Chapelle), as "what now belongs to him [the king of France] in the Low Countries."[89]

Whatever the theoretical talk about crowns not being in the marketplace, when there was a discussion in 1670 of a possible exchange of territories with Spain, Louis was not only willing to give up Bayonne and Perpignan, but even to add a part of French Navarre, and in addition to pay a *soulte* (the legal term for a payment made by one heir to another to bring shares into balance) to Spain. As if this one application of private property law was not enough to display the ease with which he saw realms and lands as in the marketplace, Louis offered a "gratification" of two million livres to the emperor, Leopold I, and one million to his minister, Lobkowitz. He was sarcastic about it, however: "When we put into one side of the scale the greatest kingdom that is for sale, we can nonetheless put into the other side so much money that it would be able not only to counterbalance the other side but even to outweigh it." Leopold did not dare tempt Madrid's wrath by picking up the suggestion.[90] But the case is significant for us. Actually, the term "for sale" (*à acheter*) is used a little loosely, for the payment would have gone to Vienna and not to Madrid (except for the *soulte*); but on the other hand, it would have been buying out Vienna's claim upon the Spanish inheritance. But the lack of embarrassment about using the language of the marketplace in a nonmetaphorical way is what is important. In the next century, the statesman Alberoni, writing of the ministers of his day, would describe such practices in a powerful image: "They cut and pare states and kingdoms as if they were Dutch cheeses."[91]

Louis XIV could shift theoretical positions as they became convenient and advantageous to him, or the contrary. In 1685, when Leopold sought to persuade Madrid to change the order of succession of the Spanish monarchy laid down in the testament of Philip IV, Louis instructed his ambassador in Spain to inform the ministers there that he was informed of the plan to have Charles II abandon "all that belongs to him in the Low Countries."[92] These rights belonged "incontestably" to his, Louis's, son.[93] Louis held that "the right of scepters

cannot be transferred, and it belongs only to Heaven to distribute it by the channels [voies] of blood and birth."[94] Two
years later, when it was reported that Vienna was sending the
emperor's second son to Madrid to be brought up as the heir
presumptive, Louis instructed Feuquières, the French ambassador in Spain, to demand a private audience with Charles to
warn him "to leave to God the burden [soin] of giving to him
such heirs as please divine Providence."[95] The admonition was
repeated three weeks later, with additional arguments that the
renunciation of Marie Thérèse was invalid because "the right
of crowns is not traded on the marketplace." Mazarin had told
this to Don Luis de Haro when the latter had raised the renunciation proposal in the Pyrenees negotiations.[96]

That princes did indeed look upon states and realms as objects of barter was shown in the statement of Elector Maximilian Emmanuel of Bavaria to the French envoy Villars in
1688: "If the Emperor gave me immediate possession of some
considerable state, I would be willing, without falling out with
the king, to become a greater lord [seigneur] than I am now,
and one day, if the king of Spain were to die without children,
I could in turn give that country to the king [of France], providing he put me in possession of the kingdoms of Naples and
Sicily."[97]

The principles of dynastic proprietorship are clearly enunciated in a proclamation that Louis XIV gave to Rébenac, who
replaced Feuquières as ambassador at Madrid in 1688, to be
published whenever Charles II died.[98] A decade later, with
Charles still alive although obviously much nearer death, Louis
realized that the attempt to gain all of the Spanish heritage for
his own family would embroil France in another immense,
costly, and dangerous war.[99] The Peace of Ryswick (Rijswijk)
which ended the Nine Years' War (the War of the League of
Augsburg, in older terminology) in 1697 was therefore followed by two treaties of partition, negotiated however not
with Austria, the other major contender and claimant, but
with the maritime powers, England and the Dutch Republic.

The centrality of the property concept of kingship was obvious throughout the negotiations.

In March 1698 Lord Portland, the closest adviser of William III, came to France to discuss a treaty of partition. During the first meeting with Pomponne, the minister of foreign affairs, and Torcy, the secretary of state for foreign affairs, talk soon turned to the testament of Philip IV on the succession to the Spanish monarchy. He did not know the details, Portland said, and asked if the Salic Law was observed in Spain. The Frenchmen replied that the emperor's children had no right to the Spanish crown. Not only was the Salic Law not observed in Spain, it was through women that the Spanish monarchy had been united with the House of Austria; and a testament could not change the fundamental laws of a kingdom. When Portland said that in England Henry VIII had changed the order of succession several times, they replied that the normal order had in fact been followed, with the son first and then the two daughters in the sequence of their birth. (It will be recalled that the succession acts under Henry VIII involved not the order of succession but the legitimacy of Mary and Elizabeth.) In Spain, in the early sixteenth century, Ferdinand of Aragon had not been able to change the order of succession. When his wife, Isabella of Castile, died, he failed in his efforts to remain king of Castile, because "the crown had belonged to that princess by right of succession." The Castilians had forced him to allow his daughter Joanna to take the throne, and her son Charles had been compelled by the Castilians to reign jointly with his mother even after she went mad.

Nonetheless Louis XIV, "not wishing for himself anything that could give umbrage to the rest of Europe," was willing to promise to arrange the succession so that it could never be joined to the crown of France. Portland replied that the duke of Anjou would remain a French prince, and the French interests would carry greater weight than those of Spanish Bourbons. There was less peril in a Habsburg succession, since the Spanish monarchy could not be joined to the imperial crown. The French rejoinder was that the experience of the Burgundian house showed that branches of the House of France went their own way. Finally, Portland suggested that under the testament of Philip IV, Elector Maximilian Emmanuel of Bavaria was the legitimate heir and should be allowed to succeed. To this they replied, as before, that the testament was null and void.[100] Louis XIV was willing to promise that the monarchy of Spain would never be annexed to his own crown, and also to have the elector of Bavaria keep the sovereignty of the Low Countries, which the Dauphin would cede to him. But the rest of the Spanish monarchy belonged to the Dauphin as "legitimate heir." For this the Dauphin was ready to cede his rights to his second son, the duke of Anjou, to be brought up in Spain as a Spaniard.[101]

D'Harcourt, who had become the French ambassador in Madrid, warned Louis that under the 1668 treaty of partition with the emperor, the advantage would have gone to the latter. It would be better to obtain cession of all Flanders than of the whole Spanish monarchy, for a French prince on that throne would "soon forget the impressions of his birth."[102] This put the contrast between narrow dynastic interests and broad political interests very well; it was the same point that Louis had made to Tallard, but with the consequences clearly drawn out. There would be another Bourbon on a throne, but no advantage to the French state. Louis's very point was turned on itself. Furthermore, if the Spanish crown was inalienable, then the Spanish king could not permit partition of the monarchy. It was the political equivalent of putting the monarchy in the marketplace, except that it would be done not by the monarch himself but by outsiders, one of whom had at least the color of a claim but the rest of whom had none whatsoever. At least the lapsed partition treaty of 1668 had been made by the two principal claimants.

When Louis XIV agreed to renunciation of the Spanish crown by the Dauphin on behalf of himself and of his son Anjou, the English became interested. Nonetheless Portland, meeting with Tallard in Holland, noted the problem of "transporting the rights of heredity of a crown," and suggested that this be done between the Dauphin and the elector of Bavaria, and not in the general treaty. Tallard's reply, in view of the whole fuss over inalienability, is remarkable: the French king "had no scruple" in so doing; he believed the Dauphin's right to be incontestable, so that "the crown of Spain would belong to him" when Charles II died, "and since it was his own he could dispose of his property as he wished."[103] Louis XIV had learned the lesson of two hard wars (the War of Devolution being one in which he had been thwarted by threat, not combat): he preferred not to engage in one even if it had as good prospects as he thought a war for Spain would give him. As he wrote Tallard, "We know when we begin it, but we do not know how it will end. What is more certain than anything else is the misfortunes it will bring in its train and the sufferings of the people."[104] He swung around to accepting the testament of Philip IV if the throne of Spain would go to the duke of Savoy, another claimant, in the event that the elector of Bavaria died without children; since it was Louis's son who was "transporting" his rights, he could do so to the duke of Savoy as well as to the elector of Bavaria.[105]

A treaty of partition therefore became possible, and one was made on October 11, 1698, between Louis XIV, William III as king of Great Britain, and the States General. Joseph Ferdinand, the six-year-old son of Elector Maximilian Emmanuel, was given Spain itself, shorn of portions for the French Dauphin and Archduke Charles of Austria.[106] It was rejected by Emperor Leopold and Charles II, but that did not matter, for Joseph Ferdinand died in 1700. France and the sea powers came together again in another treaty of partition, this time assigning Spain to Archduke Charles minus Naples-Sicily and Lorraine for the Dauphin. The emperor still turned his back on any arrangement between France and the maritime powers. It was not that he refused any thought of a partition. England and

France, an imperial minister told the French envoy at Vienna, "have been freehanded with what does not belong to them." If there had to be a partition, it should be negotiated only among the claimants themselves.[107] But Charles could do more about the proposed partition than the emperor. Before he died on November 1, 1700, he drew up a testament giving the Spanish monarchy to the duke of Anjou, as "king and natural lord proprietor," provided he accepted the whole of the monarchy. If he insisted upon its partition, in accordance with the treaties, then the whole of the monarchy would go to Archduke Charles. If Philip of Anjou accepted the throne, he could not remain on it if he later succeeded to the crown of France; in that case, it would pass to his younger brother, the duke of Berry. The two crowns would be "forever separate."[108]

The news of the testament and the king's death arrived at Fontainebleau on November 9. When the imperial envoy came to Torcy to propose beginning negotiations over the succession, the French foreign minister (Pomponne had died the year before) replied that Louis XIV was now in a position to make a choice and was not bound to anything.[109] The royal council met the next day. According to Saint-Simon, Torcy and Beauvilliers, another member, argued that the interests of France should come first and that France would benefit more by accepting the treaty of partition, which gave it Lorraine, Guipuzcoa, the key to Spain, Tuscany, Naples, and Sicily, than by accepting the testament. Philip of Anjou was only seventeen, and his descendants could become more Spanish than even the Habsburgs had been. Pontchartrain, favoring acceptance, rejoined that the Spanish kings had been enemies of France because they were Habsburgs. The Dauphin then spoke up with a passion that surprised those accustomed to his usual sloth. He told the king that he was taking the liberty of "asking for his heritage, because he was in a position to accept it; the monarchy of Spain was the property of the Queen his mother, and consequently his own, and, for the sake of the tranquility of Europe, that of his second son, to whom he ceded it with all his heart; but he would not abandon an inch to anyone else."[110]

On November 14, the decision was taken to accept the testament, and two days later the king presented Philip to his court. "Gentlemen, here is the king of Spain. His birth called him to this crown, as well as the late king's testament."[111] The inconsistency of the two rights must have been obvious to Torcy, and Louis himself at other times had argued strongly against the right of a king of Spain to decide his succession by testament.[112] The French monarch managed to work almost everything in. The Spanish nation insisted upon Philip's having the crown, and Louis XIV had given it "with pleasure." "It was the order of Heaven." To Philip he gave instructions to be a "good Spaniard" as his first duty, but to remember too that he had been born a Frenchman, and to "maintain the union of the two countries" as a way to keep the peace of Europe. A world of tensions that decades would not solve! How much simpler the cry of Castel del Rios, the Spanish envoy: "God be praised! The Pyrenees are melted. We are henceforth only one."[113]

On December 1, Louis submitted to the Parlement of Paris for registration the Dauphin's renunciation of the Spanish crown, but he maintained the right of succession to the French throne for Anjou, after the Dauphin "the true and legitimate successor and heir of our crown and our states," and after him of his first son, the duke of Burgundy. The renunciation was motivated not by fundamental law but by "our special grace, full power, and royal authority." But the affirmation of Anjou's right of succession in France was, in fact, a violation of the provisions of the testament of Charles II.[114] When Anjou was about to leave for Spain to become that country's king as Philip V, his grandfather repeated to him that France and Spain would be as one. "The two nations now should consider each other as only one nation. They should have the same interests."[115] ("Nation" here meant, of course, a political, not a linguistic-ethnic entity.) And after he reached Spain, Philip was treated by Louis not just as a grandson needing advice, but as a subject: the king of France was "the master [who] must decide," he informed the French ambassador.[116]

Publication of the testament of Charles II brought arguments against its validity. Even before the Spanish monarch's death, Pope Innocent XII had warned him that sovereigns should not consider their kingdoms as their own property. Even renunciations, he added, were null and void because they implied a proprietary conception of the royal office.[117] A Habsburg pamphleteer argued that the Spanish succession was not "a succession among commoners [*une succession bourgeoise*], but a royal succession, which followed different principles."[118] The Spanish monarchy was an "entailed estate [*majorat*]," which was "a right to succeed in such a way that the property [*les biens*] remains wholly and in perpetuity in the family." Hence the entail of the crown was in the family of Philip I and could not be alienated so long as it subsisted in the males of his descendance.[119] All the kings of Spain had sought to maintain this entail.[120] This had been true even of Philip III when he ordained the return of the Low Countries to Spain if Isabella and Albert died without heirs, declaring in his last codicil that the Low Countries belonged to him as his own by an ancient entail.[121] Clearly the issue on the Habsburg side was not whether the Spanish crown was property, but only what kind of property it was and whose. In these passages the term "entail" is not at all used in a metaphorical sense.

Once Philip of Anjou was on the Spanish throne, Torcy made for Spain the crucial distinction between the interests of rulers and those of the state, which he could only intimate at home. What was wrong in the Spanish monarchy, he wrote in confidence to the duke of Medina-Celi, was that the "principal persons [*les principaux*]" there were more concerned with their claims, their interests, and their private passions, than with the good of the state.[122] What is significant in this statement is that Torcy, as he became more and more autonomous in the conduct of French foreign policy, was helping to bring into existence an "abstract" (that is, nonpersonal) state. For, more or less at the same time, Louis XIV was writing to Marie Louise, the queen of Spain: "To put his glory ahead of any other consideration is to give true love to the king, my grandson."[123] Louis could distinguish, however, between the good of private individuals and that of the state: but that was when he was urging Philip V to act as a master in Sicily.[124]

In a significant letter to Philip in 1707, Louis described his own relationship to France, "which is to pass to my children, perhaps to yours, as our ancestors left it to me." He could silence the ministers if need be, but he could not and ought not "silence the voice of my people which rises to God, if I neglect to relieve them when they are in trouble."[125] The king of Spain, in collecting taxes, should keep in mind that he should not seize without right the property of individuals to use in his service.[126]

Meanwhile France's war against a coalition of Britain, the United Provinces, and the emperor, which resulted from the French acceptance of the testament of Charles II and the subsequent seizure of the Low Countries, went its way. France had been for more than half a century the outstanding military power in Europe, but now its prowess barely sufficed to stave off disaster. In Spain, however, Philip V was able to hold on to his crown against the attacks of Archduke Charles, who became Emperor Charles VI in 1711. A majority of the Spanish people supported the Bourbon who accepted the testament of 1700 against the Habsburg who declared it invalid.

Proprietary attitudes were just as evident during the war as they had been before. Indeed, Louis's passionate devotion to the principle of a hereditary monarchy that was beyond the ability of men to touch was one of the precipitants of the English decision to go to war against France in 1702. On September 16, 1701, the exiled James II died at Saint-Germain. Five days before, his queen, Mary of Modena, beseeched Louis to recognize her son as his father's successor as king of England. Louis called his council into session to advise upon what would be a fateful decision. All the ministers of state opposed such an action as a violation of the Peace of Ryswick which would make war with England inevitable. Nonetheless Louis, supported only by the Dauphin, decided to acknowledge the prince of Wales as the new king of England. William III would remain king of England de facto, as the Ryswick peace required, but the prince would become James III de jure because his crown was hereditary. "It was a right given to him by Nature, and it could be taken from him only if he ceased to be the son."[127] The anticipated war came on May 15, 1702, with simultaneous declarations at Vienna, The Hague, and London. The emperor's declaration was forthright in its proprietary attitude. On the pretext of the supposed testament of Charles II, it said, and in violation of all the preceding marriage contracts, renunciations, cessions, peace treaties, and oaths, "the king of France has taken hold of all the kingdoms and lands of his said Majesty (among which there are some that belonged to our archducal House before they came to the crown of Spain, as well as some that are properly dependencies of the Empire)."[128] In England, on the other hand, the argument that Charles's testament was invalid was based on the rejection of the proprietary concept of kingship. A famed pamphlet against Philip V's claim to the Spanish throne, the *Letter of Mylord on the Necessity and Justice of the Complete Restitution of the Monarchy of Spain,* spoke for the Marlborough-Godolphin ministry, although it was written in French and published in Holland in February 1710. It set forth as a "fundamental maxim" that kings "do not hold their kingdoms *in dominio,* and that consequently they have no right to dispose of them. . . . Everyone knows that kingship is an office, an administration, giving kings no proprietary possession."[129]

When, in 1711, Philip ceded the Low Countries—most of which were in the hands of his foes—to the elector of Bavaria, the sole French ally, who had lost his own lands in Germany, he required the elector to agree to give to the Princess Des Ursins, an influential member of his court, "a state as property and independent sovereignty, for herself and her heirs."[130] In 1713, despite her insistence upon getting the duchy of Limburg, she had to settle for a monetary award. Torcy was furious: Philip was sacrificing "the property of the kingdom of Naples, the duchy of Milan, and the Low Countries," and renouncing his claims upon the French succession for the sake of peace, and this princess, "whom ambition has made so stubborn," sought a sovereign principality for herself.[131]

In 1712 the Dauphin died (he had been duke of Burgundy until the death of his father, the "Grand Dauphin," the year before), and Louis had to write Philip V that the new Dauphin, his great-grandson, who was only two years old, was sickly and might not live. Philip was therefore regarded "by all Europe as the closest heir of my crown." The French king called upon him to support France more strongly than ever, because it was "a kingdom that may belong to you one day."[132] How can anyone say that Louis XIV did not think the state belonged to him?

But the English now had the upper hand in the war, and Louis could speak no more of his "special grace, full power, and royal authority," as he had in 1700. Still he continued to resist English demands that he compel Philip of Spain to renounce all rights to the French throne for himself and his heirs in perpetuity. He appealed to the fundamental laws of France. When the English demand was put to the French negotiator at Utrecht by the English negotiators, Torcy informed a special English envoy to Versailles that measures were possible to prevent the union of France and Spain, but, according to the fundamental laws of France, "the prince closest to the crown is the necessary heir. It is a patrimony that he receives neither from the king, his predecessor, nor from the people, but by benefit of the law. . . . He succeeds not as heir, but as master of the kingdom whose lordship [seigneurie] belongs to him, not by choice, but solely by the right of his birth. He owes his crown neither to the testament of his predecessor nor to any edict or other writing, nor to anyone's liberality, but to the law. This law is regarded as the work of Him who established all monarchies, and we are convinced in France that only God can abolish it. No renunciation can destroy it, therefore." If the king of Spain were to renounce the French throne, even for the sake of peace and because his grandfather commanded it, it would not be a means of avoiding the evil they had in mind.[133] It was a very important restatement of principles. We observe that the crown is called a patrimony, although transmitted by right of birth, not bequest (and hence not a patrimony in the Roman sense of the term). The proprietary concept of the state is overwhelming in this declaration, for all its denial of testamentary force and renunciations.

The argument was to no avail, however. The English were triumphant on land and at sea and insisted upon their terms for peace. They were not bound by French fundamental laws. Bolingbroke, the chief minister in England, wrote bluntly to Torcy: "We are ready to believe that you are persuaded in France that only God can abolish the law on which the right of your succession is founded. But you will permit me to be persuaded in Great Britain that a Prince can part with his right by voluntary surrender, and that he in whose favor this renunciation is made can be justly supported in his claims by the powers which became the guarantors of the treaty." Renunciation was a sine qua non of peace.[134] To the English plenipotentiaries he was even blunter. The French proposed that Philip V (whom he still called the duke of Anjou) would choose between the French and Spanish crowns if the occasion arose. How could he choose between them if he could renounce neither? "And can he renounce the Crown of France, and not the right to use it?" This was all "gross absurdity."[135] A quarter of a century later, when he wrote his famous book, *The Idea of a Patriot King*, Bolingbroke looked back to this time. It was the office of kings that was "of right divine," he wrote, although hereditary succession of kings was preferable to elective monarchy for the utilitarian reason that it averted the peril of civil war notoriously attached to the latter. As for Louis XIV himself, he had been a tyrant without even knowing it, for he had been brought up "to look upon his kingdom as a patrimony that descended to him from his ancestors, and that was to be considered in no other light."[136] Bolingbroke still did not accept Torcy's argument.

On November 5, 1712, faced with the adamantine determination of the English to make peace only on their own terms, and with a warning from Louis XIV that he could not carry on the war any longer and would make peace whatever his grandson decided to do,[137] Philip V made a formal renunciation of "all rights and titles that belong to me . . . to the succession to the crown of France," and specifically of those he held under the letters patent of December 1700.[138]

On March 15, when the Parlement of Paris, under orders from Louis XIV, registered Philip's renunciation, the duke of Berry protested that it was a violation of the fundamental law of the succession. In a formal statement before notaries, he affirmed that "the right of succession to the crown depends only on God . . . and that it belongs successively to the princes of the royal house of France, each according to the order and rank of his birth."[139] Even the first president (presiding judge) declared to the king that what the court was doing was invalid, but Louis replied that it was a sacrifice that had to be made for the sake of the state.[140] He hoped, to be sure, that if the succession actually ever fell to Philip or one of his line, the allies would permit the heir according to the old law to occupy the throne once he had passed on the Spanish crown (with the approval of the Cortes) to one of his sons. But that was speculating on the future—in the immediate present the Spanish Bourbons were effectively barred from the throne of France.

To say, as one historian does, that the issues of the interest of Europe and the balance of power had prevailed over the

private interest of families[141] is to miss that what was involved
was a changing character of the state. It was a victory of the
office theory of kingship. The study of dynasticism concerns
personal and family ownership of the state power, and there
can be no doubt that family commitments could be enormously powerful. Yet, counterbalancing such ties, ruling dy-
nasts often looked to their own individual interests even when
these had to be sought at the expense of other members of the
family. Selfishness and rivalries within families had been observed long before François Mauriac made them central in his
twentieth-century novels. We may only cite here the remarks
of Wicquefort, who had lived for decades in France as a minor
diplomat and major news reporter, regarding the 1668 peace
of Aachen: it was not necessary to seek its true causes in
"feelings of blood and kinship, which kings neither possess nor
know."[142] Louis XIV did more than bring the self-serving
character of proprietary dynasticism to a high point. By making this supremely evident and putting the French state into
an enormously difficult and costly enterprise, he had also
brought to the fore the difference between the interests of
rulers and those of peoples. The argument of strict state
interest—that Spain in the hands of a Bourbon meant the end
of the Habsburg encirclement of France—was not used, it may
be noted. It was not accidental that the political thinkers of
Louis's own time, those who were royalist as well as those who
turned against the absolute monarchy, formed a kind of pre-
Enlightenment. For the political thought of the eighteenth
century was shaped in large degree by the experience of the
age of Louis XIV—not in the special sense of Voltaire's great
history, which is a work of admiration and adulation, but because it embodied so many of the things the Enlightenment
was to oppose. It was like the relationship between a mold and
the thing formed in it, which has its very shape but inverted.

CHAPTER VI

THE CRITIQUE OF DYNASTICISM IN THE ENLIGHTENMENT

THE INSTITUTIONS of proprietary dynasticism remained intact in the eighteenth century. Many of the major and minor wars in this period were contests over royal successions, most notably the great mid-century wars on the continent. In most countries the strengthening of the bureaucratic apparatus of government redounded in the immediate present to the advantage of the dynastic rulers, whatever the long-term consequences in the creation of an abstract state. It was a century remarkably little touched by civil war until the final decade: the Jacobite risings in Britain, the palace revolts and the Pugachev rebellion in Russia are the chief ones that come at once to mind. Succession to the throne was central to these, although other interests were obviously also involved. François de Callières, who was chief clerk to Torcy and had observed diplomacy from the inside, wrote that to know the principal interests of princes, it was necessary to treat genealogies of sovereigns and their marriage alliances seriously, because they were "the principal source" of their rights and claims. Also important were various laws and customs in different countries about succession to sovereignty.[1] Dynastic monarchy seemed in its heyday. Even in the United Provinces, the restoration of the hereditary stadholdership in the principal provinces in 1747[2] brought the most important of the few European republics in existence halfway into the ranks of the dynastic monarchies.

Yet it was in this same century that the principle of dynastic monarchy came under the most furious assault. It would be a

one-sided exaggeration to maintain that the heart of Enlightenment political theory consisted in the rejection of proprietary
dynasticism, for such rejection occurs only sporadically, here
and there, and most of the time is located on the byways of
theoretical interest. But dynastic monarchy, as the principal
existing form of European government, was a fact of political
life of which everyone was aware, and it was one that could
not easily be fitted into the political theory (or theories) of
the Enlightened thinkers. Yet, until late in the century the
philosophes and their friends, who were not political revolu-
tionaries, did not care to attack dynasticism face on.[3] On the
one hand, the utilitarian doctrine implicit throughout their
discussions sustained an office theory of public power as
totally as it undercut any assertion of a birthright in the possession of the state sovereignty. On the other hand, the presenta-
tion of the principle of the sovereignty of the nation in the
form of the social contract theory meant that political power
was still envisioned in proprietary terms. Such thinkers as
Locke and Rousseau postulated an origin, either historical or
logical, for the state that has proved difficult to take literally;
it has been assumed ever since that the word "contract" was
used in a metaphorical sense. Historians and political scientists
brought up in an age in which property in political power has
long since ceased to be accepted cannot imagine that it once
meant just what it said. Once this dimension is restored to the
Enlightenment political debate, certain problems fall into
place. Proprietary dynasticism was hardly the keystone of
eighteenth-century political thought, but it was a not unimportant, even if somewhat hidden, stone in the arch.

The century began in the shadow of Louis XIV. One of the
results of his long reign was that the critical views that had
been difficult or even dangerous to express while he lived were
voiced with all the force of a repressed explosion. The reign
of Louis XV began with a juridical act that overturned the late
monarch's attempt to bypass the fundamental laws. Only days
after the death of the Sun King, his edict legitimizing his bas-

tards and inserting them in the line of succession was revoked by the Parlement of Paris. The new edict of revocation declared that the king could not modify by his own action the fundamental laws of the kingdom; he had "a fortunate inability [*une heureuse impuissance*]" to alienate the domain, and still less to dispose of the crown itself. Louis XV was made to declare that "we know it [the crown] belongs to us [*est à nous*] only for the good of the state." Characteristically, Olivier-Martin tries to take the sting out of this declaration, so fatal to his theory that the kingship was office and only office, by asserting that the fundamental laws implied that the state did *not* belong to the king but was only confided to him by the law under specific conditions.[4] But what the words put here into the young king's mouth do reveal is the vision of the monarchy held by its own servants—that it was at one and the same time both property and office. The tension between the two conceptions cannot be removed by a simple affirmation that one was true and the other false; it took political action of the most fundamental sort to achieve that.

Outside the halls of justice, the critique of the spirit of Louis XIV was even sharper. Boulainvilliers called the belief that the king was superior to the state "the most odious maxim of the past reign." Boulainvilliers—an aristocrat of distinguished family, note—enunciated the principle that the state was "all individuals taken together [*l'ensemble des particuliers*]."[5] The shift of emphasis characteristic of the eighteenth century may be seen in the court preacher Massillon, giving a sermon before Louis XV. Adhering to the same basic idea of the monarchy as Bossuet and Fénelon, he gives more emphasis to the king's duties and is plain in his sympathy for the people. "You are the master of the life and fortunes of your subjects," he told his royal listener, "but you can only dispose of them according to the laws. . . . You do not command slaves; you command a free and warlike nation, as jealous of her liberty as of her fidelity. . . . It is not the Sovereign, it is the Law, Sire, which should reign over the people: You are only its minister, the first depositary of that law." He even emphasizes the elective origins of the hereditary monarchy.[6] Yet Marshal Villeroy, the governor of Louis XV, showing him as a child from the windows of Versailles the country and the people, said, "Sire, this is all yours," and he meant it literally.[7] The child learned at least this lesson well. On a little printing press he composed a maxim: "A king owes his most precious moments to the governance of his state: this is his principal obligation, and God will one day call him to rigorous account for it."[8] He may have put the letters together, but that the words were put into his mind is obvious. There is, however, nothing in them of Massillon's equation of state and people; if there is also not directly an equation of prince and state, there is certainly that ever-dominant possessive adjective. Lessons taught that early are not easily unlearned.

What Louis XV himself thought as an adult was made clear in the famous *lit de justice* sitting of the Parlement of Paris on March 3, 1766: "It is in my person that the sovereign power resides, . . . it is to myself alone that the legislative power belongs, without dependence and unshared. . . . The entire public order emanates from me, I am its supreme guardian; my people are only one with me, and the rights and interests of the nation . . . are necessarily united with my own and rest only in my hands."[9] Again the presence of both the property and the office notions of kingship, but here the latter is dependent upon the former.

Meanwhile, off in Spain, Philip V still considered, despite his renunciation, that the throne of France would belong to him if his nephew died. In 1728, when Louis XV was suffering from smallpox, Philip wrote a letter to be read to the Parlement of Paris if the French monarch succumbed: "I will leave to take possession of the throne of the kings my fathers, which would incontestably belong to me in that sad event."[10]

D'Argenson, noting in his *Journal* that the use of the words "nation" and "state" had become current, commented ironically that they had never been pronounced under Louis XIV, "and there was not even the idea of them."[11] This may be set alongside the remonstrance of the Parlement of Paris of April 9, 1753, which distinguished royal from despotic government and spoke of the "indissoluble engagement" between the king and his subjects, such that "the King, the State, and the Law form an inseparable whole."[12]

It was during the reign of Louis XV, which lasted almost sixty years, that the Enlightenment thinkers grappled with the problem of dynastic monarchy, which bore so strongly upon many of the questions in which they were interested. In Voltaire the two ideas of kingship, office and proprietary, were still both present, although the tension between them is sometimes immeasurably heightened by his gift for ironic intensification. In his early work, the *Henriade* of 1723, the very first words accept the proprietary approach at least by implication:

> Je chante ce héros qui régna sur la France
> Et par droit de conquête et par droit de naissance . . . [13]

The point is, of course, that the right of conquest contradicts the right of birth. There is, on the other hand, the plain statement that the throne is a piece of property which the king "enjoys." He has Henry III say to Henry of Navarre:

> Mon trône vous attend, mon trône vous est dû:
> Jouissez de ce bien par vos mains défendu . . . [14]

In June 1745, in a verse epistle to Frederick II of Prussia, he wrote:

> Lorsque deux rois s'entendent bien,
> Que chacun d'eux défend son bien,
> Et du bien d'autrui fait ripaille . . . [15]

In the *Philosophical Dictionary* of 1764, in his article entitled "War," Voltaire satirizes the dynasticism out of which succession wars arise:

A genealogist proves to a prince that he is the direct descendant of a count whose parents had made a family compact three or four hundred years ago, with a house that has disappeared even from memory. This house has far-fetched claims to a province whose last proprietor died of apoplexy: the prince and his council conclude without difficulty that the province belongs to him by divine right. . . . [War results], all for the alleged interest of a man whom we don't know.[16]

What is significant here is not only the attack upon dynasticism but also the implicit acceptance of the notion that a province (or a state in general) can be the property of a prince. Yet, of course, the central thrust of the passage is directed against the very notion that such ownership should have as its consequence war for the personal and family interests of the prince.

In his *Dialogues among A, B, and C* of 1768, Voltaire is more explicit. A man can own his house, his children (a notion that would hardly have been acceptable in its ordinary sense), his servants when he calls upon them (which indicates something other than ordinary ownership), "but by what right would my fellow citizens belong to me?"[17]

The way Voltaire's attitude toward monarchy swung between the office and the proprietary notions is particularly clearly displayed in his relations with Frederick of Prussia. Sometimes the two men, poet and prince, each in his own way a *philosophe*, seem to hold the principle that kingship is an office as the only sensible and moral view of the royal state; but then the age-old habits and the realities of political life take over, and they treat the state as the king's own property.

Before Frederick came to the throne, when he was still crown prince, Voltaire wrote to him, reflecting on the events of the day, "I begin to believe that everything took place between the crowns almost as I see affairs treated between private persons."[18] In Frederick's *Anti-Machiavelli*, the refutation of the Florentine political classic written just before his accession and published anonymously, with Voltaire's assistance, while the king was opening the great wars with Maria Theresa over the Austrian succession, the crown prince takes a somewhat similar view. Inheritance in monarchy when combined with ancient superstition can be a "yoke." But he does not advocate the abolition of dynastic monarchy.[19] A sovereign should put the good of the people ahead of any other interest. Far from being absolute master of the people he rules, he "is himself only the first servant and should be the instrument of their happiness, as the peoples are of his glory."[20] But wars against usurpers and defensive wars are just wars.[21] Indeed, Frederick treats the state as a dynastic possession.[22] Is it justified then to say that his dynastic sense was very weakly developed, as does Ritter?[23]

When Voltaire called a king "who loves only his throne and his states" unworthy of the *philosophes* and proclaimed himself a disciple of the Abbé de Saint-Pierre, Frederick replied that his statement was platonic and again defended war for the defense of the king's rights.[24] But Frederick could be critical of "barbarousness" in the "buying and selling" of territories in the Holy Roman Empire in the late medieval period.[25]

He recognized that in his own time religion as the mainspring of politics had been replaced by "rights of inheritance, succession, or rather suitability [*bienséance*]."[26] Duke Francis Stephen of Lorraine received Tuscany under the 1737 treaty ending the War of the Polish Succession as "an equivalent of his patrimony."[27] Frederick approved the action of his father, Frederick William I, in going to Prussia in 1714 without being crowned; coronation as a ceremony was more fitting to elective than hereditary kings.[28] Frederick William I wanted to act effectively to sustain his claims on the succession of the duchy of Berg.[29] The dynastic pretensions of other houses were something else. Frederick II scoffed at Louis XIV's devolution claim of 1667 as less persuasive in Madrid than in Paris.[30] At another time, however, he defended Louis XIV's waging wars of succession.[31]

Although he saw no need to defend divine right monarchy,[32] in his "Critical Examination of the System of Nature" he defended hereditary monarchy as the least bad of political systems, although succession did not ensure the ruler's ability. A prince whose sons would succeed him believed he worked for his family and therefore devoted himself with more zeal "to the true good of the state which he considers his patrimony."[33] In an "Essay on the Forms of Government," he repeated the defense on even more explicitly proprietary grounds. "Men attach themselves to what they own; the state does not belong to these ministers; they do not therefore have its good truly in their hearts." But the sovereign, as the representative of the state and its head, did.[34] He did not apply to them his cynically pessimistic evaluation of human character: "We continue to deceive ourselves if we seek the principle of men's actions elsewhere than in the passions and the human heart."[35] Or should we conclude that he believed that the interests of states and sovereigns were identical so that kings more truly served the interest of state when they were most selfish?

Unlike Voltaire, who looked primarily to the French monarchy to engage in the work of reform from above, his great contemporary Montesquieu was a believer in limited and constitutional monarchy who saw the courts of Parlement as playing in France a role equivalent, if not identical, to that of Parliament in England. He was powerfully critical of the equation of the prince and the state. One can hardly doubt that he had Louis XIV in mind when he wrote, in The Spirit of the Laws, that the monarchy is "lost" when the prince, "bringing everything to himself, . . . calls the state to his capital, the capital to his Court, and the Court to his sole person."[36]

Montesquieu was more realistic than the Physiocrat Mercier de la Rivière, the theoretician of an enlightened despotism, who preferred a hereditary to an elective sovereign because, as "the owner of sovereignty, [his] interests are the same as those of the nation." Being the coproprietor of the net product of all land, his cause was indissolubly tied to that of all proprietors, that is, the cause of the nation.[37] There is more ambiguity in the discussion of the ownership of the state by another Physiocrat, Victor Riqueti, marquis de Mirabeau. France belongs to the king as the king belongs to France, Mirabeau proclaimed in his *Friend of Men* of 1757, but this does not mean that he also owns the private property of individuals.[38] But this was no more than repeating an accepted doctrine centuries old. The question was not whether the king owned subjects' property in the same way that they owned it, nor even whether he had eminent domain while they had useful domain over it; it was whether he had a right to take portions of their property for public purposes (or presumed public purposes: it would have been difficult to justify Louis XV's expenditures on the royal bordello at Le Parc aux Cerfs as for a public purpose!) without their consent. (In his letters on legislation, published a decade later, Mirabeau tacitly makes this very point. Subjects have no right to refuse the king the taxes he needs for public purposes, but to use their money for his own "dissipations, liberalities and fantasies" is to violate "the law of title" and be a tyrant. But he suggests no remedy for such abuse.)[39] Elsewhere, in a manuscript entitled *Perfection of the Monarchy*, Mirabeau agrees with his friend Quesnay that the king is not the owner of the nation, "nor of that which belongs to the nation."[40] Yet, following another thread in the long discussion of the origins of the monarchy, Mirabeau also holds that the dynasty or reigning house acquires its power by conquest, and "from conquest derives the spirit of the property of sovereignty and that of hereditary monarchy." A prince, he goes on, "can conquer sovereignty and *political* property from another ruler," but he adds at once that "*civil property*"—the private property of individual subjects—remains in their hands despite the transfer of political power.[41] Yet kings are not absolute owners of their kingdoms, but only usufructuaries who owe an account of their administration "to society."[42]

The best modern student of Mirabeau's thought, Elizabeth Fox-Genovese, thinks that in his attempt to "invalidate the more presumptuous claims of absolutism (that the kingdom is the property of the prince) and to avoid the pitfalls of proprietorship of public office . . . [he] has been led into repudiating property altogether." By this she means his use of the notion of usufruct, which she describes as "a means of guaranteeing the responsible conduct of property-holders."[43]

The critique of proprietary dynasticism becomes very explicit with Diderot. He takes up the problem in the article on "Political Authority" in the *Encyclopédie*. Government may be hereditary in a family and in the hands of a single person, but it is not "individual property but public property [*non un bien particulier, mais un bien public*], which consequently can never be taken from the people, to whom it essentially belongs in full ownership [*en pleine propriété*]. It is always the people who puts it out to lease; it always intervenes in the contract that determines who will exercise it. It is not the state that belongs to the prince, it is the prince who belongs to the state." Thus far what is striking is that Diderot, while attacking the royalist conception of the ownership of the state, does not at all reject the proprietary theory of political power. But his very next words dilute the impact of this admission, for he shifts the meaning of the word "belongs" (*appartient*) from a literal sense to a derived one: "But it belongs to the Prince to govern the state, because the state has chosen him to do so." This ambiguity of the key word "belong" is one that the historian of proprietary dynasticism must watch with extreme care; ordinarily context makes clear which meaning is intended, but sometimes either fits, and he must beware lest he assume the one that is most convenient to his argument. But Diderot does not leave us in the dark about what he intends. He repeats the traditional principle of French fundamental law that the king can abdicate but cannot put the crown on anyone else's head. He then adds to it the principle that embodies the quite contrary idea of the sovereignty of the people, "except with the consent of the nation which put it on his."[44] "In a word," he continues, "the crown, the government, and political authority are goods that are owned by the body of the nation, of which the princes are usufructuaries and ministers the depositaries."[45]

A historian of political ideas who began his study with the Enlightenment, or was unaware of the long debate between the office and the proprietary conceptions of kingship, might take all these phrases to be imaginative metaphor, reflecting no doubt the dominance of bourgeois property principles in the *philosophe's* thought. But all that is there, in fact, is Diderot's quite traditional acceptance on the one hand of the proprietary notion and on the other of the office theory. For the moment he does not give us any solution of the conflict at all, but the necessity of a solution would become greater as the century wore on.

When Diderot goes on to affirm the principle of male primogeniture—"The scepter of Louis XIV necessarily passed on to his eldest son [it passed to his great-grandson!], and there is no power that can oppose it, neither that of the nation, because it is the condition of the contract, nor that of his father, for the same reason"[46]—there is no need to think that he is being unduly cautious: the contract is two-sided, between people and king, and Diderot does not forget it. He cites a passage from Sully's *Memoirs* in which God, not the king, is called "the true proprietor of all kingdoms" (this is actually the speech of Henry IV to the Rouen assembly of notables of November 4, 1596),[47] and repeats a truism of royalist theory that equates direct vassalage under God with freehold.[48] It is interesting that this passage follows one at the beginning of the article in which Diderot, having denied that any man received from nature the right to command others, describes this right as a "gift of Heaven" and aligns it with paternal power. Authority has its origin not in nature but only in conquest or consent; and conquest, which Voltaire had praised, is for Diderot "only usurpation," although it may become legitimate rule by "explicit consent" of the subjugated,[49] and not therefore by prescription, which is the usual way of giving implicit consent. Venturi believes that in this article Diderot "made a great concession to the monarchy" and states that Diderot, in affirming that the crown and political authority were goods of which the nation was owner, the princes usufructuaries, and the ministers depositaries, was evidently following English models. Unfortunately, by this assertion, the Italian historian, so learned in the Enlightenment, betrays his own lack of familiarity with the centuries-old French tradition.[50]

Diderot was more explicitly critical of dynastic monarchy when after a visit in the United Provinces, he wrote of the hereditary stadholdership. By establishing the dignity in a single family, he says, the Dutch have found the secret of having a long series of "incompetents" (*ineptes*) at the head of their armies. (Diderot apparently did not realize that the stadholderate was not a military but a civil office, although the stadholder was always also named the captain general.) But the point is made for democracies as well as for monarchies: in all well ordered societies, there is no place for hereditary posts; "it is for talent to give the place."[51] That this applied to the France of Louis XV and Louis XVI (the work was published in 1774, when one reign was ending and the other beginning) was only too evident.

Despite the traditionalism of Diderot's article in the *Encyclopédie*, it caused a scandal by its assertion that the Frankish conquest was not legitimate unless it had been explicitly accepted by the conquered Gallo-Romans. Malesherbes, the royal director of the press, protected the author, and two years later, in 1753, when volume 3 appeared, either D'Alembert or Diderot admitted in the errata that the article was not taken from a supposed English work, as had been alleged, but added that it had been intended only to distinguish the

French crown from that of usurpers, and that the people were always obliged to obey legitimate princes, even if they were in disgrace. In fact, the article was based upon Bilain's *Treatise of the Queen's Rights* (which Diderot did not possess; he was relying upon the remonstrance of Parlement of April 9, 1753, which drew directly on Bilain).[52] We may take Diderot's attack upon the first partition of Poland as more truly expressive of his viewpoint: "Although in our own day we have seen sovereigns sell their subjects and exchange countries, a society of men is not a herd of beasts: to treat them as one does beasts is to insult the human race."[53]

The dangers that lurked in too clear a statement of the functional theory of politics could be seen in the Abbé de Saint-Pierre's *Political and Diplomatic Annals*, in which he attacked as baneful to the state the custom of making the dignity of a duke hereditary. "For it is obvious that giving more distinction to a man who is often without talents, virtue, with no merit whatever, than is given to a general of an army whose merit is greater, is ridiculous and a great offense against good government."[54] What holds of dukes holds even more, of course, of kings, but it is a conclusion that Saint-Pierre, political moralist though he was, does not draw. He criticizes Louis XIV on the occasion of the War of Devolution because he did not listen to those who held that he should not enrich himself by taking more cities at the expense of the people, when doing so would neither raise their standard of living or win him their blessing.[55] In criticizing the abandonment of the Spanish Bourbon renunciation of the French throne after the death of Philip V, Saint-Pierre does not argue against the proprietary notion but only against violation of the given word.[56]

Rousseau is of course particularly important in this study because he combines the theory of the sovereignty of the people with that of the political (social) contract, and in so doing carries on the proprietary tradition. Indeed, I would suggest, as Michel implies, that Rousseau eliminates the office theory of the state when he makes the people instead of the king the state.[57]

Rousseau confronted the question of political rights as a form of property in his first major theoretical treatise, the *Discourse on the Origin of Inequality* of 1754. To the assertion of Pufendorf that men could divest themselves of their freedom in the same way that they could transfer their property to someone else, he replied not with a blunt statement that personal freedom and personal wealth are two utterly different things (as Locke had replied to Filmer about property and political power), but by observing that once we give away property it does not matter to us whether or not it is put to bad use, but that this is not true of our own liberty. Even if liberty could be alienated, fathers could not deprive their children of it, as they could of their property.[58] He was aware, however, as were few other thinkers of the time, that the very concept of ownership is ambiguous. "Some have spoken of the natural right that each one of us has to preserve what belongs to him, but without explaining what they mean by 'belonging.' "[59]

When he published the *Social Contract* nine years later, however, Rousseau used the proprietary concepts for his central doctrines. Government, he wrote, was distinguished from the state because it had a subjective carrier—the prince—to whom the "rights, titles, and privileges . . . belong exclusively."[60] The legislative power (for him the essence of sovereignty) belonged to the people and only to the people. The governors who held the executive power, whether magistrates or kings, did not receive their powers by contract, but only by commission.[61] Sovereignty itself could not be alienated, and Rousseau used the term deliberately in its juristic sense of "transfer."[62] Individuals, in transferring their "goods" (*biens*) to the community, thereby assured themselves of "legitimate possession," changing usurpation into a true right and "enjoyment into property."[63] Rousseau denied Grotius's claim that just as an individual could alienate his freedom and become a slave, so a people could alienate its freedom to become subject to a king. Rousseau replied by expanding his argument in the *Discourse*. The term "alienate" was ambiguous. It meant to give or sell, and while an individual might sell himself for his subsistence, a people could not do so, because it was not the king who fed his subjects but they who fed him, "and according to Rabelais a king does not live on little." Even if an individual could alienate himself, he could not do so with his children, whose liberty "belongs to them."[64]

In all the pages of the *Social Contract*, this is all we find that treats of political power explicitly in terms of ownership. Nonetheless, the work is permeated with a proprietary spirit. Rousseau simply gave a twist to the old theory, putting the people in place of the king as the owner of the state. More important, he set no bounds upon the action of the people as sovereign, even discarding the notion of accountability to God which had always accompanied the idea of the king-proprietor. Gierke, with his deep familiarity with medieval law and political thought, easily accepted Rousseau's conception that individuals are each "in part, the joint-owner of a sovereign authority to which, at the same time, the whole of himself is subject."[65] There remains, of course, the mystery of what use it is to be part owner when the right of use and abuse is not given, but only total obedience is exacted—obedience even greater than that given a king who is at least bound by fundamental laws, divine laws, and natural laws.[66] Rousseau is an opponent of tyranny, but his reply to it is to turn the proprietary theory on its head by making the people and not the king the owner of the state.[67] This rests, of course, upon the simple notion that no man acts against his own self-interest. However oversimplified as psychology, it can provide an adequate basis for a political theory, although it has been abandoned by all who, while preaching the doctrine of popular sovereignty, have advocated control of the people by some superiors—in wisdom if not in formal rank—on the grounds that the people do not know their "real interest."

Michel Cantalauze, writing in defense of the Parlements in 1764, touched upon the problem that interests us. He observes that feudalism had been hollowed out: "Only the husk of feudal authority has been retained, but nothing of its reality."[68] The importance of the Parlements was shown by the fact that kings, as their first act of state, "have always come into this Court to take possession of their crown."[69] Under the first two races of kings, the kingdom had been subject to partition, but not under the third; still the Princes of the Blood were "the great Proprietors of France."[70]

The remarks of René Voyer d'Argenson as they relate to the proprietary dynasticism issue hold particular interest because he was both a foreign minister of Louis XV during the period of the War of the Austrian Succession and a friend of the *philosophes*. In his *Considerations*, he could argue the equivalence of the interests of a monarch who thought only of government, who would then be "good by passion," and those of the state,[71] taking therefore the line of moralist uplift represented by Bossuet and Fénelon. But the question remained whether such paragons actually existed. Hereditary monarchy was instituted not for the sake of the ruler but for that of the people, he affirmed, repeating one of the standbys of political theory. It therefore had to be kept from "falling into the marketplace" or being obtainable by marrying a woman. The rule of succession gave preference to eldest sons of a deceased king over sons of earlier kings through their descendants.[72] Yet kingship rested always on a contract between king and people, a conditional one that implied the primacy of the needs of the people.[73] Monarchy was government by one who "considers only his right of ownership over the states he governs," but escapes the temptation to tyranny by considering "less his right of ownership than the welfare of the state he governs, of which he considers himself to be only the first magistrate."[74]

We find here both the proprietary and the office theories, but merged in such a way that the demand upon the king is only moral and affects his character, not his power.

The strange royalist theoretician Linguet in his *Theory of Civil Rights* rested the rights of kings upon the same property principle as that of subjects, although it was not as limited as theirs. To attack hereditary monarchy was to attack all property. "The Prince is the keystone of the arch. In moving it we necessarily cause the destruction of the whole edifice."[75]

———•———

The final crisis of the absolute monarchy came during the reign of Louis XVI. Although it is not customary to number him among the benevolent despots because he did not espouse the principles of the Enlightenment, he probably was more benevolent in the ordinary sense of the word, without quotation marks, than almost any of his predecessors for eight hundred years. Indeed, it was his good nature, his distaste for conflict, his lack of authoritarian personality that undercut in large part whatever possibility of success there was in the reform efforts with which his reign began and ended. Furthermore, although "despot" in the political jargon of the Physiocrats meant no more than "absolute monarch," he was the least tyrannical of kings, despite his total commitment to the inherited traditions and institutions of absolute monarchy. The story of his failure has been told too many times to bear any repetition here; what interests us is the element of proprietary dynasticism that continued to operate in the politics and political thought of the late eighteenth century.

The distinguished historian of the Revolution Godechot has written that where Louis XIV could still consider that he had the free disposition of the property and life of his subjects, Louis XVI would no longer have been able to say such a thing. The reason for this change in the notion of the state, he suggests, probably lay more in the change of hard economic facts than in that of philosophical ideas.[76] But what economic facts had changed? The rural property-holding system remained the same, and the urban likewise. Manorialism had long since become a system of drawing revenues from the land rather than an agronomic system, and no significant change occurred in it during this period.[77] The changes that did occur lay rather in the idea of the state, that is, in political theory, and in political hard facts: in the former, in the weakening of the property concept of the state at the same time as the king and his court were unwilling to give up any whit of the king's property in state and crown; and in the latter, in the inability of the crown to solve its political and financial problems, so that the king and his officialdom achieved little but to thwart each other.

As for the critics, they brought the theory of proprietary dynasticism into clearer focus as a target of analysis and condemnation. D'Holbach, who was so revolutionary in his religious ideas, was less so when it came to politics. He did not call monarchy itself into question, as he did Christianity. He would have been satisfied if the king had merged his interests with those of his people: that was the object of politics.[78] In his *Universal Morality* of about 1776, he put the principles of enlightened despotism in the most extreme form, and thereby sought to make the kings servants of the people in accordance with the office theory of the crown. If the "principles of true policy . . . are only the art of making men happy," as D'Holbach says, he is only restating the old Augustinian view of the state in secular and hedonist rather than transcendental and ascetic terms. These principles, he holds, are "known and felt by all enlightened Princes." Everything proved that "their real interests, their real glory, their true grandeur, their own preservation, and their safety, are inseparably bound up with the prosperity [*bien-être*] and virtues of the peoples."[79] Secularization of Christian thought is even more evident in his statement that rulers had the right to use the force put into their hands by society "to oblige all its members to conform to the duties of Morality" as set forth in the social compact.[80]

But where he broke most clearly with the existing absolute authority was in his mode of legitimizing political power. Political authority ("the superiority of one man over another") could be founded only upon the greater advantage that subjects gain thereby; this meant that "legitimate authority" had to be recognized by those over whom it was exercised, because of the benefits they felt from it.[81] A prince could "revolt" against "equitable laws"—although D'Holbach does not define what this means in specific terms—but then he was "inviting" his subjects to revolt against him. In that case, of course, the meaning of revolt is evident and normal—and "inviting" carries with it implications not just of incitement and encouragement, but of justification as well.

The drive of D'Holbach's ideas was made clear in his definition of "truly sacred" legislation: laws that "consulted the interests of all and not the interests of a few leaders or those whom they favor." "Useful and just" laws were defined in the limited way to be made famous in the early nineteenth-century version of the policeman state: they were the laws that "maintain each citizen in his rights and guarantee him against the malice of others."[82] How strong this could be was indicated in his affirmation that a ruler who was oppressive was guilty of a crime; obviously a just king could not give in to courtiers' demands to be able to oppress the "rights, freedom, property, and interests of all." The monarch was "the defender and not the proprietor of the wealth of his subjects," and taxation was "stealing when it does not have as its object the preservation of the state." The state treasury belonged to the state and could not be used "without prevarication" for the satisfaction of the monarch's "own pleasures."[83] Kings should be taught from childhood, but rarely were, that the peoples are not toys provided for them by nature.[84]

Another critic, Mably, does not go as far as D'Holbach. Taking up the question of prescription as a historically significant form of political legitimization, he notes that Henry IV in the peace of Vervins in 1598 maintained his claim to all rights that "belonged" to him in Spanish Navarre, despite the lapse of time and the principle of prescription, and that the claim was not withdrawn until 1659 at the Peace of the Pyrenees. But, Mably writes, all writers on international law agree to the wisdom of the rule of prescription: the difficulty lies in knowing how it works. He suggests that it is "the silence of the injured party when he negotiates with the Prince who possesses his property [*bien*], or when the latter sells, cedes, or alienates it in any other manner."[85] Here the property notion of kingship is still taken for granted. Mably does not question the king's ownership of the state, but only whether, like private property, it is subject to the rule that undisputed possession over a long period constitutes authentic ownership.

The littérateur Louis Sebastien Mercier (not to be confused with Mercier de la Rivière) attacked the Physiocrats for their notion of "enlightened despotism." They were defending the "property of the monarchy," amounting to a third of the income of the kingdom; but this "so-called property" was the origin of all abuses. Despotism was "an eternal attack upon personal property."[86] Mercier here fails to observe the ambiguity of the term "property" as it applies to the state and the king. It is one thing for the king to have the state, the public power, for "his own," another for the king, or any sovereign— in fact, the state in general—to own lands in the country either as the residual proprietor of unclaimed places or just as a property holder like any other, and still another for the king to have a share in subjects' property through the system of taxation. Each form of ownership presented different problems for analysis, judgment, and decision, but it is the first—the king as the owner of the public power—that constituted the specific phenomenon of proprietary dynasticism. The others were essentially independent of it and continued into the modern age, long after proprietary kingship had ceased to exist in the Western world.

One of the most widely read and admired of eighteenth-century legal theorists, Burlamaqui, took up the question of proprietary dynasticism at some length. Although a Genevan, he may be cited here, like his fellow citizen Rousseau, because he was one of the most important spokesmen for the Enlightened view of the law of nations. For him the aim of sovereignty is "the felicity of the peoples," and those rulers who forget this and follow their private interests and their whims become tyrants and lose their legitimacy.[87] The claim that sovereignty is given directly by God rests only upon adulation and flattery, for it makes the ruler's power independent of all human conventions. But even if this were true, it would be given only for the welfare of society in general and of the individuals composing it, so that the people would be justified in resisting a king who worked to make them wretched.[88]

It was absurd, Burlamaqui held, to distinguish between a "real sovereignty" residing eternally in the people and a "present [actuelle] sovereignty," which belongs to the king." Even a people that has conferred sovereign authority upon a king remains "in possession" of this authority.[89] Here Burlamaqui still adheres to the property terminology. Some kings, he continues, possess their sovereignty as a patrimony, because they can share it out or transfer it as they wish; others only as a usufruct or entail, transmitting it to their descendants by fixed laws of succession. The jurists who enunciate this rule also distinguish between, on the one side, those kings who conquer countries and possess sovereignty "in full ownership," as do also those to whom a people has given itself to avoid greater harm, and on the other side, those kings who are established by the free consent of the people, and so possess sovereignty only in usufruct. This is stated by Grotius and followed by Pufendorf and most other commentators, but it does not correspond to fact, says Burlamaqui. Nothing prevents the sovereign power from "entering the marketplace," like any other right; there is nothing in it contrary to the nature of the "thing," and the people can grant the crown to the king as patrimony; but such conventions are rare, almost the only case being that of the Egyptians with their king, mentioned in Genesis (47:18–26). The sovereign power, however absolute, does not carry with it a right of property and hence of alienation. "These are two totally distinct ideas and have no necessary relation." True, such alienation seems to have occurred quite often; but in fact they were either ineffectual, or they had received the assent, express or tacit, of the people, or they rested on mere force. "Let us conclude therefore as an incontestable principle that wherever there is doubt a kingdom must be considered as nonpatrimonial so long as it has not been proved in one way or another that a people subjected itself to a sovereign in this way."[90] Although at one point Burlamaqui appears to be repeating the blunt and specific denial by Locke in his *Two Treatises of Civil Government* that there can be any property in the sovereign power, since these are two utterly different things,[91] he slipped quickly into using the property framework for the discussion of royal power. Yet his commitment to the office theory is at least equally plain. The tension between the two theories of kingship continued unabated in him, as in his predecessors.

When we come to defenders of the monarchy, we find no thinkers of the first order, none indeed who can even match such secondary figures as Mably. But this is no handicap in our study. In the estimation of the role of ideas in political life, there is an advantage in studying thinkers of less than the first rank, even the penny-a-line hacks, precisely because their lack of originality and their prosaic ability to reflect everyday habits of mind and assumptions, give us a better clue to what ideas meant to contemporaries than do thinkers who sparkle with genius and individuality. It may be the immensely gifted thinkers who help to shape the thought of generations to come, but their very outsize quality and the greatness of their subsequent influence tend to distort for us the character of their contemporaries. Compared to the Bodins and Bossuets, the Loyseaus and Diderots, who have risen large in our account because of the inherent importance of their intellectual achievement, a figure such as Jacob Nicholas Moreau is a pygmy who quite deserves the oblivion into which he has fallen. But he is vastly important in our study of proprietary dynasticism because he was the royal historiographer of Louis XVI and therefore represents the official view of kingship.[92]

The first work of Moreau's we shall review is a tract for the education of the Dauphin, the future Louis XVI, published in 1773, just a year before the prince's accession to the throne. These *Lessons* set as their goal not to persuade the young man that the authority he would wield was absolute, although that was true, but that "the experience of all centuries" taught that "there does not exist in Nature any all-powerful authority to do evil." Not even God himself possessed that "frightful power." Even the most independent sovereignty, "like all things human," was strengthened by being used well, changed by being used badly, and destroyed by being used contrary to its purpose.[93] The intention of the warning, of course, was only to bring home to the king-to-be the age-old lessons that came down across the centuries from Aristotle; but the modern reader cannot escape noting that the possible destruction of the French monarchy is set forth so easily only two decades before it actually happened.

Moreau went on with the commonplace truisms of political theory: the king reigned not for his own benefit but for that of others (*jouir*, "to enjoy," is the verb he uses, but it carries in French a tone of seriousness lacking in English).[94] Entering then into the history of France, he describes the legitimate Merovingian kings in the language of property. Clotaire II was the "usurper" of his royal nephews' "heritage."[95] He was supported by the mayors of the palace of Austrasia and Burgundy, who betrayed their legitimate sovereigns, for "they sold to him an authority that did not belong to them."[96] Soon the mayors left the descendants of Clovis with only the title and honors of kingship. Their scepters fell into the hands of the mayor, who knew that the kingship did "not belong to him [*il n'est point à lui*]," so that he called the lesser magistrates to his councils because he needed them.[97] Usurpation led to mis-government: the lesson is clear. The other lesson that the young man is being taught is to think of the crown in terms of property; it was certainly a lesson he had been learning since he was a child. Ownership of the crown was crucial: even under the Merovingians, because the crown was hereditary, it had been difficult to take it from its "legitimate possessors."[98]

The authority to make laws could belong only to the sovereign, who had the right to say, "You will do this or I will punish you." It was "the essential attribute of Sovereignty; it belongs to the King and can belong only to him."[99] Here the use of "belong" is ambiguous, but even if it is taken in the narrow, logical sense, the overtones are still, in the general context, those of property.

To preserve the idea of such absolute sovereignty, Moreau, unlike Loyseau, rejects the equation of *seigneurie* (lordship) with sovereignty, and he describes how, with the accession of the weakling Louis II, the Stammerer, in 877, "*seigneurie* rose upon the ruins of sovereignty."[100] What is being rejected here, however, is not the proprietary element of kingship but the feudal component of the French kingship as it had arisen historically. The French king is no longer seen as the capstone of the feudal pyramid; he might be, in Richelieu's words, "the first gentleman (nobleman) of France," but for Moreau the distinction between noble and royal is complete. Moreau lets himself get caught in the trap of self-contradiction, indeed, because, in order to condemn feudalism, he has to bemoan the fact that under the later Carolingians the "power of government" was transformed into "a power of property." This disorder was "the greatest scourge that could threaten mankind." This was because the "public power" lost its revenues to "property"—which now clearly means private property, *seigneurie*.[101] Not until the reign of Louis IX, Saint Louis, three centuries later, did "a correct idea of public law" begin to take hold.[102]

Yet there creeps into even such a work as this the spirit of "citizenship," with its perilous implications for royalty. For Moreau stresses to the Dauphin the importance of "knowing and holding the happy medium separating irreligious indocility from blind and superstitious obedience."[103] At the level of abstraction a fine principle—but one that in the world of political reality conflicted with another, much more powerful principle, to which monarchs held fast. This was that subjects owed them blind obedience. They could not leave it to subjects to answer the question of where the happy medium lay. Moreau's lesson was a dangerous one to teach if it should be heard not just by the king but also by those he ruled. This was the danger always lurking in the office theory of kingship, especially to the extent to which divinity was depersonalized and kingship was desacralized.

Moreau's handling of taxation is important, because it was the political question that affected subjects continually and directly. He admits that estates were rarely called into session in France unless kings needed revenues greater than those that came from the royal domain. In the older provinces ("*l'intérieur de ses possessions*," in Moreau's strange phrase), he simply "took and demanded." In the newer ones ("*au dehors*"), it was necessary on occasion to treat with assemblies, especially when mistakes and reverses multiplied what was needed.[104] Taxation, Moreau recognized, was probably the central source of conflict in all the principal states of Europe, because it immediately concerned the law of property, "so ancient and fundamental in any civil society." "Strictly speaking," these broils were "only combats between the power of Government which demanded and the power of Property which defended itself."[105] The right to set and collect taxes belonged essentially to the public power, but abusing that right could lead to disaster. "The right is clear, what is very difficult to determine and very dangerous to go beyond is its limit."[106]

Moreau may not be the greatest thinker of political thoughts in his time, but there is a hard realism in this passage that surpasses many a lofty proclamation of principle. The king may own the state absolutely and possess therefore the sole right of taxation; but he cannot with impunity set his property rights above those of his subjects. There lies behind Moreau's words an obvious awareness that subjects pressed too hard by the tax collector may not leave to God the judgment and punishment of royal excesses. Men pressed too hard in their own property rights might turn against the king's. It was not only the upsurge of resistance to royal taxation in the British colonies in North America in these years that Moreau no doubt had in mind, but also the persistent, never-flagging resistance of the Parlements of France to arbitrary and ever-growing taxation, imposed without either the assent of the estates or the approval of their surrogate, the Parlements. The task of absolute power, after all, was to assure freedom and secure the property of subjects (as Moreau demonstrated from the "sad era" of Charles VI, when power was neither "one" nor "absolute").[107]

Moreau considered fiefs as both "estates" (*terres*, that is, landed property) and offices at the same time, although power as such belonged to office. The result was a confusion and obfuscation of public law, resting on an essential difference between the laws of inalienability regarding the domain as power and those regarding it as property.[108] But feudalism had ceased with the government of Henry IV; all power was the king's, except for justice, which was still connected with the ownership of estates (that is, manorial justice).[109]

Nature had created two moral powers in man: one, the power of property, was applied to things; the other, the power of government, to persons. "Man is made to own property but no less to be governed; for without government, his freedom is that of the bear, who owns nothing but his prey, which the lion can steal from him."[110] Here, of course, in words less gripping than Hobbes's, is the essence of the state of nature as set forth in social contract theory. But Moreau goes on. A study of history easily shows that it was the inversion of the two powers, property and government, that had caused more statesmen's errors and most of the resulting calamities for the people.[111] "Inanimate things are made to be owned; man, by his nature, does not belong to man but to God; it is impossible for him to be owned, but it is necessary for him to be governed; and despotism was born in the world the day a madman took it into his head to say, 'I am the owner of my fellowmen.'"[112]

Yet, when Moreau wrote the first volume of his *Principles of Morality and Politics* only a year later, he began by affirming that sovereignty was property, belonging to the people, the king, or a small number of persons. But, whatever the number, sovereignty itself was absolute.[113] Absolute, but not arbitrary: "the constant authority and . . . uniform exercise of rule," not "the fleeting whim and unjust caprices of the prince."[114] The heir to the throne should be told, "Yes, your power is absolute; yes, you are the only person in France who has the right to say, 'I wish to be obeyed, and I shall punish those who stray from the rule that I impose.'" But he should be told at the same time:

> Your power is not at all property but a power of government, and its essence therefore is to protect and to do good. It is destined to maintain the rights that existed before it. It cannot do anything that is unjust, and by the nature of things it destroys itself when it runs counter to its own purpose. There is no written and promulgated law that is not your will, but your will is not always law: for there are laws to which you yourself are subject, which you cannot but in vain seek to compel your subjects to break.[115]

The purpose of all governments is to protect certain "goods" (*biens*), and these are spelled out: liberty, property, succession, transmission of property, and security and fidelity of contracts.[116]

Is there any difference, then, between Moreau and Locke on the purpose of government? Moreau was defending absolute monarchy, but not what he called the bizarre system of government in which a ruler with arms always at his disposal and obeying only his own whims "believes that he governs because he commands" and claims to be the "owner" of the life, liberty, and fortune of his subjects, with which he can do whatever he wants. This is not really government at all.[117] The language is certainly no longer that of Louis XIV: but if it is the king alone who decides what reason commands, what the interest of his subjects is and what the public weal is, how then in practice does this differ from despotism and tyranny? The implied answer, faced by Fénelon and ultimately taught by all the theologians who supported the absolute monarchy, was that the difference lay in the king's obedience to the moral law; he would be called to account by God and punished in the hereafter if he erred.

But Moreau, like so many of the other theorists of absolute monarchy we have read, could not easily abandon the property theory. He equated the mastery of the king of France in his country with that of the Habsburgs in their hereditary lands, and that of the duke of Bavaria, the king of Prussia, and the elector of Saxony "in the countries that belong to them."[118] The Merovingian kings, he recognized, considered the sovereign power their patrimony.[119] But it was a different kind of property, for the "unique goal" of all government was the happiness of the people.[120] Moreau saw that the Merovingians had two concepts of the crown, one patrimonial and the other a "right of Blood," and that this was not at all what the emperors of Rome had considered their monarchy to be.[121] They therefore accepted as normal the partition of this "vast patrimony" among all the king's heirs.[122] The realm of France was also given to them by conquest.[123]

Despite all that he had said about the Merovingian concept of the kingdom as a patrimony, two volumes later Moreau affirms that it "was still true that the supreme magistrate was not at all the owner but only the depositary of authority."[124] Property in land had preceded the establishment of the first throne in the world, and all civil laws had been made on its behalf. This was an unvarying rule imposed by God himself. Not only subjects but sovereigns too had been told, Thou shalt not steal.[125] Charlemagne had been the proprietor of the state, although under the obligation of eternal laws of the natural order to use his sovereignty in conformity with his position.[126] The king could share his power with magistrates, but he was the owner of the power itself.[127] Yet magistrates had a subordinate right of property in power, a precarious possession that was more than a simple executor of orders had.[128]

Moreau saw the advent of the Capetian dynasty almost as a usurpation. It was a "memorable and awesome revolution" because it resulted from the destruction of all laws except the inherent law of sovereignty. It was a dangerous thing because the new kings at first received their crown from those to whom it did not belong, and they had to make sure of it for their heirs.[129] But the Capetian kings, he suggested, were not conquerors in the ordinary sense of the word, for they increased their possessions by "all the means that the laws indicated for the transmission of property."[130] But they could not give away their subjects without their approval to a family that was foreign to them.[131] Charlemagne had ruled as both master and possessor, that is, as owner of things for his own use (*jouissance*), and as governor over persons. "He administered his properties as a father of a family by orders given to his officers; he governed his state by laws whose execution belonged to the magistrates."[132] Moreau went on:

This power of government—to whom does it really belong? It was not at all the heritage of the Roman Emperors, but they were elective; yet, as long as they were upon the throne, they considered it at least as their property; and our Kings who succeeded them in Gaul equally considered it as the patrimony of their Family. This title of *Dominus*, which has been badly translated by *Seigneur* [Lord] and which among the Romans signified a master or proprietor [*Dominium jus utendi & abutendi*] in possession of his own thing, belonged exclusively to the Emperors, and our Monarchs took it after them. It designated power, but a power belonging to him who was invested with it as his own.[133]

Under the Capetians, that which had been only *potestas* became *dominium*. The right to command became the right to enjoy.[134]

Returning to his distinction between the power of proprietors, which was "the right to enjoy whatever belongs to them, notably the ground that they cultivate, with confidence in its transmission to their posterity," and the right of government, he went on to define the latter as "that kind of property that by itself produces no enjoyment other than that of the good that it procures for others, and which itself is nothing but the right to govern joined to the duty to preserve." This was called "public power," to distinguish it from "the private power which is that of proprietors."[135]

Moreau, like all the others, continued to be trapped: if he maintained this distinction absolutely, he invalidated the whole proprietary element in monarchy and reduced hereditary transmission of the crown to a utilitarian device for the common good, and hence subject to revision if the common good seemed to require it; worse, if applied strictly, the distinction would imply the necessity to limit all the enjoyment of kingship which so obviously was part of the institution. But once having enunciated the principle (and it should be noted that this is *not* the question of the distinction between patrimony and entail, which are both forms of property, but has to do rather with the principle that property means the right of use and abuse, the right of enjoyment, the legitimacy of self-advantage), then the question comes up whether the subjects are in fact well served. And in the later eighteenth century there were powerful intellectual and political forces ready and eager to call the crown and its ministers to account. This is, of course, what is involved in such episodes as Louis XV's

Parc aux Cerfs and the pensions that Louis XVI granted to persons who were not servants of the crown: once the question of their legitimacy is raised, they are difficult to include within any ordinary notion of the welfare of subjects but obviously fall within that of the welfare of kings. Utilitarian argument on behalf of the crown was dangerous because it cut too deeply; but the sacral argument too was pretty much undercut by this time. The property theory of the kingship in the feudal period had rested upon the sharing of property-in-power between kings and the landowning (or landholding) class; now only the king had property-in-power, while the landowners' interest in his rule lay in his ability to preserve *their* property as a source of *their* revenue. It became necessary and possible to judge the king—but kingship is one of those magical things that lose their magic under too close scrutiny,

After having denied that the public power is proprietary, Moreau faced the difficulty of explaining how it is transferred by conquest. Public power may be acquired by war. The conqueror "certainly becomes the proprietor of the authority of which the vanquished are despoiled." But the obligation of public power remains the same, and the property of the subjects of the conquered state may not be seized.[136] What the prince acquires by conquest is therefore only "the ownership of the public power, and the funds attached to it as belonging to the state."[137] This difficulty is also reflected when Moreau returns to the question of the two distinct powers, "that which governs and commands, that which enjoys and cultivates." The first "belongs to the state or to its chief; it is a true property in the person of the Sovereign, whoever he may be." The other belongs to each member of society and is "natural or civil property."[138]

As for Grotius's distinction between patrimonial and non-patrimonial kings according to whether or not they can alienate the sovereignty, Moreau found it meaningless or at least inadequate to prove what it was intended to prove. Grotius would have been correct if, even in the most patrimonial sovereignty, it were "a free property of which he alone had the enjoyment, which concerned only himself, and the possession of which was related only to his own welfare." Then it would be as if he were a lord who could alienate his own estate. But if "sovereignty is a property, it is not at all a property to be enjoyed [*propriété de jouissance*, meaning property legitimately used for self-advantage] but a property in power [*propriété de pouvoir*]." It was power exercised over free men and the sovereign had the weightiest of duties toward them. He could not alienate his sovereignty because it would mean giving away his subjects who were "not his property."[139] Again we come to the straining point of analysis. The king possesses the power of command over men and their property, but he does not own them. The distinction holds so long as he commands them in their interest and to their advantage, and not in his own. The office theory of kingship was leading even the defenders of traditional monarchy to slough off its proprietary character, and so it was becoming a threat to the crown—a threat all the greater because the willingness to entrust judgment and punishment to God alone was also being lost.

Moreau goes on:

In France, Spain, and a great number of other states of Europe, sovereignty is patrimonial, that is, it belongs to the Prince by the same title as all other properties belong to ordinary individuals [*simples particuliers*]; it devolves by right to the heir to the throne, or rather he holds it by a law as ancient as the state and the most inalterable of any. But this law that makes power patrimonial does not make it infinite and arbitrary: the Prince receives it only as it is by nature. Nature itself has made men free, however, and because it made men free, it was not able to give anyone whatever the right to possess his fellowmen and to give them away.[140]

As for the claim that the prince was only the usufructuary of the crown, Moreau says that this holds true only of elective kings.[141] In patrimonial sovereignty, it is subject to "substitution," that is, entail. The sovereign, "although the proprietor of the crown, is essentially obliged to preserve it for his family and cannot transmit it in any way whatever except to the person called to succeed him by the law." In a footnote, Moreau explains that the "best jurists" are in agreement that the proprietor may be encumbered by entail of his property, but still he is not reduced to the condition of a usufructuary.[142] A king can abdicate even though he cannot alienate his throne; it simply passes to his successor by law. He cannot "treat the Nation as his own thing."[143]

Moreau believed in freedom, but his definition was a royalist one. A nation never loses its right to liberty, but it is a right to royal rather than feudal rule. Hence the Capetian takeover had been a revolution for freedom.[144] Moreau disagreed with a friend who argued that the Capetian monarchy had had its origin in the feudal conditions of the times and that its strength had lain in its proprietary character. It is "the immutable law of property" which, according to his friend, had become "the first of our fundamental laws, and the Crown is among us a property that protects, assures, and defends all the others."[145] This final maxim Moreau admitted was true, but it had been true under the Merovingians and Carolingians. They had always been administrators, but administrators "by virtue of an absolute power of which they were the proprietors and which they had the right to transmit to their descendants." This was "the only idea that we can form of sovereignty." Sovereignty is "only a right, an authority over persons and things, a right alongside a duty that spares it from arbitrariness . . . the greatest of all powers and the least of all rights of enjoyment [jouissances], for it is constituted not by the right to enjoy [jouir] but by duty and the means to enable everyone else to enjoy." It is not ownership of subjects' persons and property, and no French king has claimed it was.[146]

Moreau cites Loyseau to show that the feudal vassals had never had anything but private property, not "property in the public power." But "all property in the public power is essentially reduced not to the private advantage [*jouissance*] of the proprietor but to that of subjects, for whose protection and defense it had first been instituted."[147] This was true, although Hugh Capet thought of himself in feudal terms and of the kingship as "a great fief."[148] Yet the royal authority had become by eight hundred years of possession "the patrimony of a House that all Europe hopes will last forever [*à qui toute l'Europe souhaite l'éternité*]."[149]

Moreau was a bitter foe of the Enlightenment. He saw the necessity to instruct the people, but did not approve of "that vain and dangerous philosophy which so long now has numbered Religion itself among the prejudices of which they must be cured."[150] "What will become of society if they ever succeed in persuading the people that they owe nothing either to God or to Caesar, that the worship of the former is superstition and the power of the latter is tyranny?"[151] Still, he was an advocate of governmental reform of a kind. His model of a reformer was Richelieu, whose "tyranny of a few moments destroyed the tyranny of several centuries."[152] Some reform was now needed to complete Richelieu's work by returning to authority the "security" it had possessed under Charlemagne, that is, not to pass fiscal edicts but to have the means to do without them. The king needed a secure revenue, one that was not dependent upon the whim of the taxpayers, so that he could "make the people free."[153] There had been a long and secret struggle over taxation between the power of government and the power of possessors. If they could not be conciliated, the war between them would become more dangerous, "and which of them shall be promised victory? Oh Kings! never forget that the rights of proprietors are even more ancient than those of Sovereigns!"[154] The first Capetians had erred, although understandably, in thinking that the right of taxation inhered in the ownership of land; it properly belonged to the public power.[155] On the basis of the distinction between public power and private property, Moreau approved the use if need be of the domain of the crown for alienation so as to reduce taxation.[156]

The product of taxation was the king's to use as administrator, but the public power itself was his "true property."[157] "It is not at all as the proprietor of his subjects and their goods, but as their protector, that the Sovereign raises taxes."[158]

Valuable as Moreau's work is in enabling us to grasp the dynastic, proprietary monarchy as seen from within, the events that were to decide its fate were being shaped outside, as the conflict between the crown and the Parlements peaked, with each able to thwart the other but not to win for itself the ability to act effectively.

The penetration of allodial notions and the principle that property embodies the right to use and abuse were reflected in the royal declaration on freedom of the grain trade on June 17, 1787, which was drawn up by Loménie de Brienne as controller general of finances. Such liberty of the grain trade, the declaration argued, was in conformity with the principles of justice, "since the right to dispose as one wishes of the products created by one's investments [avances] and one's labor is an essential part of property."[159] In the royal session of the Parlement of Paris on November 19, 1787, Lamoignon, the keeper of the seals, asserted that the right to convene the Estates General "belongs only to the king." This was because "the sovereign power in his kingdom belongs only to the king," who is responsible for the exercise of supreme power "only to God." To this he added the usual description of the king as indissolubly bound to the nation, whose interests and duties were his as his were theirs.[160]

In that same year, as the French pre-Revolution was beginning, Guyot, on the first page of his *Treatise on Offices*, wrote that the king exercised "the most important of all offices in union with his people."[161] What this meant was indicated the next year when the Parlement of Paris, in a remonstrance accusing the ministers of overturning legality, denied that the king's will had the effect of law. "Could he by a law dispose of the crown, choose his heir, cede his provinces, deprive the Estates General of the right to grant taxes, distort [dénaturer] the peerage, make the magistrates subject to recall, reverse the order of tribunals, invest himself with the right to judge by himself or to choose judges in criminal cases, to declare himself finally coproprietor of the wealth of his subjects and master of their freedom?"[162] Yet a Parlement could also cite the succession to the throne as a form of property in arguing for the protection of the private property of citizens. Both were, argued the Parlement of Besançon on January 29, 1789, "the most sacred of rights."[163]

Four months later, the Estates General assembled and the character of political debate, including the question of the proprietorship of the power of the state, changed in the cauldron of revolution.

CHAPTER VII

THE FRENCH REVOLUTION AND AFTER

W ITH THE OVERTHROW of absolute monarchy in 1789 and then of monarchy itself in 1792, the terms of the question we are studying changed. On both sides of the ideological barricades, arguments for and against monarchy came to be expressed in terms drawn from different intellectual armories than that used in the debate over the ownership of political power. We may perhaps sum them up as the contest between republican democracy and antidemocratic monarchy, although we need not enter here into the difficult and subtle question of whether democracy flowed from a primary republicanism or vice versa. In any case, from the monarchist side there was no choice between the two; they were for it the same thing. Nonetheless the view of the legitimate power of the state as something in some sense owned, whether by the king or the people, persisted for some time. Not until well into the nineteenth century did this vision of politics disappear except among a few stray dwellers in political nostalgia. Both republicanism and democracy were put forward in quite new terms and upon the basis of a quite new experience. By the twentieth century, the proprietary notion had vanished from the intellectual experience of politics so that historians and political scientists, meeting it in the source materials and narrative accounts of the prerevolutionary age, were unable to accept it on its own terms. They either saw it as a metaphor or, if they took the debate between the proprietary and the office theories seriously, they accepted hook, line, and sinker the views of the office theorists, which corresponded so exactly with their own conceptions.

Underlying this evolution was a change in the legal conception of property. The hollowing out of feudalism and manorialism that had been going on for centuries had resulted, it has
been argued in these pages, in an implicit allodialism. Land
was owned outright, as freehold, from the time of the abolition of feudalism and manorialism in the fundamental decisions of the National Assembly on the night of August 4,
1789. But the ethical definition of property also changed. The
old scholastic notion that property should be used according
to its proper inherent purpose was cast aside; instead the only
moral boundary set upon what one owned consisted in observance of the forms of law. The Civil Code inscribed in its
article 544 the return of the Roman formulation of property
as an absolute right: "Property is the right to make use of
[jouir] and dispose of things in the most absolute manner,
provided that it is not used in a way prohibited by law or
ordinance."[1] The right of abuse—that is, use of property in a
way harmful either to itself or to its owner—is not explicitly
stated, but falls squarely within the range of the right to "dispose of things in the most absolute manner."

The proprietary way of looking at political power did not
cease all at once, however. In his famed inflammatory tract,
What Is the Third Estate?, Sieyès used the terminology of
ownership of political power, even if only to undermine the
old political system. Government, he proclaimed, should no
longer be the "apanage" of a separate order of society, "the
patrimony of a particular class." When that happened, government had swelled out of all reason and posts had been created
"not for the need of those governed but of those who did the
governing."[2] It was not the monarchy that he accused of such
monopolistic exploitation of the public power but the aristocracy. The "noble caste" had treated "all good places" as
"patrimonial property" (un bien patrimonial), which it had
exploited to its own advantage.[3] Attacking the very idea of
patrimonial courts which lay at the heart of the manorial
system, Sieyès denied that "public functions" should be con-

fused with property, for this was to slip into "this undefined word, *property*," the right to do harm to others, "which of all things is most opposed to true property." Yet he did not direct the same criticism at the monarchy itself. Quite the contrary! To treat lesser public functions as property was to break the scepter into a thousand pieces and to make the thieves legitimate proprietors.[4] Yet he went on to describe political rights in general as a kind of "legal property" distinct from "real property": the former was equal for all, rich or poor; the latter was different for different individuals.[5] (This was, of course, the seed of the later distinction between active citizens, with the rights to vote and to be elected, and passive citizens, who had civil but not political rights.)

It is no surprise to find Sieyès directing his assault against the nobility and the manorial system rather than against the monarchy. He was writing on the eve of the transformation of the pre-Revolution, led by the privileged class of France, into a broader democratic revolution not yet embittered and frightened into republicanism. But it is significant to see how naturally he employs the terminology of ownership to express his thoughts.

The constitutional transformation of the king into a limited monarch was expressed by describing him as no longer the owner of the French state but the servant of the French people. The hereditary character of the French kingship was not called into question as yet. Merlin de Douai, in a commentary on Guyot's *Treatise on Offices*, accepted the customary way of evading the proprietary implications of inheritance by calling the monarchy successory. The king obtained his crown not as the heir but as the successor of the late king, "because the succession to the crown is conferred by a perpetual entail. It would be otherwise if the king were the owner of his crown, because every man can dispose of what belongs to him."[6] This was the basis of the distinction that Merlin made between the (implicit) former and the present character of the kingship in his report to the National Assembly on October 28, 1790, on the claims made by the German princes owning seigneurial properties in Alsace. Were the rights of France to sovereignty in Alsace based on the Treaty of Münster of 1648, he asked, "or, what amounts to the same thing, [does] the Alsatian people owe the benefit of being French to diplomatic parchments?" Only recently kings had acted like "true owners" of their flocks. "To sell, exchange, give away, or cede by force cities, cantons, and whole provinces . . . was the principal object of their policy." But now kings were no longer the owners and masters of the nations but their delegates. The agreements made in the time of despotism did not bind the people of Alsace.[7] The firmness of the allodial idea of property in the first statement is striking. Merlin is familiar with the debate over the character of the royal succession. But what is important to us is that he cannot present the principle of succession except in the form of property, as entail.

With the revolution, the personal and public property of the king were scrupulously separated, as they had not been before. The decree of November 22–December 1, 1790, provided that the public domain (the former royal domain) belonged to the nation: the nation was taking the place of the king. But no claim was made upon his private property.[8]

The change of the king's title in the constitution of 1791 from King of France and of Navarre to King of the French implied the abandonment of the notion that the king had a property right upon the public power.[9] As Godechot says, it was no longer the king who owned the wealth of the state, but the nation which owned the king's. The king was given a "civil list," a kind of salary that clearly treated him as an officeholder-administrator.[10]

Even as it proclaimed the sovereignty of the nation, the constitution of 1791 continued the use of proprietary concepts. The sovereignty is "one, indivisible, inalienable, and imprescriptible. It belongs to the nation." The use of the terms "inalienable"[11] and "imprescriptible" taken directly from property law shows clearly that the verb "belong" is used to indicate that ownership of the state was no longer the king's but the people's. But when, in the section on ministers, the constitution says that the choice and dismissal of ministers "belong only to the king," the same term is obviously used in the looser, nonproprietary way.[12]

Proprietary terminology continued to be used now and then during the course of the Revolution. Jacques Roux, the enragé ex-priest, denouncing monarchy in his newspaper Le Publiciste as the most degrading of regimes, argued that "sovereignty belongs only to the people, and someone who seizes the supreme power is therefore a usurper, a monster, who should be smothered in his cradle."[13] The first words are wholly familiar, if the later ones carry a new spirit. The Committee of Public Safety used similar terminology in explaining to a representative on mission why measures could and should be taken to expropriate suspects. Someone who violated the social contract could not benefit by its protection. Society was "the only true proprietor, and it has distributed fortunes under the express condition of contributing to the greater advantage of all members. Someone who violates this sacred clause is dispossessed; society reserves its rights, which it can never consent to lose by prescription."[14] But none of this carries the weight of the proprietary component that was present in the dynastic monarchy of the old regime.

It was not until Napoleon stepped backward and forward at the same time in the creation of his own monarchy—the purest usurpation in origin, but deftly mingling old and new regimes in structure and spirit—that the proprietary element began to be looked at again with appreciation and even envy. Thibaudeau, Napoleon's confidant, writing about 1801, saw two different ways to govern France. The first was one that had long been practiced, that "in which the people is considered only as the property of the monarch"; the other, of more recent vintage, was that in which government was only the delegate of the people and the defender of its rights.[15] This was early in the consulate, when its republican trappings were emphasized rather than the monarchical powers given to (or taken by) the first consul.

Napoleon was soon looking back at the Bourbon times with envy, although without any intention whatever of restoring the Bourbon claimant. He told Thibaudeau about a year later that hereditary monarchy was a theoretical absurdity which had created stability in the state. Now, with the passing of the institutions on which it had rested, it had become politically impossible. "Heredity derives from civil law; it presupposes property and is established in order to assure its transmission. But how are we to reconcile inheritance of the first magistrate's office with the principle of the sovereignty of the people? How are we to persuade people that this magistrate's office is a property? When the crown was hereditary, there were also a large number of public offices [magistratures] that were too; the fiction was almost a general law. None of that exists any more."[16] But it is clear what he was yearning for. "Keep clearly in mind," he told Thibaudeau after the Peace of Amiens, "that a first consul does not resemble the kings by the grace of God, who regarded their states as an inheritance. Their power had old habits as its auxiliary. But for us, on the contrary, old habits are obstacles."[17]

When Napoleon was offered hereditary rule in 1804, he saw what he had to avoid and declared: "The citizens will not become *my subjects*; the French people will not become *my people*."[18] But he was less bound by the distinction than he seemed, for he gave sovereignty a definition that the old kings would not have found too strange: "Sovereignty resides in the French people in the sense that everything, everything without exception, should be done in their interest, for their honor and for their glory."[19] The first part of the sentence is an obeisance to popular sovereignty; the second picks up the whole theme of interest, honor, and glory so familiar to the monarchs of the old regime. Whose honor and glory he had in mind may be debated. Nor need we belabor the obvious by depicting the monarchy and the empire he created, in which dynasticism was intensified by all the clannish passion of the Corsican and an arrant personalism more than worthy of Louis XIV at his most arrogant.

The Bourbon who came back in 1814 had, despite the old jest, learned much and also knew how to forget much. But Louis XVIII considered the theoretical basis of his kingship to be the same as his father's. His chancellor proclaimed on June 4 that the king held his authority of God, but would not be an absolute monarch. "In full possession of his hereditary rights over this beautiful realm, he does not wish to exercise the authority which he holds from God and his fathers without himself setting the limits of his power."[20]

Louis XVIII was the legitimate owner of the kingdom of France—that was the ultimate reason he was brought back to rule the country by the allies. Any other solution would have been to deny the stated principles upon which they had waged their battle: a denial all the more dangerous since Austria itself, for the best reasons of state, had violated the principle in giving an archduchess as wife to the usurper. But legitimacy became a powerful argument for Talleyrand as Louis's representative at the Congress of Vienna. He used it to safeguard the integrity of France, but not the dynasties that lost their power, like that of Saxony and the mediatized princes.[21]

Some political theorists continued to argue the proprietary element of royalist doctrine. Bonald and De Maistre insisted that the interest of the king who sat on the throne he inherited was the same as the nation's.[22] Benjamin Constant could argue that divine right was replaced by utility as the origin of the king's power, but he could not gainsay the fact of inheritance and that the king's crown was a "family patrimony." His liberalism was satisfied, though, if the proprietary king entrusted actual rule in his constitutional monarchy to elective government.[23] Tocqueville characteristically viewed the matter from the broadest philosophical perspective. Succession laws were crucial in human affairs, he held, and should be placed at the head of all political institutions, "because they have an incredible influence upon the social state of peoples, of which political laws are only the expression."[24]

The replacement of the direct Bourbon line by the Orleans branch in 1830 was an obvious infringement of the strict rules of proprietary inheritance of the crown. Nonetheless, Louis Philippe sought to act the part of a legitimate monarch in the old style to the best of his (and Guizot's) ability. But the pretension was wearing thin. In 1847, the opposition leader Garnier-Pagès criticized the foreign minister for basing France's territorial policies upon prerevolutionary treaties. "How can we still speak of these treaties as if the peoples belonged to the kings?" he asked.[25]

The next year Louis Philippe was swept away by another revolution, and a new republic came to France. It was less long-lived than the first, and a new Napoleon came to power four years later. Like his uncle he sought as emperor to reconcile old dynasticism with new economic and social institutions, but found legitimacy not in inheritance, not even a spurious one, but in popular plebiscites. If anything, the memories of proprietary monarchy only became an embarrassment. Explaining in 1861 why he had introduced the reforms that created the liberal empire, he said he wanted to destroy the notion held abroad that "my government is so absolute that I hold all the wealth of France in my hands, and that I can dispose of it as I please even for my personal needs."[26]

Nine years later Napoleon III went the way of his predecessors into exile, and a third republic came to France. It was a republic for want of better—the monarchy that Thiers, the creator of the republic, preferred was impossible, not only because the royalist contenders canceled themselves out, but also because the count of Chambord, the Bourbon pretender, wanted to return at least to the symbolism of the old regime. The fleur-de-lys flag was not an idle symbol for "Henry V" and his followers. They reaffirmed their proprietary views of the French state with a purity of thought and intensity of feeling that were not marred by any consideration of reason of state. They would rather not have France at all than have it on terms not their own. In them silly politics and quaint honor merged.

In the first decade of the Third Republic one of the strangest of these purist royalists, Blanc de St. Bonnet, spoke the ancient doctrines with a tongue undefiled by new thoughts. Hereditary kingship was not a property that the prince could dispose of at his pleasure; he was merely the depositary of a principle that was the patrimony of the nation. Kings cannot abdicate their rights.[27] The old principles were thrown into a jumble when Chambord died in 1884. A rivalry for the succession followed between his French successor, the count of Paris, and a Spanish Bourbon, Don Juan. The Spaniard's supporters argued back to the time when Philip V forswore the French crown for the sake of the Spanish. This he could only do for himself, they said, not for his descendants. The French crown was not patrimonial and not under the control of a living monarch. The French royalists countered with their own fundamental law, that only a Frenchman could be king of France.[28] While they squabbled, the French republic had time to consolidate itself, and there ceased to be a throne to return to.

The issue of the Bourbon succession was revived in 1914 when Prince Sixtus of Bourbon-Parma, who was descended from Philip V, wrote a book, *The Treaty of Utrecht and the Fundamental Laws of the Kingdom*,[29] to reassert the claims of his line. Louis XIV had tampered with the law of succession of the Capetian dynasty by disbarring Philip from the succession, and this was the ultimate undoing of the monarchy. The rule had been infringed that those "capable of the crown" had a right to it beyond human interference.[30]

With this sigh of regret by a royalist who tried to employ his ties to the various royal houses of Europe to bring about a settlement of World War I,[31] we may put down our study of proprietary dynasticism. It had utterly ceased to be a matter of living politics and had slipped into the tomb of history, where things live only when historians revive them by enquiry and analysis. But it yields matter for our understanding of even deeper aspects of the rule of man over man.

AFTERTHOUGHTS

What have we shown in the preceding 168 pages of this book? I have demonstrated, I think, the existence of what, with some slight exaggeration, I treated in the introduction as an invisible dimension, to which I gave the name "proprietary dynasticism." The very texts I cite indicate that historians across the decades have remarked upon a certain proprietary aspect to early modern monarchy; but the very way I used their statements required that I take them out of their own context and put them into mine. These historians have almost always treated proprietary dynasticism as an aberration, not the ordinary practice of the time. I believe that I have shown that they were wrong in this, and that our general picture of the monarchy of old regime France (and of other European countries) must be revised to include this dimension, no longer dimly seen, but, I hope, bright and explicit.

To this I must add that it would be a grave distortion of the historical reality to paint proprietary dynasticism as more than only one among many elements in the picture. The view that the public power was dynastic property never blinded men to the existence of other notions of the actuality and purpose of the state. If anything, the proprietary principle met opposition from beginning to end, and its eventual demise does not come as a surprise. The office theory of the rulership, insisting that it was the duty of service to the ruled that justified and legitimized the violence of the state, triumphed because it represented not what men did, but what they thought they were doing and ought to do.

These two attitudes did not confront each other in total

hostility across a chasm of mutual incomprehension. In practice they interacted constantly, each working its wiles upon the other. The proprietary principle, based upon the insistent selfish force in the human personality, nonetheless seldom was set forth in unabashed nakedness. Its proponents in practice and theory almost always accepted the principle of service at the heart of the office theory of public power. To some extent, of course, this was mystification and obfuscation, a decking out of concern for one's own advantage in the trappings of idealism. But there was more to this than just the deception of others. There was also a subtle double effect. On the one hand, kings, by accepting the service theory of their rule, directed their policy toward its goals as they understood them. But that last proviso, on the other hand, could trap them into the worst kind of self-deception: believing that they were serving a higher cause, they could find good reason to justify to themselves conduct that others would see as its violation.

This complex relationship is by no means limited to dynastic monarchy. It pervades, I suspect, all politics. What is distinctive about its role in dynastic monarchy is that it is played out in terms of the conflict between the proprietary and office principles. We therefore understand early modern monarchy better with the principle of ownership of the state in our picture. It may well be, too, that with this picture in mind, we can see more clearly the mutuality of the diabolic and the angelic in the politics of other places and other times.

NOTES

INTRODUCTION

1. To take only one example from among many, and not the most extreme, we read the following in A. de Saint-Léger et al., *Louis XIV, La fin du règne*, "Marriages among the houses of Burgundy, Austria, and Spain in the fifteenth and sixteenth centuries, the Franco-Spanish marriage of 1660—these were unions between persons who were the owners of peoples and which engendered terrible misfortunes that were not necessary and created nothing useful to anyone" (p. 75). The same attitude is more calmly stated by G. R. Elton: "the dynastic arrangements often resembling purely private settlements of property, which really determined the fate of nations" (*The Reformation*, p. 14).
2. Ernst H. Kantorowicz, *The King's Two Bodies: A Study in Mediaeval Political Theology*.
3. Johan Huizinga, "Patriotisme en Nationalisme in de Europeesche Geschiedenis tot het einde der negentiende eeuw," pp. 528–529.
4. William Farr Church, *Constitutional Thought in Sixteenth-Century France: A Study in the Evolution of Ideas*, p. 3. Some fifty years ago, Marc Bloch deplored the absence of any "truly satisfactory" general synthesis of the doctrines of absolutism "considered not as a theory of social philosophy belonging to one or another writer but as the expression of a movement of ideas or feelings common to an entire epoch" (Marc Bloch, *Les Rois thaumaturges: Etude sur le caractère surnaturel attribué à la puissance royale particulièrement en France et en Angleterre*, p. 344, n. 2). The intellectual side of Bloch's complaint has been met by Church's study, but, as a constitutional history, it does not attempt to explore in depth the informal side of intellectual events, the half-expressed and uncertainly formulated feelings that are not quite ideas, but often help determine what was the true intent of explicit ideas. Bloch also noted the importance of studying political thought in the authors of the second order rather than in the giants of thought —in summaries of public law and panegyrics of the monarchy, dull

works but closer to the common conception. Even if paid propagandists, they tell us what those who paid for them wanted to have believed (ibid., pp. 346–347).

5. F. Olivier-Martin, *Histoire du Droit Français des origines à la Révolution*, p. 307.

6. See Rudolf von Albertini, *Das politische Denken in Frankreich zur Zeit Richelieus*, pp. 5–6, for the importance of extralegal factors in understanding political thought.

7. Otto Brunner, with his usual penetration, makes the point that to handle a phenomenon that seems to us confused "as if" (*als ob*) it were something else with which we are already familiar, is to reveal the inadequacy of our terminology (Otto Brunner, *Land und Herrschaft: Grundfragen der territorialen Verfassungsgeschichte Südostdeutschlands im Mittelalter*, p. 44, n. 3, p. 147).

8. See Michael Walzer, ed., *Regicide and Revolution: Speeches at the Trial of Louis XVI*, p. 26.

CHAPTER I

1. This chapter, lying outside the author's research competence, is unabashedly based on secondary sources. It is designed to set the framework for what will follow, for which I accept full responsibility.

2. André Aymard and Jeannine Auboyer, *L'Orient et la Grèce antique*, p. 3.

3. Aristotle, *The Politics of Aristotle*, p. 1.

4. Ibid., p. 236.

5. Olivier-Martin, *Histoire du Droit Français*, p. 76; Fritz Schulz, *Classical Roman Law*, p. 338; Félicien Challaye, *Histoire de la Propriété*, p. 86.

6. Schulz, *Classical Roman Law*, pp. 335–336, 338.

7. Ibid., p. 338.

8. Robert Derathé, *Jean-Jacques Rousseau et la science politique de son temps*, p. 382; Brunner, *Land und Herrschaft*, p. 281.

9. Schulz, *Classical Roman Law*, pp. 89–90.

10. Ibid., p. 340.

11. Ibid., p. 91; Olivier-Martin, *Histoire du Droit Français*, p. 37.

12. Olivier-Martin, *Histoire du Droit Français*, p. 77.

13. Fritz Kern, *Gottesgnadentum und Widerstandsrecht im früheren Mittelalter: Zur Entwicklungsgeschichte der Monarchie*, p. 4, n. 5; Jacques Boussard, "La France féodale," p. 970.

14. Ewart Lewis, *Medieval Political Ideas*, vol. 1, p. 141. John Neville

Figgis, *The Divine Right of Kings*, p. 22, describing developments in England after the Norman conquest, wrote that the succession of the crown was "assimilated . . . to the developing law of the inheritance of fiefs." Johan Huizinga observed that feudalism was "much more effective in creating than in destroying states" and provided "the true constitutive, formative, and creative principles of late medieval life" ("Abelard," p. 104).

15. Richard Schlatter, *Private Property: The History of an Idea*, pp. 64–65.
16. Albert Hyma, *Renaissance to Reformation*, pp. 39–40.
17. Charles Howard McIlwain, *The Growth of Political Thought in the West from the Greeks to the End of the Middle Ages*, p. 368.
18. Ibid., pp. 198–199; Friedrich August Freiherr von der Heydte, *Die Geburtsstunde des souveränen Staates: Ein Beitrag zur Geschichte des Völkerrechts, der allgemeinen Staatslehre und des politischen Denkens*, p. 410.
19. McIlwain, *Growth of Political Thought*, p. 181.
20. Helmut Scheidgen, *Die französische Thronfolge (987–1500): Der Ausschluss der Frauen und das Salische Gesetz*, pp. 30–32. I am grateful to Professor Ralph E. Giesey for the loan of his copy of this work.
21. Marc Bloch, *French Rural History: An Essay on Its Basic Characteristics*, p. 129, n. 22.
22. See McIlwain, *Growth of Political Thought*, p. 181, n. 2.
23. Otto Gierke generalizes this to the whole of the modern state, and observes the allodial ("patrimonial") element in the medieval period (*Political Theories of the Middle Age*, p. 82).
24. Kantorowicz, *The King's Two Bodies*, pp. 272, 354; Lewis, *Medieval Political Ideas*, vol. 1 pp. 146, 162; Peter N. Riesenberg, *Inalienability of Sovereignty in Medieval Political Thought*, pp. 3, 29–30, 47, 95, 178; Fritz Hartung, *Die Krone als Symbol der monarchischen Herrschaft im ausgehenden Mittelalter*, p. 3.
25. Leonardo Olschki, *The Genius of Italy*, pp. 166–167; Percy Ernest Schramm et al., *Herrschaftszeichen und Staatssymbolik: Beiträge zu ihrer Geschichte vom dritten bis zum sechzehnten Jahrhundert*, vol. 3, pp. 1,066–1,067.
26. Gierke, *Political Theories*, p. 99.
27. Kantorowicz, *The King's Two Bodies*, pp. 177–180, 188–189; Riesenberg, *Inalienability*, p. 155.
28. McIlwain, *Growth of Political Thought*, pp. 189–190, esp. p. 190, n. 1; Brunner, *Land und Herrschaft*, p. 280; G. von Below, *Der deutsche Staat des Mittelalters: Ein Grundriss der deutschen*

Verfassungsgeschichte, vol. 1, p. 175; Riesenberg, *Inalienability*, p. 151; Marcel David, *La souveraineté et les limites juridiques du pouvoir monarchique du IXe au XVe siècle*, p. 44, n. 1; Cecil N. Sidney Woolf, *Bartolus of Sassoferrato: His Position in the History of Medieval Political Thought*, pp. 22–24.

29. Lewis, *Medieval Political Ideas*, vol. 1, p. 92.
30. Brunner, *Land und Herrschaft*, p. 178; Scheidgen, *Die französische Thronfolge*, pp. 10–16.
31. Lewis, *Medieval Political Ideas*, vol. 1, p. 148; Figgis, *Divine Right of Kings*, p. 27; Edouard Perroy, *La guerre de Cent Ans*, p. 51; J. M. Wallace-Hadrill, *The Barbarian West, 400–1000*, p. 143.
32. Kantorowicz, *The King's Two Bodies*, pp. 373, 383.
33. Brunner, *Land und Herrschaft*, pp. 281–282.
34. J. L. L. van de Kamp, *Bartolus des Saxoferrato, 1313–1357*, pp. 62–64; Woolf, *Bartolus of Sassoferrato*, pp. 164–169.
35. Olivier-Martin, *Histoire du Droit Français*, p. 37.
36. Ibid., pp. 38–39; Ferdinand Lot, *Naissance de la France*, pp. 48, 135, 202; Louis Halphen, *Charlemagne et l'Empire carolingien*, pp. 4–5, 8; Edouard Perroy et al., *Le Moyen Age: L'expansion de l'Orient et la naissance de la civilisation occidentale*, p. 19; J. Hitier, "La Doctrine de l'Absolutisme," pp. 45–46; François L. Ganshof, *Le Moyen Age*, p. 12; F. L. Ganshof, "Het tijdperk van de Merowingen," p. 264.
37. Jean de Pange, *Le roi Très Chrétien*, pp. 96–97.
38. Robert Folz, *The Coronation of Charlemagne: 25 December 800*, p. 9; Henri Regnault, *Le Royaume de France et ses Institutions*, p. 39.
39. Folz, *Coronation of Charlemagne*, p. 40.
40. Lot, *Naissance de la France*, p. 111.
41. Louis Dollot, *Les Cardinaux-ministres sous la Monarchie Française*, p. 203.
42. Halphen, *Charlemagne*, pp. 35–36; Olivier-Martin, *Histoire du Droit Français*, p. 41.
43. Olivier-Martin, *Histoire du Droit Français*, pp. 41–42.
44. Pange, *Le roi Très Chrétien*, p. 171.
45. Marc Bloch, *La société féodale. Les classes et le gouvernement des hommes*, p. 157.
46. Paul Viollet, *Histoire des institutions politiques et administratives de l'ancienne France*, vol. 2, p. 23; Paul Viollet, "La question de la légitimité à l'avènement de Hugues Capet," p. 262.
47. Viollet, *Histoire*, p. 23; Viollet, "La question de la légitimité," p. 263.

48. André Lemaire, *Les lois fondamentales de la monarchie française, d'après les théoriciens de l'Ancien régime*, p. 8.
49. Olivier-Martin, *Histoire du Droit Français*, pp. x, 127.
50. Garrett Mattingly, "Some Revisions of the Political History of the Renaissance," pp. 10–11.
51. It is possible to take Olivier-Martin's paean to the national role of royalty (*Histoire du Droit Français*, p. 108) in this light, although this would be to overlook the backward-looking nationalism characteristic of him (see p. ix).
52. Hitier, "La Doctrine de l'Absolutisme," p. 118.
53. Viollet, *Histoire*, vol. 2, p. 45; Olivier-Martin, *Histoire du Droit Français*, p. 357; Percy Ernest Schramm, *Der König von Frankreich: Das Wesen der Monarchie vom 9. zum 16. Jahrhundert*, vol. 1, p. 107.
54. It is used in this precise sense by Olivier-Martin: "Property is not entirely patrimonial unless it passes to the heirs of him who enjoys it and provided he has free disposal of it during his lifetime" (*Histoire du Droit Français*, p. 263). Viollet uses it loosely and imprecisely when he calls the royal domain a "patrimony," although in law it could not be alienated (*Histoire*, vol. 2, p. 163). However, to assert, as does Paul Watrin (*La tradition monarchique dans l'ancien droit public français*, p. 14), that the Merovingian royalty had been patrimonial while the Capetian was not, although correct about the latter in this specific sense, fails to see that Clovis and his successors treated the kingdom as collective family property.
55. Viollet, *Histoire*, vol. 2, p. 164.
56. Hedwig Hintze, *Staatseinheit und Föderalismus im alten Frankreich und in der Revolution*, p. 514, n. 7.
57. Olivier-Martin, *Histoire du Droit Français*, pp. 213–214.
58. Ibid., p. 203. Regnault, on the other hand, speaks of the king as a "feudal lord who annexed the crown to his personal possessions" (*Royaume de France*, p. 145).
59. Olivier-Martin, *Histoire du Droit Français*, p. 205.
60. Bertrand de Jouvenel, *On Power: Its Nature and the History of Its Growth*, p. 30.
61. Viollet, *Histoire*, vol. 2, pp. 54–55; Olivier-Martin, *Histoire du Droit Français*, p. 211.
62. Bloch, *Les Rois thaumaturges*, pp. 19–20; Schramm, *Der König von Frankreich*, vol. 1, p. 260.
63. Schramm, *Der König von Frankreich*, vol. 1, p. 111.
64. Hitier, "La Doctrine de l'Absolutisme," p. 47.

65. Olivier-Martin, *Histoire du Droit Français*, p. 209.
66. Regnault, *Royaume de France*, p. 174.
67. Kantorowicz, *The King's Two Bodies*.
68. Cf. Viollet, *Histoire*, vol. 2, p. 84.
69. Paul Viollet, "Comment les femmes ont été exclues, en France, de la succession à la couronne," pp. 125–139; Pierre Ronzeaud, "La femme au pouvoir ou le monde à l'envers," p. 11; Philippe du Puy de Clinchamps, *Le Royalisme*, p. 108.
70. Viollet, "Comment les femmes," pp. 148–154; du Puy de Clinchamps, *Royalisme*, p. 108; Watrin, *Tradition Monarchique*, p. 20; Elizabeth A. R. Brown, "The Ceremonial of Succession in Capetian France: The Double Funerary Service of Louis X."
71. The treatise, *Tractatus de iure legitimi successoris in hereditate regni Galliae*, was first published in 1526; it was reprinted by François Hotman in 1585 in his *Disputatio de controversia successionis regiae*. See Hartung, *Krone als Symbol*, p. 29. The treatise is also called *Contra Rebelles Suorum Regum*. See Ralph E. Giesey, "The French Estates and the Corpus Mysticum Regni," p. 158.
72. John Milton Potter, "The Development and Significance of the Salic Law of the French," pp. 244–246; Lemaire, *Lois fondamentales*, pp. 54–62; Church, *Constitutional Thought*, pp. 28–29; Giesey, "French Estates," p. 159.
73. Robert Holtzmann, *Französische Verfassungsgeschichte*, p. 184; Viollet, *Histoire*, vol. 2, p. 83; Pange, *Le roi Très Chrétien*, p. 29. Paul Ourliac ("Souveraineté et lois fondamentales dans le droit canonique du XVe siècle," p. 29) and Denis Richet (*La France Moderne: L'Esprit des Institutions*, p. 47) present Terre Rouge's treatise as written specifically to rebut the treaty of Troyes.
74. Pange, *Le roi Très Chrétien*, p. 29.
75. Ibid., pp. 24–25.
76. Lemaire, *Lois fondamentales*, p. 62; Hartung, *Krone als Symbol*, pp. 29–30; Paul Saenger, "Burgundy and the Inalienability of Appanages in the Reign of Louis XI," pp. 6–7.
77. Perroy, *La guerre de Cent Ans*, p. 292.
78. Viollet, *Histoire*, vol. 2, p. 73.
79. Watrin, *Tradition monarchique*, pp. 120, 144; Lemaire, *Lois fondamentales*, p. 66; Regnault, *Royaume de France*, p. 161; John S. C. Bridge, *A History of France from the Death of Louis XI*, vol. 1, pp. 77–80.
80. The comments of Henri Lemonnier (*Histoire de France*, ed. Ernest Lavisse, vol. 5, pt. 1, p. 7) on the political background of

the Italian campaign of Charles VIII are instructive. In France, England, and Spain, he writes, "the sovereigns instinctively mingled with their private greed the conception of the state, which was higher than themselves and enduring"; the Italian princes, on the other hand, confused the state with their own persons or subordinated it to themselves. One wonders what "instinctively" means here. "Subconsciously" perhaps? There can be few historical affirmations harder to prove than such a subconscious.

81. Bridge, History of France, vol. 5, pp. 106–107; Lavisse, Histoire de France, vol. 5, pt. 1, p. 137.
82. Olivier-Martin, Histoire du Droit Français, p. 323.
83. Gaston Zeller, Les institutions de la France au XVIe siècle, p. 71.
84. Lavisse, Histoire de France, vol. 5, pt. 1, pp. 68–71; Edouard Perroy et al., Histoire de France pour tous les Français, vol. 1, p. 241.
85. Scheidgen, Die französische Thronfolge; Giesey, Ralph E., The Juristic Basis of Dynastic Right to the French Throne. The contrary case for dating the use of the term "Salic Law" for succession to the throne as early as the fourteenth century is given in Perroy et al., Histoire, vol. 1, pp. 167–168.

CHAPTER II

1. Zeller, Institutions de la France, p. 71.
2. Church, Constitutional Thought, p. 5; Olivier-Martin, Histoire du Droit Français, pp. 307, 325.
3. J. H. Hexter, The Vision of Politics on the Eve of the Reformation: More, Machiavelli, and Seyssel, pp. 150–172.
4. Henri Hauser, La Modernité du seizième siècle, p. 62; Perroy et al., Histoire, vol. 1, p. 246.
5. Dombes, which Francis seized from Bourbon, although effectively an independent principality, was nominally a fief of the French crown. It was returned to the house of Bourbon-Montpensier in 1561 and did not again become part of the French monarchy until 1762.
6. The term "eminent domain" has come to mean in English and American law the right of the state to take subjects' property for public use upon the payment of fair compensation.
7. René Gonnard, La propriété dans la doctrine et dans l'histoire, p. 21; Roger Doucet, Les institutions de la France au XVIe siècle, vol. 2, pp. 458–459; Roland Mousnier, Les XVIe et XVIIe

siècles: Les progrès de la civilisation européenne et le déclin de l'Orient (1492–1715), p. 64.

8. Doucet, *Institutions,* vol. 2, p. 455.

9. Ibid., pp. 503–504, 509.

10. Bloch, *French Rural History,* p. 167. Ralph Giesey, who has been studying the legal structure of property in early modern France, has pointed out to me that a majority of Frenchmen still do not make wills.

11. Bloch gets himself caught in this trap of misplaced definitions when he describes the seigneurial system in France and England until the end of the middle ages as "preventing us from speaking of property" (Marc Bloch, *Seigneurie française et manoir anglais,* p. 15).

12. N. Tommaseo, ed. and trans., *Relations des Ambassadeurs Vénitiens sur les affaires de France au XVIe siècle,* vol. 1, pp. 504–506.

13. R. Carré de Malberg, *Contribution à la Théorie générale de l'Etat,* vol. 1, p. 78.

14. Albert Buisson, *Michel de l'Hospital,* p. 107.

15. Olivier-Martin, *Histoire du Droit Français,* p. 357.

16. Maurice Deslandres, *Histoire constitutionnelle de la France de 1789 à 1870,* vol. 1, p. 12.

17. Church, *Constitutional Thought,* pp. 22–26; Ronzeaud, "La femme au pouvoir," pp. 12–13.

18. Claude de Seyssel, *La Monarchie de France et deux autres fragments politiques,* p. 190.

19. Hintze, *Staatseinheit,* p. 501, n. 131, citing Claude de Seyssel, *Les Louenges du bon Roy de France, Louis XII de ce nom, dict Pere du Peuple, et de la felicité de son Règne,* ed. Godefroy [Paris, 1615], p. 137.

20. Tommaseo, *Relations des Ambassadeurs,* vol. 1, p. 152.

21. P. Dupuy, *Traitez touchant les droits du Roy tres-Chrestien sur plusieurs Estats et seigneuries possedées par divers Princes voisins,* p. 90.

22. Ibid., p. 172.

23. Doucet, *Institutions,* vol. 1, p. 81; Vittorio de Caprariis, *Propaganda e pensiero politico in Francia durante le guerre di religione,* vol. 1, p. 203.

24. Church, *Constitutional Thought,* p. 81.

25. For venality of office, see Chapter 3.

26. Myron Piper Gilmore, *Argument from Roman Law in Political Thought, 1200–1600,* pp. 64–68; Church, *Constitutional Thought,* pp. 122–123, 182.

27. See Gilmore, *Argument from Roman Law*, p. 105: "A learned tradition can obscure the perception of contemporary fact."
28. Pierre Mesnard, *L'essor de la philosophie politique au XVIe siècle*, pp. 446–447.
29. Ibid., p. 443.
30. Georges Weill, *Les théories sur le pouvoir royal en France pendant les guerres de religion*, p. 7; Maurice Duverger, *Manuel de droit constitutionnel et de science politique*, pp. 53–54.
31. Hitier, "La Doctrine de l'Absolutisme," p. 521. This affirmation of Poyet's contradicts Michel François's statement that Francis I, "placed by right of natural succession at the head of the king-dom . . . knew that he was only the depositary of a public func-tion, although by divine right, 'the grace of God.'" (Michel François, "La formation de l'Etat moderne [1515–1598]," p. 341).
32. Church, *Constitutional Thought*, p. 166.
33. Lavisse, *Histoire de France*, vol. 6, pt. 1, p. 36.
34. Church, *Constitutional Thought*, p. 170.
35. Lavisse, *Histoire de France*, vol. 5, pt. 1 (Henri Lemonnier), p. 116. Lemonnier's statement that "it is quite strange to observe how little place France held in the foreign policy of this king of France" tells more about the assumptions of modern nationalism that this historian shared with virtually all his contemporaries than it really does about Francis I and his contemporaries. See also Lucien Romier, *Les origines politiques des guerres de religion*, vol. 1, p. 3; Perroy et al., *Histoire*, vol. 1, pp. 244–245.
36. Perroy et al., *Histoire*, vol. 1, p. 254.
37. Jean Seznec, *La survivance des dieux antiques: Essai sur le rôle de la tradition mythologique dans l'humanisme et dans l'art de la Renaissance*, p. 27.
38. Roland Mousnier, *L'Assassinat d'Henri IV: 14 Mai 1610*, p. 72.
39. Schlatter, *Private Property*, pp. 101–102.
40. Mesnard, *L'essor de la philosophie politique*, p. 320.
41. Weill, *Théories sur le pouvoir royal*, p. 73, n. 5.
42. Ibid., p. 79.
43. Philippe du Plessis-Mornay, *Mémoires et Correspondances Pour servir à l'histoire de la Réformation et des Guerres Civiles et reli-gieuses de France, sous les règnes de Charles IX, de Henri III, de Henri IV et de Louis XIII, depuis l'an 1571 jusqu'en 1623*, vol. 2, pp. 21–22, 24.
44. J. H. M. Salmon, *The French Religious Wars in English Political Thought*, p. 7.
45. François Hotman, *Francogallia*, pp. 247, 253.

46. Ibid., p. 467.
47. Ibid., p. 256.
48. Mesnard, *L'essor de la philosophie politique*, p. 334. Another legist, R. Choppin, used the same language of the marriage contract to express the same idea: "The patrimony and the domain of the crown are, as it were, the inseparable dowry of the public state" (Hartung, *Krone als Symbol*, p. 33).
49. Hotman, *Francogallia*, pp. 273–274; Julian H. Franklin, trans. and ed., *Constitutionalism and Resistance in the Sixteenth Century: Three Treatises by Hotman, Beza, & Mornay*, pp. 21, 62–64.
50. Franklin, *Constitutionalism and Resistance*, pp. 142–143; Gerhard Oestreich, "Die Idee des religiösen Bundes und die Lehre vom Staatsvertrag," pp. 172–173; Albert Elkan, *Die Publizistik der Bartholomäusnacht und Mornay's "Vindiciae contra Tyrannos,"* pp. 138–139.
51. Franklin, *Constitutionalism and Resistance*, pp. 167–168, 171–179; Weill, *Théories sur le pouvoir royal*, pp. 110–113, 116; Mesnard, *L'essor de la philosophie politique*, p. 345; Elkan, *Publizistik der Bartholomäusnacht*, pp. 127–128, 155–156.
52. Weill, *Théories sur le pouvoir royal*, p. 91, citing *Résolution claire et facile sur la question tant de fois faite de la prise des armes par les inférieurs* (Reims, 1577).
53. On the question of whether Bodin was of Jewish (Marrano) ancestry on his mother's side, see Roger Chauviré, *Jean Bodin, auteur de la République*, pp. 16–18, and J. Guttmann, "Jean Bodin in seinen Beziehungen zum Judentum." Christopher R. Baxter ("Jean Bodin's Daemon and His Conversion to Judaism") argues not that Bodin became a Jew, but that he accepted a form of Judaism, without ceasing to be a Catholic in public.
54. There are instances, especially in federal republics like the United Provinces of the Netherlands and the United States of America, where the effort to apply Bodin's definition leads to insoluble theoretical problems; but what is significant is the absence of any important alternative definition.
55. Jean Bodin, *Six Books of the Commonwealth*.
56. Ibid., pp. 26–27.
57. Church, *Constitutional Thought*, p. 238, n. 122.
58. Bodin uses the same proprietary analogy in distinguishing between offices and commissions in government, although denying that offices were "personal property" (Bodin, *Six Books*, pp. 82, 93). Albertini therefore goes too far in declaring that Bodin carries through a sharp division between what is covered by public and

private law (Albertini, *Das politische Denken*, p. 37). See also Otto Gierke, *Natural Law and the Theory of Society, 1500 to 1800*, vol. 1, p. 59; Mesnard, *L'essor de la philosophie politique*, p. 499; Gilmore, *Argument from Roman Law*, pp. 104, 109, 111.

59. Bodin, *Six Books*, pp. 56–57.
60. Ibid., pp. 59–60. See also Mesnard, *L'essor de la philosophie politique*, p. 501.
61. Bodin, *Six Books*, p. 62. Bodin makes the same point in his *Method*, using the Lothair-Azo controversy as his case. Jean Bodin, *Method for the Easy Comprehension of History*, pp. 173, 205; Jean Bodin, *Méthode pour faciliter la connaissance de l'histoire*, pp. 175, 360. McIlwain (*Growth of Political Thought*, p. 386) discusses the common misapprehension of Bodin's attitude. See also Gilmore, *Argument from Roman Law*, pp. 97, 105, 108.
62. Bodin, *Six Books*, pp. 64–65.
63. Ibid., p. 67.
64. See Church, *Constitutional Thought*, p. 10, for the implications of the League doctrines.
65. Richet (*La France Moderne*, p. 49) states the relationship as the twenty-first degree.
66. Mousnier, *Assassinat*, pp. 91–92; see also Frederic J. Baumgartner, *Radical Reactionaries: The Political Thought of the French Catholic League*, pp. 63–65.
67. A good description of the Guises' claim is in Baumgartner, *Radical Reactionaries*, pp. 59–61. The claim was set forth in a work by François de Rosières, archdeacon of Toul, entitled *Stammata Lotharingiae ac Barri ducum* (Paris, 1580).
68. Henry of Navarre to Duke Henry of Anjou, July 12, 1569, *Henry IV, Recueil des lettres missives de Henri IV*, vol. 8, p. 15. The editor of volume 8, J. Guadet, did not think this letter was actually written by Henry, but its significance remains the same, for he read and signed it.
69. See Henry of Navarre to Capitaine d'Espalunge, March 6, 1573, in ibid., vol. 1, p. 50, for an early example.
70. Duplessis de Mornay, Cahier général presented to Henry III, 1583, Mornay, *Mémoires et Correspondance*, vol. 2, p. 357.
71. Henry of Navarre to Messieurs de la Noblesse, April 15, 1580, *Henry IV, Recueil des lettres missives*, vol. 1, p. 294. See also Henry of Navarre to Henry III, February 8, 1584, ibid., p. 657.
72. Mornay, "Estat du Roy de Navarre et de son parti en France, envoyé audict sieur de Valsingham, en mai 1583," Mornay, *Mémoires et Correspondance*, vol. 2, pp. 244–245.

73. Mornay, "Lettre de discours sur les divers jugements des occurences du temps," ibid., pp. 562, 564.
74. Donald R. Kelley, *François Hotman: A Revolutionary's Ordeal*, pp. 295–297. This is a correction of Dodge's view that Hotman now accepted the Salic Law (Guy Howard Dodge, *The Political Theory of the Huguenots of the Dispersion: With Special Reference to the Thought and Influence of Pierre Jurieu*, p. 4). See also Giesey, *Juridical Basis*, pp. 30–36, and Salvo Mastellone, *Venalità e Machiavellismo in Francia (1572–1610): All'origini della mentalità politica borghese*, pp. 112–113.
75. Henry of Navarre to Elizabeth I, c. April 5, 1585, to Lord Treasurer Burghley, April 20, 1585, Henry IV, *Recueil des lettres missives*, vol. 2, pp. 31–32, 283.
76. Henry of Navarre to Duke Christian of Saxony and King John III of Sweden, July 25, 1585, ibid., pp. 104, 108–109.
77. Henry of Navarre to Monseigneur de Ségur, c. March 25, 1585, ibid., p. 20.
78. Henry of Navarre to Henry III, December 1, 1585, ibid., p. 149.
79. See Church, *Constitutional Thought*, pp. 249–250, 267–268.
80. "Association de Bergerac," November 1585, Mornay, *Mémoires et Correspondance*, vol. 2, pp. 218–220.
81. "Déclaration du roy de Navarre, au passage de la rivière de Loire, dressée par M. Duplessis," ibid., vol. 3, p. 358.

CHAPTER III

1. Baumgartner, *Radical Reactionaries*, pp. 133–134, 153, 222.
2. See Olivier-Martin, *Histoire du Droit Français*, p. 315, on this point in general.
3. To say, as does Albertini, that the king, as the just ruler, "does not consider the kingdom as his private property and hence protects the personal freedom of the individual" (Albertini, *Das politische Denken*, p. 200), is to confuse the proprietary character of the French kingship with patrimonialism on the Turkish model, which no French king, certainly from the time of the Carolingians, ever claimed. The key term, it must be repeated, is "private." The crown was not private property, but dynastic property, property under special limitations of descent and entail. Albertini correctly emphasizes, in another respect, that divine right theory was not at all identical with monarchical absolutism (ibid., p. 22, n. 1).

4. Ibid., p. 21.
5. Ibid., p. 35.
6. See, for instance, Louis Madelin, *Histoire politique (De 1515 à 1804)*, p. 226: "the will of the king, that is, of the nation [*la volonté royale, c'est-à-dire nationale*]."
7. Gerhard Ritter, *Friedrich der Grosse: Ein historisches Profil*, p. 10.
8. Olivier-Martin, *Histoire du Droit Français*, pp. 334–335.
9. Henry IV to principal cities of France, August 2, 1589, Henry IV, *Recueil des lettres missives*, vol. 3, pp. 2–3.
10. Henry IV to François de Montholon, seigneur d'Aubervilliers, August 2, 1589, ibid., p. 4.
11. Henry IV to duke of Nevers, August 2, 1589, ibid., pp. 7–8.
12. Henry IV to Duplessis-Mornay, August 24, 1589, ibid., p. 28. Similar phrases occur so frequently in Henry's correspondence over the next two decades that individual citations become pointless.
13. Henry IV to Michel Colas, seigneur de la Borde, ibid., p. 38.
14. Ernest Hinrichs, *Fürstenlehre und Politisches Handeln im Frankreich Heinrichs IV. Untersuchungen über die politische Denk- und Handlungsformen im Späthumanismus*, p. 188. Both usages are to be found in Henry IV to Queen Elizabeth I of England, 1590, Henry IV, *Recueil des lettres missives*, vol. 3, p. 331.
15. For the use of "scepter," see Henry IV to duke of Orleans, 1589, Henry IV, *Recueil des lettres missives*, vol. 2, p. 491.
16. Paul Viollet, *Le Roi et ses ministres pendant les trois derniers siècles de la monarchie*, pp. 61, 65–68; Olivier-Martin, *Histoire du Droit Français*, p. 323.
17. Henry IV to Provost of Merchants, aldermen, councillors, residents, and inhabitants of Paris, July 16, 1590, Henry IV, *Recueil des lettres missives*, vol. 3, pp. 216–217. See also Henry IV to sultan Murad III, April 6, 1591, ibid., p. 363.
18. Henry IV to duke of Nemours, c. July 20, 1590, ibid., p. 226.
19. Henry IV to Queen Elizabeth I of England, 1590, ibid., p. 320; to governor and people of Besançon, April 30, 1595, ibid., vol. 4, p. 352. See also Henry's description of John Bodan, prince of Moldavia, as "robbed" of "states" that "belong" to him (ibid., vol. 3, pp. 427, 429).
20. Murad (Amurath) III to Henry of Navarre (Henry IV), ibid., p. 346, n. 2.
21. Henry IV to Messieurs des Ligues Grises, August 13, 1592, ibid., p. 660.

22. Jacques-Auguste de Thou, *Histoire Universelle*, vol. 2, p. 179.
23. Lavisse, *Histoire de France*, vol. 6, pt. 1, p. 378.
24. Regnault, *Royaume de France*, p. 176.
25. Henry IV to Pope Clement VIII, November 24, 1594, Henry IV, *Recueil des lettres missives*, vol. 4, pp. 54-55.
26. Henry IV, "Circulaire sur la réduction de Paris," March 22, 1594, ibid., p. 120.
27. Henry IV to Monsr. de Sioujac, April 23, 1594, ibid., vol. 8, p. 511.
28. Henry IV to cities of Arras, Mons, Lille, and Douai, etc., December 17, 1594, ibid., vol. 4, pp. 280-281.
29. Henry IV to Rosny (Sully), April 15, 1596, ibid., p. 564. This letter exists only in the citation in Sully's *Oeconomies royales*, and the passage I refer to may be an interpolation by Sully or his editor. Its significance for us remains the same, however. Maximilien de Béthune, duc de Sully, *Mémoires de Sully, Principal Ministre de Henri-le-Grand*, vol. 2, p. 300).
30. Henry IV, "Les paroles que le Roy a tenues à Messieurs de la Court de Parlement le VIIᵉ Fevrier 1599," Henry IV, *Recueil des lettres missives*, vol. 5, p. 90.
31. Henry IV to De Brèves, February 16, 1600, to Constable of France, July 12, 1600, to Marie de Médicis, September 3, 1600, ibid., pp. 203, 250, 296.
32. Henry IV to Cardinal d'Ossiat, December 24, 1601, ibid., p. 519.
33. Henry IV to De Beaumont, March 27, 1603, ibid., vol. 6, p. 62.
34. Henry IV to De Fresnes Canaye, January 20, 1603, ibid., vol. 5, p. 18.
35. Mornay, *Mémoires et Correspondance*, vol. 7, p. 198.
36. Mousnier, *Assassinat*, p. 192.
37. See Roland Mousnier, *La Vénalité des offices sous Henri IV et Louis XIII*.
38. Zeller, *Institutions de la France*, pp. 132-141; Ralph E. Giesey, "Rules of Inheritance and Strategies of Mobility in Prerevolutionary France," pp. 281-283.
39. Zeller, *Institutions de la France*, pp. 23-24; Doucet, *Institutions*, vol. 2, pp. 453-455.
40. See Mastellone, *Venalità*, pp. 211-231, for a succinct discussion of Loyseau's ideas in a different context.
41. Charles Loyseau, *Les oeuvres de maistre Charles Loyseau, avocat en Parlement, contenant les cinq livres du droit des Offices, les Traitez Des Seigneuries, des Ordres et des Simples Dignitez, du Déguerpissement & Délaissement par Hypotheque, de la Garantie*

des Rentes, & des Abus des Justices de Village, "Traité des seigneuries," p. 12. The pagination for each treatise is separate.

42. Loyseau, Oeuvres, "Traité des offices," pp. 1, 131.
43. Ibid., p. 99.
44. Ibid., p. 214.
45. Ibid., pp. 3, 100.
46. Ibid., p. 8.
47. Ibid., pp. 96–97.
48. Ibid., p. 98.
49. Ibid., p. 99.
50. Ibid., pp. 100–101.
51. Ibid., p. 101.
52. Ibid.
53. Ibid., pp. 101–102.
54. Ibid., p. 102.
55. Ibid., p. 102; "Traité des seigneuries," p. 4.
56. Ibid., "Traité des offices," pp. 104, 281, 303.
57. Ibid., p. 302.
58. Ibid., p. 152; "Traité des seigneuries," pp. 2–3.
59. Ibid., "Traité des seigneuries," p. 16.
60. Ibid., "Traité des offices," p. 41.
61. Ibid., "Traité des seigneuries," p. 77.
62. Ibid., p. 18.
63. "Traité des offices," p. 278.
64. Ibid.
65. Ibid., p. 279.
66. Ibid., "Traité des seigneuries," p. 3.
67. Ibid.
68. Ibid.
69. Ibid., p. 4.
70. Ibid., pp. 6–7.
71. Ibid., p. 11.
72. Ibid., p. 12.
73. Ibid., pp. 8, 10.
74. Ibid., p. 8.
75. Ibid.
76. Ibid., p. 15.
77. Church, Constitutional Thought, pp. 318–320.
78. See G. d'Avenel, Richelieu et la monarchie absolue, vol. 2, p. 131.
79. Albertini, Das politische Denken, p. 58.
80. See ibid., p. 53, for instance: "Nor is the French king the owner but only the administrator of the state."

81. Iehan Savaron, *De la Sovveraineté dv Roy, et qve Sa Maiesté ne la peut souzmettre à qui que ce soit, ny aliener son Domaine à perpetuité*, pp. 3–5.
82. Ibid., p. 8.
83. Ibid., p. 10.
84. Ibid., p. 85.
85. Ibid., p. 117.
86. For instance, Heinrich Ritter von Srbik, *Der Westfälische Frieden und die deutsche Volkseinheit*, p. 9.
87. Avenel, *Richelieu*, vol. 1, p. 229.
88. For this statement, see Louis XIV, *Mémoires for the Instruction of the Dauphin*, pp. 29–30.
89. Cardinal de Richelieu, *Maximes d'Etat et Fragments politiques*, p. 60.
90. Avenel, *Richelieu*, vol. 1, p. 176, citing the Latin dedication: "Haec prima mea cogitatio majestas Regis, altera magnitudo regni."
91. Richelieu, *Maximes*, p. 55; see also p. 87.
92. E.g., ibid., p. 49, n. 2.
93. Ibid., p. 47: "ceux qui ont du mérite dans l'Etat."
94. Ibid., p. 42: "En affaires d'Etat."
95. Ibid., p. 10.
96. Ibid., p. 84.
97. Cardinal de Richelieu, *Testament politique*, pp. 128, 330, 332–333, 362.
98. Fritz Dickmann, *Der Westfälische Frieden*, p. 222.
99. Dollot, *Cardinaux-ministres*, p. 226.
100. Dupuy, *Traitez*, p. 652.
101. Ibid., pp. 15, 347.
102. Ibid., pp. 34, 293.
103. Ibid., p. 221.
104. Ibid., p. 218.
105. Ibid., p. 665.
106. Ibid., p. 135.
107. On Le Bret, see Gilbert Picot, *Cardin Le Bret (1558–1655) et la Doctrine de la Souveraineté*.
108. Cardin Le Bret, *De la Sovveraineté du roy*, pp. 1–4, 66, 77.
109. Ibid., pp. 3–4.
110. Ibid., pp. 9–10.
111. Ibid., p. 27.
112. Ibid., p. 71. Albertini traces the phrase back to a Venetian rela-

tion of 1610, but no further (Albertini, *Das politische Denken*, p. 40).

113. Le Bret, *De la Sovveraineté*, pp. 33–34.
114. Ibid., p. 697.
115. Ibid., p. 623.
116. Ibid., pp. 632–633.
117. Ibid., pp. 634–635.
118. Ibid., pp. 640–641.
119. Lavisse, *Histoire*, vol. 7, pt. 1, pp. 2–3.
120. Wilhelm Mommsen ("Zur Beurteiling des Absolutismus," p. 72) misses the historical point in asserting that Mazarin, like Richelieu, helped to create absolutism under the influence of "the suprapersonal force of the idea of the state." The intensity of the idea of personal duty to the king can be seen in the statement by Duke Armand de Gramont, a marshal of France, explaining to the princess of Condé why he was not joining the Frondeurs: "I have always made known that the quality of subject of the king, joined to that of servant [*domestique*] under so many obligations, did not permit me on any occasion whatever to examine the actions of Their Majesties and gave me the liberty only to obey their orders punctually" (June 16, 1650; cited in Dina Lanfredini, *Un antagonista di Luigi XIV: Armand de Gramont, Conte de Guiche*, p. 14, n. 4).
121. Claude Joly, *Recveil de maximes veritables et importantes povr l'institvtion dv Roy. Contre la fausse & pernicieuse Politique du Cardinal Mazarin, pretendu Sur-Intendant de l'education de sa Majesté*, preface, unpaginated.
122. Ibid., pp. 18–19.
123. Ibid., p. 423.
124. Ibid., pp. 56–57.
125. Dodge, *Political Theory*, pp. 5–6.
126. Jean-Pierre Massaut, "Autour de Richelieu et de Mazarin: Le carme Léon de Saint-Jean et la grande politique," pp. 35–36, citing a sermon of Saint-Jean before the court in 1652 or 1653.
127. See Dickmann, *Der Westfälische Frieden*, pp. 296, 551, for examples.
128. Ibid., pp. 409, 552.
129. Louis André, *Louis XIV et l'Europe*, p. x.
130. Jacques Roujon, *Louis XIV*, vol. 1, pp. 131–132.
131. Lieuwe van Aitzema, *Saken van Staet en Oorlogh, in, ende omtrent de Vereenighde Nederlanden*, vol. 4, p. 50.

132. Raymond de Geouffre La Pradelle, *La Monarchie,* p. 65.
133. Roujon, *Louis XIV,* vol. 1, pp. 168–169. On the historicity of the episode and this phrase, see Robert Holtzmann, *Französische Verfassungsgeschichte von der Mitte des neunten Jahrhunderts bis zur Revolution,* p. 320; Deslandres, *Histoire constitutionnelle,* vol. 1, p. 17; Louis XIV, *Mémoires de Louis XIV pour l'instruction du Dauphin,* vol. 2, p. ccxlviii; Hitier, "La Doctrine de l'Absolutisme," pp. 43–44. In the most recent discussion of this episode, A. Lloyd Moote, on the basis of hitherto unused archival sources, denies outright that the king spoke the famous phrase (A. Lloyd Moote, "Law and Justice under Louis XIV," p. 233 and n. 29).
134. Hitier, "La Doctrine de l'Absolutisme," p. 45) notes that the formula "L'Etat c'est moi" derives from the principle of proprietary dynasticism. It goes back, he demonstrates from Mommsen, to Augustus's identification of the state with himself, resting on identification of all property in the country with the king's, and found its definitive formulation in the state of Diocletian and Constantine.
135. Aitzema, *Saken van Staet,* vol. 3, p. 902.
136. Jean-Pierre Chauveau, "Un sonnet inédit de Tristan l'Hermite," pp. 31–32. The key lines read:

> Si tousjours vostre amour n'est mon souverain bien
> Le Ciel qui me promet plus d'un sceptre en partage
> Revoque sa promesse et ne me donne rien.

137. Roujon, *Louis XIV,* vol. 1, p. 203.
138. Mazarin to Louis XIV, July 16, 1659, Jules Cardinal Mazarin, *Lettres du Cardinal de Mazarin, Où l'on voit Le Secret de la Négociation de la Paix des Pirenées,* pp. 16, 19.
139. Henri Vast, ed., *Les grands traités du règne de Louis XIV,* vol. 1, pp. 94, 98.
140. Lionne to Boineburg, June 7, 1659, J. Valfrey, *La diplomatie française au XVIIe siècle: Hugues de Lionne, ses ambassades en Espagne et en Allemagne: La Paix des Pyrénées d'après sa correspondance conservée aux archives du Ministère des Affaires Etrangères,* p. 269.
141. Ibid., p. 21.
142. Ibid., p. 35.
143. Ibid., p. 73.
144. Vast, *Grands traités,* vol. 1, pp. 178–180, 179, n. 1; Antoine Bilain, *Traité des Droits de la Reyne Tres-Chrétienne, sur divers*

Etats de la Monarchie d'Espagne, vol. 1, p. 16; A. Legrelle, *La diplomatie française et la succession d'Espagne,* vol. 1, pp. 419–420.

145. Vast, *Grands traités,* vol. 1, pp. 180–183; Legrelle, *La diplomatie française,* vol. 1, pp. 18–19, 419–423; R. B. Mowat, *A History of European Diplomacy, 1451–1789,* pp. 121–122. Vast (*Grands traités,* vol. 1, p. 180, n. 1) specifically cites inadequacies of the treaty texts in Jean Dumont, *Corps Universel diplomatique du droit des gens,* vol. 6, pt. 2, pp. 288–290.

146. Legrelle, *La diplomatie française,* vol. 1, p. 21. Vast (*Grands traités,* vol. 1, p. 180, n. 1) rebuts Legrelle, who accepts this distinction as valid.

147. Edward Kirkpatrick de Closeburn, *Les renonciations des Bourbons et la Succession d'Espagne,* pp. xii, 31. See also Vast, *Grands traités,* vol. 1, p. 183, n. 1.

CHAPTER IV

1. Hinrichs, *Fürstenlehre und Politisches Handeln,* p. 151.
2. For an interesting distinction between state absolutism and absolute monarchy, see J. A. H. J. S. Bruins Slot, "Staatsabsolutisme onder Lodewijk XIV," p. 481.
3. Hitier, "La Doctrine de l'Absolutisme," p. 122; Olivier-Martin, *Histoire du Droit Français,* pp. 292–293; Ernst Walder, "Aufgeklärter Absolutismus und Staat," p. 160, n. 56.
4. Lemaire, *Lois fondamentales,* pp. 285–286; Hinrichs, *Fürstenlehre und Politisches Handeln,* p. 151; Hartung, *Krone als Symbol,* p. 46; Fritz Hartung, "L'Etat c'est Moi," p. 22.
5. Hitier, "La Doctrine de l'Absolutisme," p. 40.
6. Ernest Barker, *The Development of Public Services in Western Europe, 1660–1930,* pp. 5–6.
7. Olivier-Martin, *Histoire du Droit Français,* pp. 307, 334.
8. Roujon, *Louis XIV,* vol. 1, p. 229; Paul Bonnefon, ed., *Mémoires de Louis-Henri de Loménie, Comte de Brienne, dit le Jeune Brienne,* vol. 3, p. 36.
9. Roujon, *Louis XIV,* vol. 2, p. 137. See also p. 147, for a similar statement in a different situation.
10. Ibid., vol. 2, p. 240. See Albertini, *Das politische Denken,* for a discussion of the personalism of Louis XIV.
11. Mousnier, *Les XVIe et XVIIe siècles,* p. 234; Hitier, "La Doctrine

de l'Absolutisme," p. 517; Bloch, *Les Rois thaumaturges*, pp. 344–345.

12. Actually, the *Memoirs for the Dauphin* were for the most part either dictated by the king to a secretary, or drafted for him by his personal historiographer, Paul Pellisson-Fontanier; but they can be taken as representing his ideas. The best edition of the *Memoirs*, based on the closest study of the manuscripts, is actually the English translation by Paul Sonnino. The citations here are to the edition of Charles Dreyss, which is not the most precise from the point of view of scholarship (see Sonnino, "Introduction" to Louis XIV, *Mémoires for the Instruction of the Dauphin*, pp. 6–7), but is the most available.

13. See Chapter 6 for the interchange between Voltaire and Frederick II of political ideas relevant to our theme.

14. Andrew Lossky, "The Nature of Political Power according to Louis XIV," p. 122. Professor Lossky has explained his argument on the status of "The Craft of Kingship" meditation in a letter to the author (April 2, 1976): "It is questionable whether the '*Métier du roi*' was meant to be a part of the Memoirs of Louis XIV (though Paul Sonnino was inclined to this view having examined the King's military Memoirs for the Dutch War). The original document in the Bibl. Nat. Mss. *fonds* is quite peculiar. First, unlike the rest of the *Mémoires* it is drawn up in its entirety in the king's own hand. Second, the accusations against Pomponne (who is directly named) are couched in the *present* tense and are more extensive and sharper than in the final (published) version. Third, the original draft was corrected, in a trembling hand, also of Louis XIV, to produce the commonly published version. All of this leads me to believe that this document is Louis's memorandum *to himself*, drawn up as he was pondering whether to dismiss Pomponne. The reason for writing is twofold: Louis's belief that one cannot trust one's advisers in matters of appointment to or dismissal from the highest offices in the state, and his contention that the best way to clear up inchoate or confused ideas is to express them in words. Hence a memorandum to himself was the most appropriate way to make up his mind on a matter of this sort. As for the later modifications of the document, I believe they date from the time when he was deciding to dismiss Chamillart and pulled out from among his papers this earlier memorandum to consult. He must have taken this occasion to strike out some of the invective against Pomponne (e.g., accusation of '*manque de*

capacité') as well as to suppress the name of his faithful old servant. A case can be made out, though it is a weak one, that he thought of dismissing Louvois shortly before the latter's death; possibly even Louvois's son, Barbezieux, and the revision of the document took place à propos of them. But this is doubtful."

15. Louis XIV, *Mémoires*, ed. Dreyss, vol. 2, p. 521; see also pp. 428–429.
16. Ibid., pp. 518–520.
17. Ibid., p. 285.
18. Ibid., p. 288.
19. Ibid., p. 230.
20. Ibid., p. 246.
21. See ibid., vol. 1, Dreyss's introduction, p. lxx.
22. Ibid., vol. 2, p. 251.
23. Ibid., pp. 10–11.
24. Ibid., pp. 14–15.
25. Ibid., p. 15.
26. Ibid., vol. 1, p. cli.
27. Ibid., p. 150.
28. Ibid., p. 163.
29. Ibid., p. 177.
30. Ibid., p. 209.
31. Ibid., p. 249. See Jean-Louis Thireau, *Les Idées politiques de Louis XIV*, pp. 87–90, for an argument that Louis XIV had only taxation in mind in this passage.
32. Louis XIV, *Mémoires*, ed. Dreyss, vol. 1, p. 250.
33. For a contrary view of this passage, see Hartung, "L'Etat c'est Moi," pp. 17–18.
34. Hitier, "La Doctrine de l'Absolutisme," pp. 520–521.
35. *Oeuvres de Louis XIV*, vol. 1, pp. 149–150.
36. Louis XIV, *Mémoires*, vol. 1, Dreyss's introduction, p. ccvi.
37. Ibid., vol. 2, p. 442.
38. Philippe de Béthune, *Le Conseiller d'Estat, ou Recveil general de la politiqve moderne, seruant au maniement des Affaires publiques,* pp. 2–3.
39. Ibid., p. 4.
40. Ibid., p. 22.
41. Ibid., p. 28.
42. Ibid., pp. 119–120.
43. Ibid., pp. 121–122.
44. Claude Fleury, *Institution au Droit Français*, vol. 1, p. 170.
45. Ibid., p. 85.

46. Jacques Bénigne Bossuet, *Politique tirée des propres paroles de l'Ecriture Sainte*, vol. 1, pp. 305–306.

47. Ibid., p. 307.

48. Ibid., p. 308.

49. Ibid., p. 320.

50. Ibid., p. 408.

51. Ibid., pp. 324–325.

52. Ibid., p. 327.

53. Ibid., p. 333.

54. Ibid., pp. 415–416.

55. Ibid., p. 417.

56. Ibid.

57. Roujon, *Louis XIV*, vol. 2, p. 211.

58. François de Salignac de la Mothe-Fénelon, *Oeuvres Choisies de Fénelon*, vol. 4, p. 283.

59. Ibid., p. 288. See also pp. 350–351, where wars of conquest are called "taking someone else's property."

60. Ibid., p. 284.

61. Ibid., p. 361.

62. Ibid., p. 354.

63. Ibid., p. 351.

64. Jean de La Bruyère, *Les Caractères de Théophraste traduits du grec avec Les Caractères ou les Moeurs de ce siècle*, p. 290.

65. Ibid., p. 291.

66. E. Préclin and E. Jarry, *Les luttes politiques et doctrinales au XVIIe et XVIIIe siècles*, vol. 1, p. 132.

67. Roujon, *Louis XIV*, vol. 2, p. 131.

68. Algernon Sidney, *Discourses on Government*, vol. 2, p. 225.

69. Ibid., vol. 3, p. 113.

70. Dodge, *Political Theory*, pp. 130–133.

71. *Les Soupirs de la France esclave*. It is cited here after an edition published in Amsterdam in 1788 under the title *Les Voeux d'un Patriote*. Richet (*La France Moderne*, p. 143), on grounds of discrepancy of tone and vocabulary from Jurieu's earlier works, doubts his authorship. Michel Le Vassor is sometimes held to be the author. In either case, the impact of *Les Soupirs* on my argument remains the same.

72. Jurieu, *Les Voeux*, p. 14.

73. Ibid., pp. 21–22; see also pp. 57–58.

74. Ibid., p. 26.

75. Ibid., pp. 36–37.

76. Ibid., pp. 53–54.

77. Ibid., p. 55.
78. Ibid., pp. 64–65.
79. Ibid., p. 42.
80. Ibid., p. 65.
81. Ibid., p. 67.
82. Dodge, *Political Theory*, pp. 78–79.
83. Derathé, *Jean-Jacques Rousseau*, p. 121.
84. Friedrich Kleyser, *Der Flugschriftenkampf gegen Ludwig XIV. zur Zeit des pfälzischen Krieges*, p. 111, n. 247, citing *La politique françoise ou les desseins artificieux du conseil de France, pénétrés & découverts au travers des dernières propositions que le Roi T. C. a fait courir en divers lieux et proposer à plusieurs princes de l'Europe* Utrecht, 1695), p. 320.
85. Holtzmann, *Französische Verfassungsgeschichte*, pp. 310–311.
86. Hitier, "La Doctrine de l'Absolutisme," pp. 420, 425–426, 437–438; Thireau, *Idées Politiques*, p. 92.
87. Louis de Rouvroy, duc de Saint-Simon, *Mémoires de Saint-Simon*, ed. A. de Boislisle, vol. 4, pp. 341–342, 356–357; Saint-Simon, *Ecrits inédits de Saint-Simon*, vol. 2, pp. 121, 148–149.
88. Saint-Simon, *Mémoires*, ed. de Boislisle, vol. 4, pp. 380–381; "Mémoires sur les légitimés," *Ecrits inédits*, vol. 2, pp. 87–88; vol. 1, p. 356.
89. Saint-Simon, ed. de Boislisle, vol. 4, pp. 381–382; *Ecrits inédits*, vol. 1, pp. 356–357.
90. Watrin, *Tradition monarchique*, p. 166.

CHAPTER V

1. Barker, *Development of Public Services*, p. 39.
2. G. Tréca, *Les Doctrines et les Réformes du droit public en réaction contre l'absolutisme de Louis XIV dans l'entourage du Duc de Bourgogne*, p. 124.
3. Werner Näf, *Die Epochen der neueren Geschichte: Staat und Staatengemeinschaft vom Ausgang des Mittelalters bis zur Gegenwart*, vol. 1, p. 360.
4. David Jayne Hill, *A History of Diplomacy in the International Development of Europe*, vol. 3, p. 358.
5. Aitzema, *Saken van Staet*, vol. 4, p. 852. See, however, the sarcastic comment of the contemporary Dutch observer Wicquefort that the duke sold and the king bought "a thing that was not for sale," because the duke was not the proprietor of the duchy

but only its usufructuary (Abraham de Wicquefort, *Histoire des Provinces-Unies des Païs-Bas, depuis le parfait établissement de cet état par la paix de Munster*, vol. 3, pp. 25–26).

6. P. de Groot to A. de Wicquefort, January 9, 1671, de Groot, *Lettres de Pierre de Groot à Abraham de Wicquefort (1668–1674)*, p. 25; to John de Witt, September 19, 1671, [Johan de Witt], *Brieven aan Johan de Witt*, ed. Robert Fruin and N. Japikse, vol. 1, p. 482.

7. Legrelle, *La diplomatie française*, vol. 1, pp. 53–54.

8. Church, *Constitutional Thought*, p. 113.

9. Vast, *Grands traités*, vol. 2, pp. 2–3.

10. Legrelle, *La diplomatie française*, vol. 1, pp. 72–74.

11. Ibid., p. 74.

12. Johan de Witt, *Brieven geschreven ende gewisselt tusschen den Heer Johan de Witt, Raedt-pensionaris en Groot-Segelbewaerder van Hollant en West-Vrieslandt; ende de Gevolmaghtigden van den Staedt der Vereenighde Nederlanden, so in Vranckryck, Engelandt, Sweden, Denemarcken, Poolen, enz. Beginnende met den jaere 1652 tot het jaer 1669 incluys* (hereafter cited as De Witt, *Brieven*), vol. 2, pp. 579–588; a French version of this letter in *Correspondance française du Grand Pensionnaire Jean de Witt*.

13. De Witt, memorandum on conference with D'Estrades, [July 27, 1663], Algemeen Rijksarchief, The Hague (hereafter cited as ARA), Staten van Holland vóór 1795, no. 2,679; D'Estrades to De Witt, July 27, 1663, ibid.; D'Estrades to Louis XIV, Godefroi comte d'Estrades, *Lettres, Mémoires et Négociations de Monsieur le Comte d'Estrade [sic] Tant en qualité d'Ambassadeur de S. M. T. C. en Italie, en Angleterre et en Hollande, Que comme Ambassadeur Plénipotentiaire à la Paix de Nimègue, Conjointement avec Messieurs Colbert et Comte d'Avaux; avec les Reponses du Roi et du Secrétaire d'Etat*, vol. 2, pp. 273–276.

14. Louis XIV, "Proiet," undated [c. September 21, 1663], ARA, Staten van Holland vóór 1795, no. 2,679.

15. D'Estrades to Louis XIV, October 11, 1663, D'Estrades, *Lettres*, vol. 2, p. 303.

16. D'Estrades to Louis XIV, November 15, 1663, ibid., pp. 313–314.

17. De Witt, memorandum, with replies of Wicquefort, undated [c. November 1663], ARA, Staten van Holland vóór 1795, no. 2,688.

18. D'Estrades to Louis XIV, November 28, 1663, D'Estrades, *Lettres*, vol. 2, pp. 329–334.

19. Louis XIV to D'Estrades, December 6, 1663, ibid., p. 336.
20. Secret resolution of the States of Holland, December 14, 1663, *Secrete Resolutien van de Edele Groot Mog. Heeren Staten van Holland en Westvriesland, genomen zedert den aanvang der bedieninge van den Heer Johan de Witt, als Raadpensionaris,* vol. 2, p. 416.
21. Legrelle, *La diplomatie française,* vol. 1, pp. 103–104; Kirkpatrick, *Les renonciations,* p. 53.
22. D'Estrades to Louis XIV, May 19, 1667, D'Estrades, *Lettres,* vol. 5, pp. 210–213. Vast attributes at least partial authorship to Duhem, secretary of Turenne (*Grands traités,* vol. 2, p. 3, n. 5).
23. Bilain, *Traité des Droits,* vol. 1, p. 3.
24. Ibid., p. 3.
25. Ibid., p. 4.
26. Ibid., pp. 6–7.
27. Ibid., p. 7.
28. Ibid., p. 12.
29. Ibid.
30. Ibid., pp. 14–15.
31. Ibid., p. 20.
32. Ibid., pp. 31–32.
33. Ibid., p. 81.
34. Ibid., pp. 83–84.
35. Ibid., pp. 89–90.
36. Ibid., pp. 93, 103, 120–121.
37. Ibid., p. 104.
38. Ibid., p. 112.
39. Ibid., pp. 115–116.
40. Ibid., p. 161.
41. Ibid., p. 168.
42. Ibid., p. 169.
43. Ibid., p. 171.
44. Ibid., pp. 174–175, 183.
45. Ibid., pp. 170–171.
46. Ibid., p. 177.
47. Ibid., pp. 181–183.
48. Louis XIV to D'Estrades, December 26, 1664, D'Estrades, *Lettres,* vol. 2, p. 582.
49. Abraham de Wicquefort, "Mémoire sur la guerre faite aux Provinces-Unies en l'année 1672," p. 117.
50. André, *Louis XIV,* p. 100.

51. Edmond Préclin and Victor L. Tapié, *Le xviie siècle: Monarchies centralisées* (1610–1715), p. 369.

52. Edmond Poullet, *Les constitutions nationales belges de l'Ancien régime à l'époque de l'invasion française de 1794*, pp. 61–62. See also Aitzema, *Saken van Staet*, vol. 6, p. 268.

53. C. A. J. Armstrong, "The Burgundian Netherlands, 1477–1521," p. 243.

54. Dickmann, *Der Westfälische Frieden*, p. 271.

55. *Actes du Colloque sur la Renaissance, organisé par la Société d'Histoire Moderne et présidé par MM. Febvre, Renaudet, Coornaert. Sorbonne, 30 Juin–1er Juillet 1956*, pp. 61–62 (F. Chabod).

56. J. A. Wijnne, "De souvereiniteit der provinciën ten tijde van de Republiek," p. 18.

57. John Lothrop Motley, *History of the United Netherlands from the Death of William the Silent to the Twelve Years' Truce–1609*, vol. 3, pp. 395–396; H. Brugmans, ed., *Geschiedenis van Nederland*, vol. 4, p. 40.

58. *Algemene Geschiedenis der Nederlanden*, ed. J. A. van Houtte et al., vol. 6, p. 221.

59. Dickmann, *Der Westfälische Frieden*, p. 271.

60. Abraham de Wicquefort, *Remarques Sur le Discours du Commandeur de Gremonville, Fait au Conseil d'Estat de Sa Majesté Imperiale*, p. 5.

61. Abraham de Wicquefort, memorandum on possessory rights in Brabant, 1668, ARA, Staten van Holland vóór 1795, box D229.

62. Aitzema, *Saken van Staet*, vol. 6, p. 296.

63. Ibid., vol. 5, pp. 623–627.

64. Pieter Stockmans, *Deductie, Waer uyt Met klare ende bondige Bewijs-Redenen getoont en beweesen wordt, Datter geen Recht van Devolutie is, in het Hertogdom van Brabandt, Noch ook In de andere Provintien van Nederlandt, ten regarde van de Princen der selfde, gelijk eenige getracht hebben te bewijsen ende staende te houden*, pp. 4–5.

65. Ibid., pp. 5–6.

66. Ibid., pp. 4–5.

67. Ibid., p. 4.

68. Johan Meerman to De Witt, December 5, 1667, *De Witt, Brieven*, vol. 4, p. 560.

69. François Paul, baron de Lisola, *Bouclier d'estat et de justice, contre Le dessein manifestement découvert de la Monarchie Universelle, Sous le vain pretexte des pretentions de la Reyne de*

France; Lisola, *The Buckler of State and Justice against the Design manifestly Discovered of the Universal Monarchy, Under the vain Pretext of the Queen of France, Her Pretensions.*

70. Lisola, *Buckler*, p. 196.
71. Ibid., p. 66.
72. Ibid., pp. 299–300.
73. Lisola, *Lettre d'un Gentilhomme Ligeois, Envoyée à l'Autheur des Remarques, qui servent de réponse à deux escrits imprimez à Bruxelles, contre Les Droits de la Reyne sur le Brabant*, p. 27.
74. Ibid., p. 205.
75. Ibid., p. 93.
76. Lisola, *Buckler*, p. 53.
77. Ibid., p. 51.
78. Ibid., p. [7].
79. Lisola, *Le Denoüement Des Intrigues du temps, Par la Responce Au Livret intitulé, Lettres Et autres pieces curieuses sur les affaires du temps*, pp. 3–4.
80. Lisola, *La France Demasquée, Ou ses Irregularitez Dans sa Conduite, & Maximes. Ent-larfftes Frankreich, Oder die Irregularitäten seiner Regierung, und Maximen*, p. 26.
81. André, *Louis XIV*, p. 78.
82. Petrus Valkenier, *'t Verwerd Europa, ofte Politijke en Historische Beschryvinge Der Waare Fundamenten en Oorsaken van de Revolutien in Europa, voornamentlijk in en omtrent de Nederlanden zedert den jaare 1664. gecauseert door de gepretendeerde Universele Monarchie der Franschen*, pp. 52–53, 131. The Salic Law actually never had anything to do with inalienability or indivisibility, in either its precise original form or its extended modern usage. Valkenier's use of the term here shows how loose its meaning had become.
83. Ibid., pp. 82, 168.
84. Olivier Lefèvre d'Ormesson, *Journal d'Olivier Lefèvre d'Ormesson, et extraits des mémoires d'André Lefèvre d'Ormesson*, vol. 2, pp. 525–526.
85. Louis XIV, *Mémoires*, vol. 1, Dreyss's introduction, p. clxiv.
86. Onno Klopp, *Der Fall des Hauses Stuarts und die Succession des Hauses Hannover in Gross-Britannien und Irland im Zusammenhange der europäischen Angelegenheiten von 1660–1714*, vol. 1, p. 177.
87. Tallard to Louis XIV, April 11, 1698, Legrelle, *La diplomatie française*, vol. 2, p. 303.

88. W. J. F. Nuyens, "De politiek van Lodewijk XIV tegenover de Staten-Generaal vóór 1672," p. 283.
89. Lionne to Rousseau, January 11, 1669, Legrelle, La diplomatie française, vol. 1, p. 227.
90. Ibid., p. 191.
91. Arthur Hassall, The Balance of Power, 1715–1789, p. 2.
92. Louis XIV to Feuquières, February 16, 1685, Legrelle, La diplomatie française, vol. 1, p. 261.
93. Croissy to Feuquières, March 23, 1685, ibid., p. 266.
94. Louis XIV to Feuquières, July 23, 1685, ibid., p. 279.
95. Louis XIV to Feuquières, November 20, 1687, ibid., pp. 303–304.
96. Louis XIV to Feuquières, December 11, 1687, ibid., pp. 306–308.
97. Ibid., p. 346.
98. Ibid., pp. 316–318. Rébenac was given another, milder proclamation to use if there was too much opposition to taking a French prince as king (p. 319).
99. André, Louis XIV, p. 281.
100. Legrelle, La diplomatie française, vol. 2, pp. 284–287.
101. Louis XIV to Tallard, March 27, 1698, ibid., p. 290.
102. D'Harcourt to Louis XIV, April 16, 1698, ibid., pp. 510–511.
103. Tallard to Louis XIV, August 25, 1698, ibid., p. 479.
104. Louis XIV to Tallard, July 15, 1698, ibid., p. 363.
105. Louis XIV to Tallard, September 2, 1698, ibid., p. 482.
106. Vast, Grands traités, vol. 3, pp. 4–7.
107. Villars to Louis XIV, June 14, 1700, Legrelle, La diplomatie française, vol. 3, pp. 285–288.
108. W. N. Hargreaves-Mawdsley, ed., Spain under the Bourbons, 1700–1833. A Collection of Documents, p. 1; Marquis de Courcy, "La renonciation des Bourbons d'Espagne au trône d'Espagne," p. 311.
109. Arnold Gaedeke, Die Politik Oesterreichs in der Spanischen Erbfolgefrage, vol. 2, p. 118.
110. Saint-Simon, Mémoires de Saint-Simon, ed. Gonzague Truc, vol. 1, pp. 789–796.
111. Marquis de Courcy, Renonciation des Bourbons d'Espagne au Trône d'Espagne, p. 9; Saint-Simon, Mémoires, ed. Truc, vol. 1, p. 800.
112. This denial was reaffirmed by D'Avaux, the French ambassador in the United Provinces, when he departed from The Hague on August 5, 1701. You cannot decide, he told the States General, that Philip IV had the right or power to change the fundamental laws of the Spanish monarchy, but that Charles II did not have

the power to reestablish them by his own testament (Vast, *Grands traités*, vol. 3, pp. 26–27).

113. Saint-Simon, *Mémoires*, ed. True, vol. 1, p. 800; Courcy, "La renonciation," p. 309.
114. Courcy, "La renonciation," pp. 320–321; Vast, *Grands traités*, vol. 3, p. 24.
115. Saint-Simon, *Mémoires*, ed. Truc, vol. 1, p. 807.
116. Louis XIV to Blécourt, June 3, 1701, Alfred Baudrillart, *Philippe V et la Cour de France*, vol. 1, p. 70.
117. Watrin, *Tradition monarchique*, pp. 47–48.
118. *Défense du droit de la Maison d'Autriche à la Succession d'Espagne. Et la Vérification du Partage du Lion de la Fable dans les conséquences de l'Intrusion du Duc d'Anjou*, pp. 184, 186.
119. Ibid., p. 40.
120. Ibid., p. 52.
121. Ibid., p. 106.
122. Torcy to duke of Medina-Celi, 1702, Baudrillart, *Philippe V*, vol. 1, p. 124.
123. Louis XIV to Marie-Louise, queen of Spain, March 22, 1702, ibid., p. 97.
124. Louis XIV to Philip V, June 7, 1702, ibid., pp. 108–109.
125. Louis XIV to Philip V, August 1, 1707, ibid., p. 300.
126. Louis XIV to Amelot, December 19, 1706, ibid., p. 280.
127. Vast, *Grands traités*, vol. 3, p. 30.
128. Ibid., p. 31.
129. Joseph Klaits, *Printed Propaganda under Louis XIV: Absolute Monarchy and Public Opinion*, pp. 254–256.
130. Courcy, *Renonciation*, p. 78.
131. Baudrillart, *Philippe V*, vol. 1, pp. 542–545.
132. Louis XIV to Philip V, March 11, 1712, Courcy, "La renonciation," pp. 322–323. See also Louis to Philip, April 22, 1712, Watrin, *Tradition monarchique*, p. 86.
133. Watrin, *Tradition monarchique*, p. 82; Courcy, "La renonciation," pp. 325–326; Kirkpatrick, *Les renonciations*, pp. 151–152, 160–161. Also see marquis de Torcy, *Mémoires du marquis de Torcy, pour servir à l'histoire des négociations, depuis le traité de Riswick jusqu' à la paix d'Utrecht*, ser. 3, vol. 8, pp. 710–711.
134. Bolingbroke to Torcy, March 23/30, 1711/12, Bolingbroke, *Lettres and Correspondance, Public and Private, of the Right Honourable Henry St. John, Lord Viscount Bolingbroke, During the time he was Secretary of State to Queen Anne*, vol. 1, p. 439.

135. Bolingbroke to Lords Plenipotentiaries, March 26/April 5, 1711/12, ibid., p. 445.
136. Bolingbroke, *The Works of the late Right Honorable Henry St. John, Lord Viscount Bolingbroke* ,vol. 3, pp. 45–50, 56–57.
137. Kirkpatrick, *Les renonciations*, pp. 166–167.
138. Courcy, *Renonciation*, p. 236; Kirkpatrick, *Les renonciations*, p. 181.
139. Watrin, *Tradition monarchique*, pp. 159–160.
140. Baudrillart, *Philippe V*, vol. 1, p. 531.
141. Watrin, *Tradition monarchique*, p. 152.
142. Wicquefort, *Remarques*, p. 10.

CHAPTER VI

1. François de Callières, *De la manière de négocier avec les souverains, De l'utilité des Negociations, du choix des Ambassadeurs et des Envoyez, et des qualitez necessaires pour réüssir dans ces emplois*, pp. 55–56.
2. William IV, prince of Orange, named hereditary stadholder by the provincial States in Holland, Zeeland, Utrecht, and Overijssel, was already stadholder in Friesland, Groningen, and Gelderland.
3. Early in the nineteenth century, in the wake of the Napoleonic triumphs in Prussia, a Prussian political writer named Buchholz observed with surprise that all "political metaphysicians" of the previous century had shied away from discussion of the inheritance of sovereignty (Friedrich Buchholz, *Der neue Leviathan*, pp. 39–40).
4. Olivier-Martin, *Histoire du Droit Français*, p. 325.
5. Henri Sée, *L'Evolution de la Pensée Politique en France au XVIIIᵉ Siècle*, p. 31.
6. Jean Baptiste Massillon, *Sermons "On the Duties of the Great,"* pp. 121–123.
7. Hitier, "La Doctrine de l'Absolutisme," pp. 51–52.
8. Olivier-Martin, *Histoire du Droit Français*, p. 334.
9. Viollet, *Le Roi*, p. 78.
10. Ibid., p. 36.
11. Sée, *L'Evolution*, p. 93.
12. Ibid., p. 320.
13. François-Marie Arouet de Voltaire, *Oeuvres complètes de Voltaire*, vol. 8, p. 43. ("I sing of this hero who reigned over France / By the double right of conquest and birth.")

14. Ibid., p. 145. ("My throne awaits you, my throne shall come to you by right: / Enjoy this thing you'll own that your own hands have defended.")
15. Ibid., vol. 10. p. 333. ("When two kings get on well, / And each defends his own property, / And feasts upon someone else's.")
16. Voltaire, *Philosophical Dictionary*, s.v. War (*Guerre*), cited from Peter Gay, ed., *The Enlightenment: An Anthology* (New York, 1973), p. 246.
17. Voltaire, "Dialogues entre A, B, C, sixième entretien," *Politique de Voltaire*, p. 179.
18. Voltaire to Crown Prince Frederick, August 5, 1738, Frederick II, *Briefwechsel Friedrichs des Grossen mit Voltaire*, vol. 1, p. 198.
19. Frederick II, "L'Anti-Machiavel," *Oeuvres de Frédéric le Grand*, vol. 8, p. 67.
20. Frederick II, "Réfutation du Prince de Machiavel," ibid., pp. 167–168; also "Histoire de mon temps," ibid., vol. 2, p. xvi.
21. Frederick II, "L'Anti-Machiavel," ibid., vol. 8, p. 160; "Réfutation," ibid., pp. 168, 295, 298.
22. Frederick II, "Réfutation," ibid., pp. 171, 173.
23. Ritter, *Friedrich der Grosse*, pp. 205–206.
24. Voltaire to Frederick II, July 1742, Frederick II to Voltaire, July 25, 1742, Frederick II, *Briefwechsel*, vol. 2, pp. 136, 138.
25. Frederick II, *Memoirs of the House of Brandenburg*, pp. 17–18; "Mémoires de la Maison de Brandebourg," *Oeuvres*, vol. 1, p. 6.
26. Frederick II, *Histoire de mon temps* (Redaction von 1746), p. 186.
27. Ibid., p. 161.
28. Frederick II, "Mémoires de la Maison de Brandebourg," *Oeuvres*, vol. 1, p. 137.
29. Ibid., p. 126.
30. Ibid., p. 65.
31. Frederick II, "Examen de l'Essai sur les préjugés," *Oeuvres*, vol. 9, pp. 144–145, 149; Frederick II to Voltaire, October 20, 1774, *Briefwechsel*, vol. 3, p. 307.
32. Frederick II, "Examen de l'Essai sur les préjugés," *Oeuvres*, vol. 9, p. 151.
33. Frederick II, "Examen critique du Système de la Nature," ibid., pp. 167–168.
34. Frederick II, "Essai sur les formes du gouvernement," ibid., pp. 199–200.
35. Frederick II, "Mémoires de la Maison de Brandebourg," ibid., vol. 1, p. 101.

36. Sée, *L'Evolution*, p. 72. It is interesting to note that the modern historian F. H. Hinsley, discussing the concept of sovereignty, wrote that Montesquieu "mistook the English principle of mixed government, based on the separation of different government powers, to be a doctrine resulting from and justifying the deliberate division of sovereignty itself among several independent *owners* [emphasis added]" (F. H. Hinsley, *Sovereignty*, p. 152). Hinsley appears to be using the term in its metaphorical rather than its literal meaning.

37. Sée, *L'Evolution*, pp. 209–210.

38. Elizabeth Fox-Genovese, *The Origins of Physiocracy: Economic Revolution and Social Order in Eighteenth-Century France*, p. 164.

39. Ibid., p. 215.

40. Ibid., p. 182.

41. Ibid., pp. 187–188.

42. Ibid., p. 189.

43. Ibid., p. 190. Fox-Genovese adds at once her discovery of a dilemma in Mirabeau: he circumscribes the proprietary rights of the prince to protect those of the members of society, yet he also circumscribes their rights in the name of society's rights, all in order to preserve "that divine distinction of *thine* from *mine*." In failing to see that private property was taken for granted in Mirabeau's time and that its protection was cited as a function of political power, an axiom of an argument rather than its Q.E.D., she reads twentieth-century concerns and ideas into the eighteenth. But her oversight is also a result of the general absence among historians of an awareness of the proprietary element in the political practice and theory of the old regime.

44. Denis Diderot, *Oeuvres politiques*, p. 14.

45. Ibid., p. 15.

46. Ibid.

47. Ibid., pp. 16–17; J. Lough, ed., *The Encyclopédie of Diderot and D'Alembert: Selected Articles*, pp. 11–12; Sully, *Mémoires*, vol. 2, p. 300.

48. The whole passage is also in *Oeuvres complètes de Diderot*, vol. 13, pp. 394–395.

49. Lough, *The Encyclopédie*, pp. 6–7.

50. Franco Venturi, *Utopia and Reform in the Enlightenment*, p. 75.

51. Diderot, "Voyage de Hollande," *Oeuvres complètes*, vol. 17, p. 389.

52. Diderot, *Oeuvres politiques*, pp. 6–7; J. Lough, "The 'Encyclopédie' and the Remonstrances of the Paris Parlement."

53. Furio Diaz, *Filosofia e politica nel Settecento francese*, p. 499, n. 2.

54. Abbé de Saint-Pierre, *Annales Politiques* (1658–1740), pp. 15–16.

55. Ibid., p. 114.

56. Ibid., pp. 118–119.

57. Henry Michel, *L'Idée de l'Etat: Essai critique sur l'histoire des théories sociales et politiques en France depuis la Révolution*, p. 39.

58. Jean-Jacques Rousseau, "Discours sur l'origine de l'inégalité," *Oeuvres complètes*, vol. 3, pp. 183–184.

59. Ibid., p. 132.

60. Rousseau, "Du contrat social," ibid., p. 399.

61. Ibid., pp. 395–396.

62. Ibid., pp. 328, 361.

63. Ibid., p. 367.

64. Ibid., pp. 355–356.

65. Gierke, *Natural Law*, vol. 1, p. 129.

66. Derathé, *Jean-Jacques Rousseau*, pp. 98–99.

67. Ibid., p. 105.

68. Michel Cantalauze, seigneur de La Garde, *Dissertation sur l'origine et les fonctions essentielles du Parlement; sur la Pairie, et le Droit des Pairs; et sur les loix fondamentales de la Monarchie Française*, p. 11.

69. Ibid., pp. 52, 63.

70. Ibid., p. 67, n. a.

71. Marquis d'Argenson, *Considérations sur le gouvernement ancien et présent de la France*, p. 189.

72. Ibid., pp. 129–131.

73. Ibid., p. 124.

74. Ibid., p. 2.

75. Diaz, *Filosofia*, p. 420, n. 1; Elie Carcassonne, *Montesquieu et le problème de la constitution française au XVIIIe siècle*, pp. 308–309.

76. Jacques Godechot, *Les Institutions de la France sous la Révolution et l'Empire*, p. 22.

77. Regnault, *Royaume de France*, p. 270.

78. Michel, *L'Idée de l'Etat*, p. 16.

79. Paul Thiry, baron d'Holbach, *La Morale Universelle ou les Devoirs de l'homme fondés sur sa nature*, vol. 2, pp. 26, 66–67.

80. Ibid., p. 32.

81. Ibid., pp. 118–119.
82. Ibid., p. 99.
83. Ibid., pp. 44–45.
84. Ibid., vol. 1, p. 246.
85. Abbé Gabriel Bonnot de Mably, *Le Droit Public de l'Europe, fondé sur les Traités,* vol. 1, pp. 1, 31–32.
86. Diaz, *Filosofia,* p. 417, n. 5.
87. Jean Jacques Burlamaqui, *Principes ou Elémens du Droit politique,* p. 41.
88. Ibid., pp. 54–55.
89. Ibid., pp. 60–61.
90. Ibid., pp. 78–81; see also pp. 132 (misprinted 130)–134.
91. See Herbert H. Rowen, "A Second Thought on Locke's *First Treatise.*"
92. Jacques Godechot, *La Contre-Révolution: Doctrine et Action, 1789–1804,* pp. 18–19; Paul H. Beik, *The French Revolution Seen from the Right: Social Theories in Motion, 1789–1799,* pp. 7–8. Beik's view of Moreau is more favorable than mine.
93. Jacob Nicolas Moreau, *Leçons de Morale, de politique, et de droit public, Puisées dans l'Histoire de notre Monarchie, Ou Nouveau Plan d'étude de l'Histoire de France, Rédigé par les ordres & d'après les vues de feu Monseigneur le Dauphin, pour l'Instruction des Princes ses Enfans,* pp. 21–22.
94. Ibid., p. 24.
95. Ibid., p. 37.
96. Ibid., p. 38.
97. Ibid., p. 42.
98. Ibid., p. 47.
99. Ibid., p. 52, n. a.
100. Ibid., p. 73.
101. Ibid., pp. 80–81.
102. Ibid., p. 91.
103. Ibid., pp. 96–97.
104. Ibid., p. 103.
105. Ibid., pp. 104–105.
106. Ibid., p. 105.
107. Ibid., p. 106.
108. Ibid., pp. 108–110.
109. Ibid., p. 123.
110. Ibid., pp. 178–179.
111. Ibid., p. 179.
112. Ibid., p. 180.

113. Jacob Nicolas Moreau, *Principes de morale, de politique et de droit public, Puisés dans l'Histoire de notre Monarchie, ou Discours sur l'Histoire de France, Dédiés au Roi*, vol. 1, pp. 2, 11.
114. Ibid., pp. 11–12.
115. Ibid., vol. 13, p. 43; see also vol. 17, p. 344.
116. Ibid., vol. 1, p. 46.
117. Ibid., p. 53.
118. Ibid., p. 105.
119. Ibid., vol. 2, p. 197.
120. Ibid., vol. 3, p. 1.
121. Ibid., pp. 160, 162.
122. Ibid., pp. 161, 165.
123. Ibid., p. 161.
124. Ibid., vol. 5, p. 109.
125. Ibid., vol. 6, pp. 188–189.
126. Ibid., vol. 7, pp. 202, 403; vol. 8, p. 113; vol. 11, p. xxviii.
127. Ibid., vol. 7, p. 271.
128. Ibid., pp. 329–330.
129. Ibid., vol. 13, pp. 1–3, 52.
130. Ibid., vol. 17, p. 418.
131. Ibid.
132. Ibid., vol. 13, pp. 226–227.
133. Ibid., pp. 228–229.
134. Ibid., pp. 232–233.
135. Ibid., vol. 6, pp. 189–190.
136. Ibid., pp. 199–200.
137. Ibid., p. 204.
138. Ibid., pp. 209–210.
139. Ibid., pp. 230–232; see also vol. 13, p. 231.
140. Ibid., vol. 6, pp. 232–233.
141. Ibid., p. 233.
142. Ibid., p. 234; vol. 16, p. 483.
143. Ibid., vol. 6, p. 235.
144. Ibid., vol. 13, p. 244.
145. Ibid., pp. 247–250.
146. Ibid., pp. 251–252.
147. Ibid., p. 260.
148. Ibid., pp. 350, 352.
149. Ibid., pp. 264, 271–273; vol. 16, p. 476.
150. Ibid., vol. 15, p. 264.
151. Ibid., p. 265.
152. Ibid., vol. 7, p. 366.

153. Ibid., pp. 368–369.
154. Ibid., vol. 16, pp. 429, 466–467.
155. Ibid., pp. 430, 432–433, 465.
156. Ibid., p. 483.
157. Ibid., p. 484.
158. Ibid., vol. 3, p. 292.
159. J. M. Roberts et al., eds., *French Revolution Documents*, vol. 1, p. 6.
160. Ibid., p. 18.
161. Olivier-Martin, *Histoire du Droit Français*, p. 329.
162. Jules Flammermont, ed., *Remontrances du Parlement de Paris au XVIIIe siècle*, vol. 3, pp. 736–737.
163. *Archives Parlementaires de 1787 à 1860*, vol. 1, pp. 531–534.

CHAPTER VII

1. Challaye, *Histoire de la Propriété*, p. 84.
2. Emmanuel Sieyès, *Qu'est-ce que le Tiers état?*, pp. 122–123.
3. Ibid., p. 124, n. d.
4. Ibid., p. 141, n. 1.
5. Ibid., p. 145.
6. Watrin, *Tradition monarchique*, p. 22.
7. *Archives parlementaires*, ser. 1, vol. 20, pp. 81–84.
8. Hitier, "La Doctrine de l'Absolutisme," p. 48.
9. Ibid., p. 49.
10. Godechot, *Institutions*, p. 79.
11. The term "inalienable" has come to mean "cannot be *taken* away," not "cannot be *given* away." For one among innumerable examples, see Christopher Lehmann-Haupt, book reviewer of the *New York Times*, August 4, 1977: "These are not your tricks and bluffs, but your inalienable rights, at least until the laws are changed." This usage probably traces back to the use of the phrase "inalienable rights" in the American Declaration of Independence; but it is significant of the loss of its primary proprietary meaning that later generations made sense out of the phrase by understanding it to mean the rights that government cannot take from citizens.
12. Roberts et al., *French Revolution Documents*, vol. 1, pp. 350, 355.
13. Jacques Roux, *Jacques Roux, Scripta et Acta*, p. 292.
14. The Committee of Public Safety to Roux-Fazillac, representative on mission in Corrèze and Puy-de-Dôme, 26 pluviôse Year II/

February 14, 1794. Roberts, et al., *French Revolution Documents*, vol. 2, pp. 180–181.

15. A. C. Thibaudeau, *Mémoires sur le Consulat. 1799 à 1804. Par un ancien Conseiller d'Etat*, p. 235.
16. Ibid., pp. 298–299.
17. Ibid., p. 391.
18. Ibid., p. 462.
19. *Archives parlementaires*, ser. 2, vol. 8, pp. 269–271.
20. Hitier, "La Doctrine de l'Absolutisme," p. 105.
21. Friedrich Brockhaus, *Das Legitimitätsprincip: Eine staatsrechtliche Abhandlung*, pp. 117–119.
22. Charlotte Touzalin Muret, *French Royalist Doctrines since the Revolution*, p. 24.
23. Ibid., p. 77.
24. Alexis de Tocqueville, *De la Démocratie en Amérique*, vol. 1, pp. 46–47.
25. Watrin, *Tradition monarchique*, pp. 150–151.
26. Theodore Zeldin, *The Political System of Napoleon III*, pp. 105–106.
27. Muret, *French Royalist Doctrines*, p. 148.
28. Ibid., pp. 178–179.
29. Prince Sixte de Bourbon de Parme, *Le traité d'Utrecht et les lois fondamentales du royaume*.
30. Ibid., p. iii.
31. See Robert A. Kann, *Die Sixtusaffäre und die geheimen Friedensverhandlungen Österreich-Ungarns im Ersten Weltkrieg*.

WORKS CITED

Actes du Colloque sur la Renaissance, organisé par la Société d'Histoire Moderne et présidé par MM. Febvre, Renaudet, Coornaert. Sorbonne, 30 Juin-1er Juillet 1956. Paris, 1958.

Aitzema, Lieuwe van. Saken van Staet en Oorlogh, in, ende omtrent de Vereenighde Nederlanden. 2d ed. 6 vols. The Hague, 1669–1671.

Albertini, Rudolf von. Das politische Denken in Frankreich zur Zeit Richelieus. Marburg, 1951.

Algemene Geschiedenis der Nederlanden. Edited by J. A. van Houtte et al. 1st ed. 12 vols. Utrecht, 1949–1958.

André, Louis. Louis XIV et l'Europe. Paris, 1950.

Archives Parlementaires de 1787 à 1860. Edited by J. Mavidal and E. Laurent. 218 vols. Paris, 1867–1913.

Argenson, [René-Louis de Voyer de Paulmy], marquis de. Considérations sur le gouvernement ancien et présent de la France. Amsterdam, 1765.

[Aristotle]. The Politics of Aristotle. Translated and edited by Ernest Barker. 3rd rev. ed. Oxford, 1961.

Armstrong, C. A. J. "The Burgundian Netherlands, 1477–1521." In The New Cambridge Modern History, vol. 1, pp. 224–258. Cambridge, 1957.

Avenel, vicomte G. d'. Richelieu et la monarchie absolue. 4 vols. Paris, 1884–1890.

Aymard, André, and Auboyer, Jeannine. L'Orient et la Grèce antique. Paris, 1953.

Barker, Ernest. The Development of Public Services in Western Europe, 1660–1930. London, 1945.

Baudrillart, Alfred. Philippe V et la Cour de France. 5 vols. Paris, 1890–1901.

Baumgartner, Frederic J. Radical Reactionaries: The Political Thought of the French Catholic League. Geneva, 1976.

Baxter, Christopher R. "Jean Bodin's Daemon and His Conversion to Judaism." In *Jean Bodin: Verhandlungen der internationalen Bodin Tagung zu München*, edited by Horst Denzer, pp. 1–21. Munich, 1973.

Beik, Paul H. *The French Revolution Seen from the Right: Social Theories in Motion, 1789–1799.* Philadelphia, 1956.

Below, G. von. *Der deutsche Staat des Mittelalters: Ein Grundriss der deutschen Verfassungsgeschichte.* Leipzig, 1914.

[Béthune, Philippe de.] *Le Conseiller d'Estat, ou Recveil general de la poltiqve moderne, seruant au maniement des Affaires publiques.* Paris, 1665.

[Bilain, Antoine.] *Traité des Droits de la Reyne Tres-Chrétienne, sur divers Etats de la Monarchie d'Espagne.* 2 vols. Paris, 1667.

Bloch, Marc. *French Rural History: An Essay on its Basic Characteristics.* Translated by Janet Sondheimer. Berkeley and Los Angeles, 1966.

———. *Les Rois thaumaturges: Etude sur le caractère surnaturel attribué à la puissance royale particulièrement en France et en Angleterre.* Strasbourg and Paris, 1924.

———. *Seigneurie française et manoir anglais.* Paris, 1960.

———. *La société féodale. Les classes et le gouvernement des hommes.* Paris, 1940.

Bodin, Jean. *Method for the Easy Comprehension of History.* Translated by Beatrice Reynolds. New York, 1945.

———. *Méthode pour faciliter la connaissance de l'histoire.* In *Oeuvres Philosophiques de Jean Bodin*, edited and translated by Pierre Mesnard. Paris, 1951.

———. *Six Books of the Commonwealth.* Abridged and translated by M. J. Tooley. Oxford, n.d.

[Bolingbroke, Henry St. John, Viscount.] *Lettres and Correspondance, Public and Private, of the Right Honourable Henry St. John, Lord Viscount Bolingbroke, During the time he was Secretary of State to Queen Anne.* Edited by Gilbert Parke. 2 vols. London, 1798.

———. *The Works of the late Right Honorable Henry St. John, Lord Viscount Bolingbroke.* 5 vols. London, 1777.

Bossuet, Jacques Bénigne. *Politique tirée des propres paroles de l'Ecriture Sainte.* In *Oeuvres*, vol. 1, pp. 299–482. 4 vols. Paris, 1870.

Boussard, Jacques. "La France féodale." In *Encyclopédie de la Pléiade: La France et les Français*, edited by Michel François, pp. 967–1,021. Paris, 1972.

Bridge, John S. C. *A History of France from the Death of Louis XI.* 5 vols. Oxford, 1921–1936.

[Brienne, Louis-Henri de Loménie, Comte de Brienne], *Mémoires de Louis-Henri de Brienne, Comte de Brienne, dit le Jeune Brienne.* Edited by Paul Bonnefon. 3 vols. Paris, 1916–1919.

Brockhaus, Friedrich. *Das Legitimitätsprincip: Eine staatsrechtliche Abhandlung.* Leipzig, 1868.

Brown, Elizabeth A. R. "The Ceremonial of Succession in Capetian France: The Double Funerary Ceremony of Louis X." *Traditio* 34 (1978): 234–252.

Brugmans, H., ed. *Geschiedenis van Nederland.* 8 vols. Amsterdam, 1935–1938.

Bruins Slot, J. A. H. J. S. "Staatsabsolutisme onder Lodewijk XIV." *Antirevolutionaire Staatkunde* 15 (1939): 481–502.

Brunner, Otto. *Land und Herrschaft: Grundfragen der territorialen Verfassungsgeschichte Südostdeutschlands im Mittelalter.* 3rd ed. Brünn, 1943.

Bruyère, Jean de La. *Les Caractères de Théophraste traduits du grec avec les Caractères ou les Moeurs de ce siècle.* Edited by Robert Garapon. Paris, 1962.

Buchholz, Friedrich. *Der neue Leviathan.* Tübingen, 1805. Reprint ed. Aalen, 1970.

Buisson, Albert. *Michel de l'Hospital.* Paris, 1950.

Burlamaqui, Jean Jacques. *Principes ou Elémens du Droit politique.* Lausanne, 1784.

Callières, [François] de. *De la manière de négocier avec les souverains, De l'utilité des Negociations, du choix des Ambassadeurs et des Envoyez, et des qualitez necessaires pour réüssir dans ces emplois.* Amsterdam, 1716.

[Cantalauze, Michel, seigneur de La Garde.] *Dissertation sur l'origine et les fonctions essentielles du Parlement; sur la Pairie, et le Droit des Pairs; et sur les loix fondamentales de la Monarchie Française.* Amsterdam, 1764.

Caprariis, Vittorio de. *Propaganda e pensiero politico in Francia durante le guerre di religione.* Vol. 1. Naples, 1959.

Carcassonne, Elie. *Montesquieu et le problème de la constitution française au XVIIIe siècle.* Paris, 1927. Reprint ed. Geneva, 1970.

Carré de Malberg, R. *Contribution à la Théorie générale de l'Etat.* 2 vols. Paris, 1920–1922.

Challaye, Félicien. *Histoire de la Propriété.* 3rd ed. Paris, 1944.

Chauveau, Jean Pierre. "Un sonnet inédit de Tristan l'Hermite." *XVIIe siècle* 61 (1963): 31–36.

Chauviré, Roger. *Jean Bodin, auteur de la République.* Paris, 1914.

Church, William Farr. *Constitutional Thought in Sixteenth-Century France: A Study in the Evolution of Ideas.* Cambridge, Mass., 1941.

Courcy, [Marie-René-Roussel], marquis de. "La renonciation des Bourbons d'Espagne au trône d'Espagne." *Revue des Deux Mondes* 88 (1888): 305–339, 872–905; 89 (1888): 266–304.

———. *Renonciation des Bourbons d'Espagne au Trône d'Espagne.* Paris, 1889. Same as preceding.

David, Marcel. *La souveraineté et les limites juridiques du pouvoir monarchique du IXe au XVe siècle.* Paris, 1954.

Défense du droit de la Maison d'Autriche à la Succession d'Espagne. Et la Vérification du Partage du Lion de la Fable dans les conséquences de l'Intrusion du Duc d'Anjou. Cologne, 1703.

Derathé, Robert. *Jean-Jacques Rousseau et la science politique de son temps.* Paris, 1950.

Deslandres, Maurice. *Histoire constitutionnelle de la France de 1789 à 1870.* 2 vols. Paris, 1932.

Diaz, Furio. *Filosofia e politica nel Settecento francese.* Turin, 1962.

Dickmann, Fritz. *Der Westfälische Frieden.* Münster, 1959.

[Diderot, Denis.] *Oeuvres complètes de Diderot.* Edited by J. Assézat. 20 vols. Paris, 1875–1877.

———. *Oeuvres politiques.* Edited by Paul Vernière. Paris, 1963.

Dodge, Guy Howard. *The Political Theory of the Huguenots of the Dispersion: With Special Reference to the Thought and Influence of Pierre Jurieu.* New York, 1947.

Dollot, Louis. *Les Cardinaux-ministres sous la Monarchie Française.* Paris, 1952.

Doucet, Roger. *Les institutions de la France au XVIe siècle.* 2 vols. Paris, 1948.

Dumont, [Jean]. *Corps Universel diplomatique du droit des gens.* 8 vols. Amsterdam and The Hague, 1726–1731.

[Dupuy, P.] *Traitez touchant les droits du Roy tres-Chrestien sur plusieurs Estats et seigneuries possedées par divers Princes voisins: et pour prouver qu'il tient à juste titre plusieurs Provinces contestées par les Princes Estrangers. . . .* New ed. Rouen, 1670.

Duverger, Maurice. *Manuel de droit constitutionnel et de science politique.* 5th ed. Paris, 1948.

Elkan, Albert. *Die Publizistik der Bartholomäusnacht und Mornay's "Vindiciae contra Tyrannos."* Heidelberg, 1905.

Elton, G. R., ed. "The Reformation." In *The New Cambridge Modern History,* vol. 2. Cambridge, 1958.

[Estrades, Godefroi comte d'.] *Lettres, Mémoires et Négociations de Monsieur le Comte d'Estrade [sic] Tant en qualité d'Ambassadeur de S. M. T. C. en Italie, en Angleterre et en Hollande, Que comme Ambassadeur Plénipotentiaire à la Paix de Nimègue, Conjointement avec Messieurs Colbert et Comte d'Avaux: avec les Reponses du Roi et du Secrétaire d'Etat.* New [actually 4th] ed. 9 vols. London [actually The Hague], 1743.

[Fénelon, François de Salignac de la Mothe-.] *Oeuvres Choisies de Fénelon.* 4 vols. Paris, 1880–1901.

Figgis, John Neville. *The Divine Right of Kings.* 2d ed. Cambridge, 1934.

Flammermont, Jules, ed. *Remontrances du Parlement de Paris au XVIIIe siècle.* 3 vols. Paris, 1888–1898.

Fleury, Claude. *Institution au Droit Français.* Edited by Edouard Laboulaye and Rodolphe Dareste. 2 vols. Paris, 1858.

Folz, Robert. *The Coronation of Charlemagne: 25 December 800.* Translated by J. E. Anderson. London, 1974.

Fox-Genovese, Elizabeth. *The Origins of Physiocracy: Economic Revolution and Social Order in Eighteenth-Century France.* Ithaca, N.Y., 1976.

Franck, Ad. *Réformateurs et publicistes de l'Europe, dix-septième siècle.* Paris, 1881.

François, Michel. "La formation de l'Etat moderne (1515–1598)." In *Histoire de France,* edited by Marcel Reinhard, vol. 1, pp. 337–419. 2 vols. Paris, 1954.

Franklin, Julian H., trans. and ed. *Constitutionalism and Resistance in the Sixteenth Century: Three Treatises by Hotman, Beza, &* Mornay. New York, 1969.

[Frederick II, king of Prussia.] *Briefwechsel Friedrichs des Grossen mit Voltaire.* Edited by Reinhold Koser and Hans Droysen. 3 vols. Leipzig, 1908–1911.

——. *Histoire de mon temps (Redaction von 1746).* Edited by Max Posner, Leipzig, 1879.

——. *Memoirs of the House of Brandenburg,* N.p.; n.d.

——. *Oeuvres de Frédéric le Grand.* 30 vols. Berlin, 1846–1857.

Gaedeke, Arnold. *Die Politik Oesterreichs in der Spanischen Erbfolgefrage.* 2 vols. Leipzig, 1877.

Ganshof, François L. *Le Moyen Âge. Histoire des relations internationales,* edited by Pierre Renouvin, vol. 1. Paris, 1953.

——. "Het tijdperk van de Merowingen." In *Algemene Geschiedenis der Nederlanden,* edited by J. A. van Houtte et al., vol. 1, pp. 252–305. 1st ed. 12 vols. Utrecht, 1949–1958.

Gierke, Otto. *Natural Law and the Theory of Society, 1500 to 1800.* Translated by Ernest Barker. Cambridge, 1934.

——. *Political Theories of the Middle Age.* Translated by Frederic William Maitland. Cambridge, 1927.

Giesey, Ralph E. "The French Estates and the Corpus Mysticum Regni." In *Album Helen Maud, I,* pp. 153–171. Louvain and Paris, 1960.

——. *The Juristic Basis of Dynastic Right to the French Throne.* Philadelphia, 1961.

——. "Rules of Inheritance and Strategies of Mobility in Pre-revolutionary France." *American Historical Review* 82 (1977): 271–289.

Gilmore, Myron Piper. *Argument from Roman Law in Political Thought, 1200–1600.* Cambridge, Mass., 1941.

Godechot, Jacques. *La Contre-Révolution: Doctrine et Action, 1789–1804.* Paris, 1961.

——. *Les Institutions de la France sous la Révolution et l'Empire.* Paris, 1951.

Gonnard, René. *La propriété dans la doctrine et dans l'histoire.* Paris, 1943.

[Groot, Pieter de.] *Lettres de Pierre de Groot à Abraham de Wicquefort (1668–1674).* Edited by F. J. L. Krämer. The Hague, 1894.

Guttman, J. "Jean Bodin in seinen Beziehungen zum Judentum." *Monatsschrift für Geschichte und Wissenschaft des Judentums* 49 (1905): 315–348, 459–489.

Halphen, Louis. *Charlemagne et l'Empire carolingien.* Paris, 1949.

Hargreaves-Mawdsley, W. N., ed. *Spain under the Bourbons, 1700–1833. A Collection of Documents.* Columbia, S.C., 1973.

Hartung, Fritz. "L'Etat c'est Moi." *Historische Zeitschrift* 169 (1949): 1–30.

———. *Die Krone als Symbol der monarchischen Herrschaft im ausgehenden Mittelalter.* Berlin, 1941.

Hassall, Arthur. *The Balance of Power, 1715–1789.* 5th ed. London, 1929.

Hauser, Henri. *La Modernité du seizième siècle.* Paris, 1930.

[Henry IV, king of France.] *Recueil des lettres missives de Henri IV.* Edited by [Jules] Berger de Xivrey. 9 vols. Paris, 1843–1876.

Hexter, J. H. *The Vision of Politics on the Eve of the Reformation: More, Machiavelli, and Seyssel.* New York, 1973.

Heydte, Friedrich August Freiherr von der. *Die Geburtsstunde des souveränen Staates: Ein Beitrag zur Geschichte des Völkerrechts, der allgemeinen Staatslehre und des politischen Denkens.* Regensburg, 1952.

Hill, David Jayne. *A History of Diplomacy in the International Development of Europe.* 3 vols. New York, 1905–1914.

Hinrichs, Ernst. *Fürstenlehre und Politisches Handeln im Frankreich Heinrichs IV. Untersuchungen über die politische Denk- und Handlungsformen im Späthumanismus.* Göttingen, 1969.

Hinsley, F. H. *Sovereignty.* London, 1966.

Hintze, Hedwig. *Staatseinheit und Föderalismus im alten Frankreich und in der Revolution.* Stuttgart, 1928.

Hitier, J. "La Doctrine de l'Absolutisme." *Annales de l'Université de Grenoble* 15 (1903): 37–137, 417–532.

[Holbach Paul Thiry, baron d'] *La Morale Universelle ou Les Devoirs de l'homme fondés sur sa nature. Théorie de la morale.* 3 vols. Tours and Angers, 1792.

Holtzmann, Robert. *Französische Verfassungsgeschichte von der Mitte des neunten Jahrhunderts bis zur Revolution.* Munich and Berlin, 1910.

Hotman, François. *Francogallia.* Latin text by Ralph E. Giesey. Translated by J. H. M. Salmon. Cambridge, 1972.

Huizinga, Johan. "Abelard." In *Verzamelde Werken*, vol. 4, pp. 104–122. 8 vols. Haarlem, 1948–1953.

———."Patriotisme en Nationalisme in de Europeesche Geschiedenis tot het einde der negentiende eeuw." In *Verzamelde Werken*, vol. 4, pp. 497–554. 8 vols. Haarlem, 1948–1953.

Hyma, Albert. *Renaissance to Reformation*. Grand Rapids, Mich., 1951.

[Joly, Claude.] *Recveil de maximes veritables et importantes povr l'institvtion dv Roy. Contre la fausse & pernicieuse Politique du Cardinal Mazarin, pretendu Sur-Intendant de l'education de sa Majesté*. Paris, 1653.

Jouvenel, Bertrand de. *On Power: Its Nature and the History of Its Growth*. Boston, 1962.

[Jurieu, Pierre.] *Les Soupirs de la France esclave qui aspire à la liberté*. 15 nos. Amsterdam, 1689.

———. *Les voeux d'un Patriote*. Amsterdam, 1788.

Kamp, J. L. L. van de. *Bartolus des Saxoferrato, 1313–1357*. Amsterdam, 1936.

Kann, Robert A. *Die Sixtusaffäre und die geheimen Friedensverhandlungen Österreich-Ungarns im Ersten Weltkrieg*. Vienna, 1966.

Kantorowicz, Ernst H. *The King's Two Bodies: A Study in Mediaeval Political Theology*. Princeton, 1957.

Kelley, Donald R. *François Hotman: A Revolutionary's Ordeal*. Princeton, 1973.

Kern, Fritz. *Gottesgnadentum und Widerstandsrecht im früheren Mittelalter: Zur Entwicklungsgeschichte der Monarchie*. Leipzig, 1914.

Kirkpatrick de Closeburn, Edward. *Les renonciations des Bourbons et la Succession d'Espagne*. Paris, 1907.

Klaits, Joseph. *Printed Propaganda under Louis XIV: Absolute Monarchy and Public Opinion*. Princeton, 1976.

Kleyser, Friedrich. *Der Flugschriftenkampf gegen Ludwig XIV. zur Zeit des pfälzisshen Krieges*. Berlin, 1935.

Klopp, Onno. *Der Fall des Hauses Stuarts und die Succession des Hauses Hannover in Gross-Britannien und Irland im Zusammenhange der europäischen Angelegenheiten von 1660–1714*. 14 vols. Vienna, 1875–1888.

Lanfredini, Dina. *Un antagonista di Luigi XIV: Armand de Gramont, Conte de Guiche.* Florence, 1959.

La Pradelle, [Raymond de] Geouffre. *La Monarchie.* Paris, 1944.

Lavisse, Ernest, ed. *Histoire de France depuis les origines jusqu'à la Révolution.* 9 vols. Paris, 1900–1911.

Le Bret, Cardin. *De la Sovveraineté du roy.* Paris, 1632.

Legrelle, A. *La diplomatie française et la succession d'Espagne.* 4 vols. Paris, 1888–1892.

Lemaire, André. *Les lois fondamentales de la monarchie française, d'après les théoriciens de l'Ancien régime.* Paris, 1907.

Lewis, Andrew W. "Anticipatory Association of the Heir in Early Capetian France." *American Historical Review* 83 (1978): 906–927.

Lewis, Ewart. *Medieval Political Ideas.* 2 vols. New York, 1954.

[Lisola, François Paul, baron de.] *Bouclier d'estat et de justice, contre Le dessein manifestement découvert de la Monarchie Universelle, Sous le vain pretexte des pretentions de la Reyne de France.* New ed. N.p., 1667.

———. *The Buckler of State and Justice against the Design manifestly Discovered of the Universal Monarchy, Under the vain Pretext of the Queen of France, Her Pretensions.* 2d ed. London, 1673. Translation of the preceding.

———. *S. I. P. P. B., Le Denoüiement Des Intrigues du temps, Par la Responce Au Livret intitulé, Lettres Et autres pieces curieuses sur les affaires du temps.* Liège, 1672.

———. *La France Demasquée, Ou ses Irregularitez Dans sa Conduite, & Maximes. Ent-larfftes Frankreich, Oder die Irregularitäten seiner Regierung, und Maximen.* The Hague, 1670.

———. *Lettre d'un Gentilhomme Ligeois, Envoyée à l'Autheur des Remarques, qui servent de réponse à deux escrits imprimez à Bruxelles, contre les Droits de la Reyne sur le Brabant.* Liège, 1668.

Lossky, Andrew. "The Nature of Political Power according to Louis XIV." In *The Responsibility of Power: Historical Essays in Honor of Hajo Holborn,* edited by Leonard Krieger and Fritz Stern, pp. 107–122. Garden City, N.Y., 1967.

Lot, Ferdinand. *Naissance de la France.* Paris, 1948.

J. Lough. "The 'Encyclopédie' and the Remonstrances of the Paris

Parlement." *The Modern Language Review* 56 (1961): 393–395.

———, ed. *The Encyclopédie of Diderot and D'Alembert: Selected Articles.* Cambridge, 1954.

[Louis XIV, king of France.] *Mémoires de Louis XIV pour l'instruction du Dauphin.* Edited by Charles Dreyss. 2 vols. Paris, 1860.

———. *Mémoires for the Instruction of the Dauphin.* Edited and translated by Paul Sonnino. New York and London, 1970.

———. *Oeuvres de Louis XIV.* 6 vols. Paris, 1806.

[Loyseau, Charles.] *Les oeuvres de maistre Charles Loyseau, avocat en Parlement, contenant les cinq livres du droit des Offices, les Traitez Des Seigneuries, des Ordres ea des Simples Dignitez, du Déguerpissement & Délaissement par Hypotheque, de la Garantie des Rentes, & des Abus des Justices de Village.* Last ed. Lyon, 1701.

Mably, Abbé [Gabriel Bonnot] de. *Le Droit Public de l'Europe, fondé sur les Traités.* 3rd ed. 3 vols. Geneva, 1744.

McIlwain, Charles Howard. *The Growth of Political Thought in the West from the Greeks to the End of the Middle Ages.* New York, 1932.

Madelin, Louis. *Histoire politique (De 1515 à 1804).* Paris, 1924.

Massaut, Jean-Pierre. "Autour de Richelieu et de Mazarin: Le carme Léon de Saint-Jean et la grande politique." *Revue d'histoire moderne et contemporaine* (1960): 11–45.

[Massillon, Jean-Baptiste.] *Sermons "On the Duties of the Great."* Translated by William Dodd. Dublin, 1770.

Mastellone, Salvo. *Venalità e Machiavellismo in Francia (1572–1610): All'origini della mentalità politica borghese.* Florence, 1972.

Mattingly, Garrett. "Some Revisions of the Political History of the Renaissance." In *The Renaissance: A Reconsideration of the Theories and Interpretations of the Age,* ed. Tinsley Helton, pp. 3–25. Madison, Wisc., 1961.

[Mazarin, Jules Cardinal.] *Lettres du Cardinal de Mazarin, Où l'on voit Le Secret de la Négociation de la Paix des Pirenées; et la Relation des Conferences qu'il a eües avec D. Loüis de Haro, Ministre d'Espagne . . .* New ed. Amsterdam, 1693.

Mesnard, Pierre. *L'essor de la philosophie politique au XVIe siècle.* Paris, 1936.

Michel, Henry. *L'Idée de l'Etat: Essai critique sur l'histoire des théories sociales et politiques en France depuis la Révolution.* 2d ed. Paris, 1896.

Mommsen, Wilhelm. "Zur Beurteiling des Absolutismus." *Historische Zeitschrift* 158 (1938): 52–76.

Moote, A. Lloyd. "Law and Justice under Louis XIV." In *Louis XIV and the Craft of Kingship,* edited by John C. Rule, pp. 224–239. Columbus, Ohio, 1969.

[Moreau, Jacob Nicolas.] *Leçons de Morale, de politique, et de droit public, Puisées dans l'Histoire de notre Monarchie, Ou Nouveau Plan d'étude de l'Histoire de France, Rédigé par les ordres d'après les vues de feu Monseigneur le Dauphin, pour l'Instruction des Princes ses Enfans.* Versailles, 1773.

——. *Principes de morale, de politique et de droit public, Puisés dans l'Histoire de notre Monarchie, ou Discours sur l'Histoire de France, Dédiés au Roi.* 21 vols. Paris, 1777–1789.

Mornay, [Philippe] du Plessis-. *Mémoires et Correspondance Pour servir à l'histoire de la Réformation et des Guerres Civiles et religieuses de la France, sous les règnes de Charles IX, de Henri III, de Henri IV et de Louis XIII, depuis l'an 1571 jusqu'en 1623.* Edited by A. D. de La Fontenelle and P. R. Augis. 12 vols. Paris, 1824–1825. Reprint ed. Geneva, 1969.

Motley, John Lothrop. *History of the United Netherlands from the Death of William the Silent to the Twelve Years' Truce—1609.* 4 vols. New York, 1860.

Mousnier, Roland. *L'Assassinat d'Henri IV: 14 Mai 1610.* Paris, 1964.

——. *Les XVIe et XVIIe siècles: Les progrès de la civilisation européenne et le déclin de l'Orient (1492–1715).* 2d ed. Paris, 1956.

——. *La Vénalité des offices sous Henri IV et Louis XIII.* 2d ed. Paris, 1971.

Mowat, R. B. *A History of European Diplomacy, 1451–1789.* London, 1928.

Muret, Charlotte Touzalin. *French Royalist Doctrines since the Revolution.* New York, 1933.

Näf, Werner. *Die Epochen der neueren Geschichte: Staat und Staatengemeinschaft vom Ausgang des Mittelalters bis zur Gegenwart.* 2 vols. Aarau, 1945–1946.

Nuyens, W. J. F. "De politiek van Lodewijk XIV tegenover de Staten-Generaal vóór 1672." *Onze Wachter,* 1877, pt. 1, 262–296.

Oestreich, Gerhard. "Die Idee des religiösen Bundes und die Lehre vom Staatsvertrag." In *Geist und Gestalt des frühmodernen Staates,* pp. 157–178. Berlin, 1969.

Olivier-Martin, F. *Histoire du Droit Français des origines à la Révolution.* 2d ed. Paris, 1951.

Olschki, Leonardo. *The Genius of Italy.* London, 1950.

[Ormesson, Olivier Lefèvre d'.] *Journal d'Olivier Lefèvre d'Ormesson, et extraits des Mémoires d'André Lefèvre d'Ormesson.* Edited by A. Chéruel. 2 vols. Paris, 1860–1861.

Ourliac, Paul. "Souveraineté et lois fondamentales dans le droit canonique du XVe siècle." In *Herrschaftsverträge, Wahlkapitulationen, Fundamentalgesetze,* edited by Rudolf Vierhaus. Göttingen, 1977.

Pange, Jean de. *Le roi Très Chrétien.* Paris, 1949.

Perroy, Edouard. *La guerre de Cent Ans.* Paris, 1945.

———. et al. *Histoire de France pour tous les Français.* 2 vols. Paris, 1950.

———. et al. *Le Moyen Age: L'expansion de l'Orient et la naissance de la civilisation occidentale.* Paris, 1955.

Picot, Gilbert. *Cardin Le Bret (1558–1655) et la Doctrine de la Souveraineté.* Nancy, 1948.

Potter, John Milton. "The Development and Significance of the Salic Law of the French." *English Historical Review* 52 (1937): 235–253.

Poullet, Edmond. *Les constitutions nationales belges de l'Ancien régime à l'époque de l'invasion française de 1794.* Brussels, 1875.

Préclin, Edmond, and Jarry, E. *Les luttes politiques et doctrinales au XVIIe et XVIIIe siècles.* 2 vols. Paris, 1955–1956.

Préclin, Edmond, and Tapié, Victor L. *Le xviie siècle: Monarchies centralisées (1610–1715).* Paris, 1943.

Puy de Clinchamps, Philippe du. *Le Royalisme.* Paris, 1967.

Regnault, Henri. *Le Royaume de France et ses Institutions.* Paris, 1942.

Richelieu, Armand Jean du Plessis, Cardinal de. *Maximes d'Etat et Fragments politiques.* Edited by Gabriel Hanotaux. Paris, 1880.

———. *Testament politique.* Edited by Louis André. 7th ed. Paris, 1947.

Richet, Denis. *La France Moderne: L'Esprit des Institutions.* Paris, 1973.

Riesenberg, Peter N. *Inalienability of Sovereignty in Medieval Political Thought.* New York, 1956.

Ritter, Gerhard. *Friedrich der Grosse: Ein historisches Profil.* Leipzig, 1936.

Roberts, J. M. et al., eds. *French Revolution Documents.* 2 vols. Oxford, 1966–1973.

Romier, Lucien. *Les origines politiques des guerres de religion.* 2 vols. Paris, 1913–1914.

Ronzeaud, Pierre. "La femme au pouvoir ou le monde à l'envers." *XVIIe siècle* 108 (1975): 9–33.

Roujon, Jacques. *Louis XIV.* 2 vols. Paris, 1943.

Rousseau, Jean-Jacques. *Oeuvres complètes.* Edited by Bernard Gagnebin and Marcel Raymond. 4 vols. Paris, 1959–1969.

[Roux, Jacques.] *Jacques Roux, Scripta et Acta.* Edited by W. Markov. Berlin, 1959.

Rowen, Herbert H. "A Second Thought on Locke's *First Treatise.*" *Journal of the History of Ideas* 17 (1956): 130–132.

Saenger, Paul. "Burgundy and the Inalienability of Appanges in the Reign of Louis XI." *French Historical Studies* 10 (1977): 1–26.

Saint-Léger, A. de et al. *Louis XIV. La fin du règne.* Histoire de France depuis les origines jusqu'à la Révolution, edited by Ernest Lavisse, vol. 8, pt. 1. Paris, 1908.

Saint-Pierre, [Charles-Irénée Castel, called] Abbé de. *Annales Politiques (1658–1740).* Edited by Joseph Drouet. Paris, 1912.

Saint-Simon, [Louis de Rouvroy, duke of]. *Ecrits inédits de Saint-Simon.* Edited by Armand-Prosper Faugère. 8 vols. Paris, 1880–1893.

———. *Mémoires de Saint-Simon.* Edited by A. de Boislisle. 41 vols. Paris, 1879–1928.

———. *Mémoires de Saint-Simon.* Edited by Gonzague Truc. 7 vols. Paris, 1953–1961.

Salmon, J. H. M. *The French Religious Wars in English Political Thought.* Oxford, 1959.

Savaron, Iehan. *De la Sovveraineté dv Roy, et qve Sa Maiesté ne la peut souzmettre à qui que ce soit, ny aliener son Domaine à perpetuité.* Paris, 1620.

Scheidgen, Helmut. *Die französische Thronfolge (987–1500): Der Ausschluss der Frauen und das Salische Gesetz.* Bonn, 1976.

Schlatter, Richard. *Private Property: The History of an Idea.* New Brunswick, N.J., 1951.

Schramm, Percy Ernest, et al. *Herrschaftszeichen und Staatssymbolik: Beiträge zu ihrer Geschichte vom dritten bis zum sechzehnten Jahrhundert.* 3 vols. Stuttgart, 1954–1956.

———. *Der König von Frankreich: Das Wesen der Monarchie vom 9. zum 16. Jahrhundert. Ein Kapitel aus der Geschichte des abendländischen Staates.* 2 vols. Weimar, 1939.

Schulz, Fritz. *Classical Roman Law.* Oxford, 1951.

Secrete Resolutien van de Edele Groot Mog. Heeren Staten van Holland en Westvriesland, genomen zedert den aanvang der bedieninge van den Heer Johan de Witt, als Raadpensionaris van den zelven Lande . . . 2 vols. Utrecht, 1717.

Sée, Henri. *L'Evolution de la Pensée Politique en France au XVIIIᵉ Siècle.* Paris, 1925.

Seyssel, Claude de. *La Monarchie de France et deux autres fragments politiques.* Edited by Jacques Poujol. Paris, 1961.

Seznec, Jean. *La survivance des dieux antiques: Essai sur le rôle de la tradition mythologique dans l'humanisme et dans l'art de la Renaissance.* London, 1940.

Sidney, Algernon. *Discourses on Government.* 3 vols. New York, 1805.

Sieyès, Emmanuel. *Qu'est-ce que le Tiers état?* Edited by Roberto Zapperi. Geneva, 1970.

Sixte de Bourbon de Parme, Prince. *Le traité d'Utrecht et les lois fondamentales du royaume.* Paris, 1914.

Srbik, Heinrich Ritter von. *Der Westfälische Frieden und die deutsche Volkseinheit.* Munich, 1940.

[Stockmans, Pieter.] *Deductie, Waer uyt met klare ende bondige Bewijs-Redenen getoont en bewecsen wordt, Datter geen Recht van Devolutie is, in het Hertogdom van Brabandt, Noch oock In de andere Provintien van Nederlandt, ten regarde van de Princen der selfde, gelijk eenige getracht hebben te bewijsen ende staende te houden.* New ed. Amsterdam, 1667.

Sully, [Maximilien de Béthune, duke of]. *Mémoires de Sully, Principal Ministre de Henri-le-Grand.* New ed. 6 vols. Paris, 1788.

[Thibaudeau, A. C.] *Mémoires sur le Consulat. 1799 à 1804. Par un ancien Conseiller d'Etat.* Paris, 1827.

Thireau, Jean-Louis. *Les Idées politiques de Louis XIV.* Paris, 1973.

Thou, Jacques-Auguste de. *Histoire Universelle . . .* 11 vols. The Hague, 1740.

Tocqueville, Alexis de. *De la Démocratie en Amérique.* Edited by J. P. Mayer. 2 vols. Paris, 1961.

Tommaseo, N., ed. and trans. *Relations des Ambassadeurs Vénitiens sur les affaires de France au XVIe siècle.* 2 vols. Paris, 1838.

[Torcy, Jean-Baptiste Colbert, marquis de.] *Mémoires du marquis de Torcy, pour servir à l'histoire des négociations, depuis le traité de Riswick jusqu'à la paix d'Utrecht.* In Nouvelle Collection des mémoires pour servir à l'histoire de France, depuis le XIIIe siécle jusqu'à la fin du XVIIIe, edited by Joseph F. Michaud and Jean F. Poujoulat, ser. 3, vol. 8, pp. 519–535. 3 series. 32 vols. Paris, 1836–1839.

Tréca, G. *Les Doctrines et les Réformes du droit public en réaction contre l'absolutisme de Louis XIV dans l'entourage du Duc de Bourgogne.* Paris, 1909.

Valfrey, J. *La diplomatie française au XVIIe siècle: Hugues de Lionne, ses ambassades en Espagne et en Allemagne: La Paix des Pyrénées d'après sa correspondance conservée aux archives du Ministère des Affaires Etrangères.* Paris, 1881.

Valkenier, Petrus. *'t Verwerd Europa, ofte Politijke en Historische Beschryvinge Der Waare Fundamenten en Oorsaken van de Revolution in Europa, voornamentlijk in en omtrent de Nederlanden zedert den jaare 1664. gecauseert door de gepretendeerde Universele Monarchie der Franschen.* 2d ed. Amsterdam, 1675.

Vast, Henri, ed. *Les grands traités du règne de Louis XIV.* 3 vols. Paris, 1893–1899.

Venturi, Franco. *Utopia and Reform in the Enlightenment.* Cambridge, 1971.

Viollet, Paul. "Comment les femmes ont été exclues, en France, de la succession à la couronne." *Mémoires de l'Institut National de France, Académie des Inscriptions et Belles-Lettres* 34, pt. 2 (1895): 125–178.

———. *Histoire des institutions politiques et administratives de la France.* 4 vols. Paris, 1890–1912.

——. "La question de la légitimité à l'avènement de Hugues Capet." *Mémoires de l'Institut National de France, Académie des Inscriptions et Belles-Lettres* 34, p. 1 (1892): 257–288.

——. *Le Roi et ses ministres pendant les trois derniers siècles de la monarchie.* Paris, 1912.

[Voltaire, François-Marie Arouet, called.] *Oeuvres complètes de Voltaire.* 52 vols. Paris, 1877–1885.

——. *Politique de Voltaire.* Edited by René Pomeau. 2d ed. Paris, 1963.

Walder, Ernst. "Aufgeklärter Absolutismus und Staat." *Schweizer Beiträge zur Allgemeinen Geschichte* 15 (1957): 156–171.

Wallace-Hadrill, J. M. *The Barbarian West, 400–1000.* London, 1952.

Walzer, Michael, ed. *Regicide and Revolution: Speeches at the Trial of Louis XVI.* Translated by Marian Rothstein. London, 1974.

Watrin, Paul. *La tradition monarchique dans l'ancien droit public français.* Paris, n.d.

Weill, Georges. *Les théories sur le pouvoir royal en France pendant les guerres de religion.* Paris, 1891.

Wicquefort, Abraham de. *Histoire des Provinces-Unies des Päis-Bas, depuis le parfait établissement de cet état par la paix de Munster.* Edited by E. Lenting and C. A. Chais van Buren. 4 vols. Amsterdam, 1861–1874.

——. "Mémoire sur la guerre faite aux Provinces-Unies en l'année 1672." Edited by J. A. Wijnne. *Bijdragen en Mededeelingen van het Historisch Genootschap* 11 (1888): 70–344.

[——.] *Remarques Sur le Discours du Commandeur de Gremonville, Fait au Conseil d'Estat de Sa Majesté Imperiale.* The Hague, 1672.

Wijnne, J. A. "De souvereiniteit der provinciën ten tijde van de Republiek." In *Geschiedenis,* pp. 16–36. Groningen, 1872.

[Witt, Johan de.] *Brieven aan Johan de Witt.* Edited by Robert Fruin and N. Japikse. 2 vols. Amsterdam, 1919–1922.

[——.] *Brieven geschreven ende gewisselt tusschen der Heer Johan de Witt, Raedt-pensionaris en Groot-Segelbewaerder van Hollant en West-Vrieslandt; ende de Gevolmaghtigden van den Staedt der Vereenighde Nederlanden, so in Vranckryck, Engelandt, Sweden, Denemarcken, Poolen, enz. Beginnende met den* jaere 1652 tot het jaer 1669 incluys. 7 vols. The Hague, 1723–1725.

———. *Correspondance française du Grand Pensionnaire Jean de Witt.* Edited by François Combes. In *Mélanges historiques, choix de documents,* pp. 123–392. Collection de documents inédits sur l'histoire de France, vol. 11, pt. 1. Paris, 1873.

Woolf, Cecil N. Sidney. *Bartolus of Sassoferrato: His Position in the History of Medieval Political Thought.* Cambridge, 1913.

Zeldin, Theodore. *The Political System of Napoleon III.* New York, 1971.

Zeller, Gaston. *Les institutions de la France au XVIe siècle.* Paris, 1948.

INDEX

Aitzema, Lieuwe van, 104
Alba, Fernando Alvarez de Toledo, Duke of, 103
Albert, Archduke of Austria (co-sovereign of Southern Netherlands), 53, 94, 103, 112, 115
Albertini, Rudolf von, 180n.58, 182 n.3
Alençon (later of Anjou), Francis, Duke of, 43–44
Anjou, Henry, Duke of, 43
Anjou, Philip, Duke of. See Philip V, King of Spain
Anne of Austria, regency government of, 67–68
Antonio, Prior of Prato, pretender to the Portuguese throne (1580), 52
Aquinas, Thomas, 9
Ardingello (papal nuncio), duchy of Milan and, 31
Argenson, René Louis de Voyer de Paulmy, Marquis d', 126–127, 138
Aristotle, on the state, 5, 6
Arlington, Henry Bennet, Earl of, 105
Arnauld, Antoine, 89
Aubéry, Antoine, 106–107
Avaux, Jean Antoine de Mesmes, Count d', 69
Azo (Azolinus Porcius), 12

Bartolus of Sassoferrato, 12
Baxter, Christopher R., 180n.53
Bayle, Pierre, 87

Beaujeu, Anne de, 24
Berry, Charles de Bourbon, Duke of, 113, 120
Béthune, Philippe de, 82
Bèze (Beza), Theodore de, 36–37
Bilain, René, 98–102, 104, 135
Bloch, Marc, 171n.4, 178n.11
Bodin, Jean, 40–42, 50, 180n.53, 180n.58
Bolingbroke, Henry St. John, Viscount, 119–120
Bonald, Louis Gabriel Ambroise, Viscount de, 165
Bossuet, Jacques Bénigne, 125, 138; divinity of royal authority and, 83–84, 85
Boulainvilliers, Henri de, Count de Saint-Saire, 125
Bourbon, Charles, Cardinal of, 44, 45
Bourbon, Charles, Duke of (Constable of Bourbon), 28
Bourbon-Parma, Prince Sixtus of, 167
Brienne, Louis Henri de Loménie, Count of, 157
Brunner, Otto, 172n.7
Brutus, Stephanus Junius, pseudonym of the author of A Defense against Tyrants, 39
Bruyère, Jean de La, 86
Buchholz, Friedrich, 200n.3
Bulgarus (Italian jurist), 11–12
Burgundy, Louis, Duke of (later Dauphin), 118. See also Louis of Bourbon, Dauphin of France, called "the Grand Dauphin"
Burlamaqui, Jean Jacques, 143–144

227